"What I like most about *The Cry for Myth* is Rollo May's ability to transform the timeless wisdom of myth into a timely and brilliant commentary upon both contemporary culture and psychotherapy. The book is lucid, deep, powerful, and, above all, wise. In a most effective manner he harnesses the power of myth and brings it to bear upon the struggle of the single individual to grow, to change and to heal."

—Irvin Yalom, M.D., Stanford University,
author of *Love's Executioner*

"[May] demonstrates his thesis . . . and keeps good his promise to provide an American audience that is currently interested in the mythic realms of other cultures . . . with insight into our own mythology." —*Library Journal*

"Thought-provoking and persuasive." —*Kirkus Reviews*

"May's thinking is supple, compassionate, and grand, aimed at those who are able to see everyday problems as reflections of universal experiences." —*Booklist*

"Rollo May's ninth book is a gem that comments cogently on today's culture, psychotherapy and both modern and ancient myths . . . tightly written, inspired, and a logical extension of Joseph Campbell's studies on myth and Jungian psychology. May gives the reader hope. . . ." —*The Pittsburgh Press*

"The latest fruit of May's constantly evolving synthesis of wisdom, erudition and compassion. . . . Rollo May has yet again set his sights as high as humanity dares." —*Applause*

THE
CRY FOR
MYTH

ROLLO MAY

Delta

A Delta Book
Published by
Dell Publishing
a division of
Bantam Doubleday Dell Publishing Group, Inc.
666 Fifth Avenue
New York, New York 10103

ISBN: 0-385-30685-7

Reprinted by arrangement with W.W. Norton & Company Inc.

Manufactured in the United States of America

Published simultaneously in Canada

August 1992

10 9 8 7 6 5 4 3 2 1

BVG

Contents

Part II: *MYTHS IN AMERICA*

THE MYTH OF THE FRONTIER • LONELINESS IN AMERICA • VIOLENCE
AND LONELINESS • THE SEDUCTION OF THE NEW • THE MYTH OF
PROTEUS

THE MYTH AND NEUROSIS OF NARCISSUS • THE NEUROSIS OF OUR
TIME • THE HORATIO ALGER MYTH • CONTEMPORARY EVIL IN
PARADISE • THE AGE OF MELANCHOLY • NARCISSISM, DRUGS, AND
MONEY

THE JAZZ AGE • TRAGIC SUCCESS • THE INABILITY TO CARE • THE
AMERICAN-STYLE GOD • CONSCIOUSNESS IN AMERICA • THE MYTH
OF SISYPHUS

Part III: *MYTHS OF THE WESTERN WORLD*

DANTE'S *DIVINE COMEDY* • VIRGIL AND TRANSFERENCE • THE
JOURNEY THROUGH HELL • THE FREEDOM TO LOVE

THE LOSS OF ONE'S SELF • THE MEANING OF TROLLDOM • THE
VALUE OF DESPAIR • THE STRANGE PASSENGER • LOVE AND
RESTORATION

FAIRY TALE AND MYTH • CREATIVE PRESENCE • REVISITING BRIAR
ROSE

Part IV: *MYTHS FOR SURVIVAL*

Foreword

As a practicing psychoanalyst I find that contemporary therapy is almost entirely concerned, when all is surveyed, with the problems of the individual's search for myths. The fact that Western society has all but lost its myths was the main reason for the birth and development of psychoanalysis in the first place. Freud and the divergent therapists made it clear that myths are the essential language in psychoanalysis.

The great interest in Joseph Campbell's television talks on myth is the most obvious demonstration of the profound need throughout Western countries for myth. But whereas Campbell's talks were almost exclusively about myths in India, Asia, China, and Asia Minor, this book is about myths as they are immediately present in the consciousness and unconsciousness of contemporary living people in the West.

We are concerned here with narratives which come up continuously in contemporary psychotherapy.

I speak of the *Cry* for myths because I believe there is an urgency in the need for myth in our day. Many of the problems of our society, including cults and drug addiction, can be traced to the lack of myths which will give us as individuals the inner security we need in order to live adequately in our day. The sharp increase in suicide among young people and the surprising increase in depression among people of all ages are due, as I show in this book, to the confusion and the unavailability of adequate myths in modern society. This book will appeal, I hope, to people in America and similar countries as part of our

endeavor to bring the problem of myths into open consciousness and to show how myths can be rediscovered as tools for
understanding ourselves.

This is especially urgent as we seek to give meaning to our
lives—in our creativity, our loves, our challenges—since we
stand on the threshold of a new century. The approach of a
new period in history stimulates us to take stock of our past and
to ask the question of the meaning we have made and are
making in our lives. It is in that mood that I offer this book.

Rollo May

Here we have our present age . . . bent on the extermination of myth. Man today, stripped of myth, stands famished among all his pasts and must dig frantically for roots, be it among the most remote antiquities.

Friedrich Nietzsche,
*The Birth of Tragedy from
the Spirit of Music*

It may perhaps seem to you as though our theories are a kind of mythology. . . . But does not every science come in the end to a kind of mythology like this? Cannot the same be said today of your own Physics?

Freud, in his correspondence
with Einstein

We hear the cry for myth, sometimes a silent cry, on the campuses of our day. Science and Humanism must join together to respond to this cry.

Matthew Bronson, biologist,
at a student conference at
the University of California, San Diego

PART I

THE FUNCTION OF MYTHS

ONE

What Is a Myth?

Studied alive, myth . . . is not an explanation in satisfaction
of a scientific interest, but a narrative resurrection of a
primeval reality, told in satisfaction of deep religious wants,
moral cravings.

Bronislaw Malinowski,
Magic, Science and Religion

A MYTH IS A WAY of making sense in a senseless world. Myths are narrative patterns that give significance to our existence. Whether the meaning of existence is only what we put into life by our own individual fortitude, as Sartre would hold, or whether there is a meaning we need to discover, as Kierkegaard would state, the result is the same: myths are our way of finding this meaning and significance. Myths are like the beams in a house: not exposed to outside view, they are the structure which holds the house together so people can live in it.

Myth making is essential in gaining mental health, and the compassionate therapist will not discourage it. Indeed, the very birth and proliferation of psychotherapy in our contemporary age were called forth by the disintegration of our myths.

Through its myths a healthy society gives its members relief from neurotic guilt and excessive anxiety. In ancient Greece, for example, when the myths were vital and strong, individuals in the society were able to meet the problems of existence without overwhelming anxiety or guilt feeling. Hence we find the philosophers in those times discussing beauty, truth, goodness, and courage as values in human life. The myths freed Plato and Aeschylus and Sophocles to create their great philosophic and literary works, which come down as treasures for us today.

But when the myths of classical Greece broke down, as they did in the third and second centuries, Lucretius could see "aching hearts in every home, racked incessantly by pangs the mind was powerless to assuage and forced to vent themselves in recalcitrant repining."*

We in the twentieth century are in a similar situation of "aching hearts" and "repining." Our myths no longer serve their function of making sense of existence, the citizens of our day are left without direction or purpose in life, and people are at a loss to control their anxiety and excessive guilt feeling. People then flock to psychotherapists or their substitutes, or drugs or cults, to get help in holding themselves together. Hence the psychologist Jerome Bruner can write, "For when the prevailing myths fail to fit the varieties of man's plight, frustration expresses itself first in mythoclasm and then in the lonely search for internal identity."†

This "lonely search for internal identity" is a widespread need which gives rise in our society to the development of psychoanalysis and the many forms and promises of psychotherapy and the multitude of cure-alls and cults, constructive or destructive as they may be.

---

*Lucretius, *The Nature of the Universe* (London: Penguin Books, 1951), p. 217.

†Jerome S. Bruner, "Myth and Identity," in *Myth and Mythmaking*, ed. Henry A. Murray (New York: George Braziller, 1960), p. 285.

''I NEVER PROMISED YOU
A ROSE GARDEN''

This autobiographical novel, *I Never Promised You a Rose Garden*, tells the experience of a young schizophrenic woman, Deborah, in her actual treatment with a psychiatrist. The stirring events in the treatment of this girl read like a contemporary extraterrestrial film. In her therapy we see a constant and gripping interplay of myths. Deborah (as she is called) lived with the mythic figures of Idat, Yr, Anterrabae, Lactamaen, the Collect, all of whom inhabited the Kingdom of Yr. Since Deborah could communicate with no one else in the world, she desperately needed these mythic figures. She writes, "the gods of Yr had been companions—secret, precisely *sharers of her loneliness.* "* She would flee to them when she was terrified or unbearably lonely in the so-called real world.

On the way to the sanatorium, as Deborah tells us, she and her parents stayed overnight in adjacent rooms in a motel.

On the other side of the wall, Deborah stretched to sleep. The kingdom of Yr had a kind of neutral place which was called the Fourth Level. It was achieved only by accident and could not be reached by formula or an act of will. At the Fourth Level there was no emotion to endure, no past or future to grind against.

Now, in bed, achieving the Fourth Level, a future was of no concern to her. The people in the next room were supposed to be her parents. Very well. But that was part of a shadowy world that was dissolving, and now she was being flung unencumbered into a new one in which she had not the slightest concern. In moving from the old world, she was also moving from the intricacies of Yr's kingdom, from the Collect of Others, the Censor, and the Yri gods. She rolled over and slept a deep, dreamless, and restful sleep.

*Hannah Green, *I Never Promised You a Rose Garden* (New York: Holt, Rinehart and Winston, 1964), p. 55. (Italics mine.)

Next morning, she tells us, she felt the great reassurance and comfort the myths had given her.

. . . it occurred to Deborah, as the car pulled away from the motel and out into the sunny day, that the trip might last forever and that the calm and marvelous freedom she felt might be a new gift from the usually too demanding gods and offices of Yr.*

Not only are these gods in Deborah's scheme remarkable for their imaginative depth, but they are remarkable as well for their great similarity to what has been shown thirty years later in *E.T.*, *The Return of the Jedi, Close Encounters of the Third Kind,* and the other extra-worldly films which attract millions of children and adults in our late twentieth century. Deborah was schizophrenic. But where one draws the line between schizophrenia and an intensely creative imagination is a perpetual puzzle. Again Hannah Green (her pen name) writes:

She began to fall, going with Anterrabe through this fire-framed darkness into Yr. This time the fall was far. There was utter darkness for a long time and then a grayness, seen only in bands across the eye. The place was familiar; it was the Pit. In this place gods and Collect moaned and shouted, but even they were unintelligible. Human sounds came, too, but they came without meaning. The world intruded, but it was a shattered world and unrecognizable.†

The psychiatrist who served as therapist for Deborah at Chestnut Lodge, Frieda Fromm-Reichmann, wisely made clear to Deborah at the outset that she would not pull these gods away against Deborah's will. Dr. Frieda, as she is called in the book, worked them into the treatment, suggesting sometimes to Deborah that she tell her gods such-and-such, or occasionally asking her what her gods say. What is most important is that Dr. Fromm-Reichmann respected Deborah's need for these mythic figures, and she sought to help Deborah to see

---

*Ibid., p. 12. This description has a curious similarity to Dante's hell, which we will describe later in Chapter 9, "The Therapist and the Journey Into Hell."
†Ibid., p. 31.

that she, Deborah, had her part in creating them. In one session,

"Our time is over," the doctor said gently, "You have done well to tell me about the secret world. I want you to go back and tell those gods and Collect and Censor that I will not be cowed by them and that neither of us is going to stop working because of their power."*

But when Dr. Frieda had to go to Europe for a summer, Deborah was temporarily assigned to a younger psychiatrist who was imbued with the new rationalism. This psychiatrist marched in to destroy the "delusions" of Deborah with no understanding whatever of Deborah's need for her myths. The result was that Deborah, her whole system of gods and their extraterrestrial kingdom in shambles, deteriorated markedly. She regressed into a completely withdrawn world. She set fire to the sanatorium, burned and maimed herself, and behaved like a human being whose humanity is destroyed. For this is literally what had happened. Her soul—defined as the most intimate and fundamental function of her consciousness—was taken away, and she had literally nothing to hold on to.

Deborah described this to Dr. Frieda when the latter returned from Europe. The other psychiatrist, she wept, "wanted only to prove how right he was and how smart." Amid her flood of tears, she continued, "He might as well have said, 'Come to your senses and stop the silliness.' . . . God curse me!" groaned Deborah. "God curse me! . . . for my truth the world gives only lies!"

We may take the rationalistic psychiatrist's behavior as an allegory of our modern age. When we in the twentieth century are so concerned about proving that our technical reason is right and we wipe away in one fell swoop the "silliness" of myths, we also rob our own souls and we threaten to destroy our society as part of the same deterioration.

Deborah's myths continued right up to the last page of *I*

*Ibid., p. 56.

Never Promised You a Rose Garden. But by then she had learned that her myths were also a product of her own rich creativity. Dr. Frieda had helped her understand that the form the myths took—allegedly schizophrenic to start with—was within her own power to mold.

Though Deborah had her part in creating the myths, it is important to state that she did not create the *need* for them. This need is part of our destiny as human beings, part of our language and our way of understanding each other. At the end of the therapy Deborah's creativity emerged in ways that genuinely contributed to herself and her society; she has written and published several excellent novels after completing her treatment at Chestnut Lodge, at least two of these novels about seriously handicapped persons.

This present book is written not chiefly about schizophrenics as such but about the need of all of us for myths arising from our character as human beings. The form these myths take will vary. But the *need* for myths, indeed, the *cry* for myths, will be present wherever there are persons who call themselves human. We are all like Deborah in this sense: though we form our own myths in various collective and personal ways, the myths are necessary as ways of bridging the gap between our biological and our personal selves.

Myths are our self-interpretation of our inner selves in relation to the outside world. They are narrations by which our society is unified.* Myths are essential to the process of keeping our souls alive and bringing us new meaning in a difficult and often meaningless world. Such aspects of eternity as beauty, love, great ideas, appear suddenly or gradually in the language of myth.

---

*The myths from China, India, Tibet, Japan, and other parts of the Orient spring out of a different culture from ours, and therefore we can understand them only partially. But they also give us a garden of flowers which we can appreciate at least from the garden gate. Joseph Campbell has given us an excellent survey of these myths of different countries in the world. I intend in this book, in contrast, to deal with the myths *of our own America,* as they are revealed in our present world, in psychotherapy, and in social and religious experience.

Myth making thus is central in psychotherapy. It is of the essence that the therapist permit the client to take his or her myths seriously, whether the myths come up in dreams or in free association or in fantasy. Every individual who needs to bring order and coherence into the streams of her or his sensations, emotions, and ideas entering consciousness from within and without is forced to do deliberately for himself what in previous ages had been done for him by family, custom, church, and state. In the therapy myths may be a reaching out, a way of trying out new structures of life, or a desperate venture at rebuilding his or her broken way of life. Myths, as Hannah Green put it, are "sharers of our loneliness."

CULTS AND MYTHS

There are frightening statistics of suicide by young people in the last decades. In the 1970s suicide among white young men increased greatly. We may try various ways to prevent suicide in these young people, like telephoning seriously depressed persons and so on. But as long as the highest goal remains making money, as long as we teach practically no ethics by example in home or in government, as long as these young people are not inspired to form a philosophy of life, and as long as television is overloaded with aggression and sex with no mentors in learning to love—as long as these obtain, there will continue to be among young people such frightening depression and suicide.

At a graduation speech at Stanford University recently, the student speaker described his class as not knowing how it "relates to the past or the future, having little sense of the present, no life-sustaining beliefs, secular or religious," and as consequently having "no goal and no path of effective action." As long as our world and society remain thus empty of myths which express beliefs and moral goals, there will be depression, as we shall see below, and suicide. We shall refer in a later chapter to some reasons for this ethical emptiness; here we only assert that the lack of myths is a lack of language even to begin to communicate on such issues.

In such directionless states as we find ourselves near the end of the twentieth century, it is not surprising that frantic people flock to the new cults, or resurrect the old ones, seeking answers to their anxiety and longing for relief from their guilt or depressions, longing for something to fill the vacuum of their lives. They also beg for guidance from astrologers.* Or they grasp at superstitions from the primitive past, however reminiscent of the age of witchcraft.†

Our twentieth century was originally heralded as the age which would be graced with rationalism, the age when enlightened education would be widespread, religion would at last be cleansed of all superstition and would be itself enlightened. Indeed, almost all the fond aims of the Enlightenment have been at least partially realized: we have great wealth for *some* people, freedom from tyranny as a goal for most people in the West, dissemination of science, ad infinitum. But what has happened? As a people we are more confused, lacking in moral ideals, dreading the future, uncertain what to do to change things or how to rescue our own inner life. "We are the best informed people on earth," Archibald MacLeish proclaims:

We are deluged with facts, but we have lost, or are losing, our human ability to feel them. . . . We know with the head now, by the facts, by the abstractions. We seem unable to know as Shakespeare knew who

*A Gallup poll indicates that "32 million people in this country believe in astrology." It is "a search for meaning in life," the president of the International Society for Astrological Research holds. "Knowing where your stars are is like having a weather forecast of problems in life." Particularly during times of stress they look for "answers for their lives" (*New York Times,* October 19, 1975).

Carl Sagan spent much effort in his television series attacking astrology as unscientific. Arguing from his position as professor of astronomy, he did not seem to realize that astrology has an entirely different basis. Astrology is a myth and requires the language of the myth. It has both the shortcomings and the positive effects of myths.

†There are dozens of these cults—led by Rajnesh, Trunghpa, Da Free John, Radachristian, Muktananda, the Moonies, etc. New ones spring up every year. I do not wish here to make judgments about the value or lack of it of these groups; I only cite them as groups to which people flock in order to get some way of handling their lives, some pattern for managing their anxiety and achieving some meaning and purpose in life.

made King Lear cry out to blinded Gloucester on the heath: . . . "you see how this world goes," and Gloucester answers: "I see it feelingly."*

Language abandons myth only at the price of the loss of human warmth, color, intimate meaning, values—these things that give personal meaning to life. For we understand each other by identifying with the subjective meaning of the language of the other persons, by experiencing what important words mean to them in *their* world. *Without myth we are like a race of brain-injured people unable to go beyond the word and hear the person who is speaking.* There can be no stronger proof of the impoverishment of our contemporary culture than the popular—though profoundly mistaken—definition of myth as falsehood.

The thirst for myth and the discouragement at the lack of adequate myths show in the use of narcotics. If we cannot make sense of our lives, we can at least temporarily check out of our boring routine by "out-of-the-body" experiences with cocaine or heroin or crack or some other drug which will take one temporarily out of this world. This is also a pattern we see not infrequently in psychotherapy: when the person finds his prospects overwhelmingly difficult, he may consider that at least he can participate in his own fate by overdosing or shooting himself. If we are going to be annihilated anyway, it is less humiliating to go out with a bang than a whimper.

The flocking to cults in our day, especially by young people but by older ones as well, is also an indication of the desperate need for myths. Any group which promises bliss and love and an inside track to whatever gods may be can get an audience, and people flock to the banner of a new cult whatever it is called. Jim Jones and the Guyana tragedy, when 980 of his followers committed suicide because the authoritarian Jones told them to, is a warning we cannot forget.

Cults have the power of myths without the social limits, without the brakes, without societal responsibility. The cry for

*Archibald MacLeish, "Poetry and Journalism," *A Continuing Journey* (Boston: Houghton Mifflin, 1967), p. 43.

myths must be listened to, for unless we achieve authentic myths our society will fill the vacuum with pseudo-myths and beliefs in magic. The sociologists inform us of a number of polls in the 1960s and 1970s which showed that the belief in God was decreasing and the belief in the Devil increasing.* This is a reflection of the passion for cults by people who feel our society is disintegrating and need to have some way of explaining it.

Instead of being viewed as random, irrational behavior, Devil-belief is an effort by the powerless to make sense of the world, to apply causality when disorder threatens, and to reduce the dissonance generated by their commitment to a social order that is incomprehensible and unresponsive to them.†

THE DENIAL OF MYTHS

It will seem confusing indeed to propose our need for myths when we have become accustomed in our culture to label myths as falsehoods. Even people of high intelligence speak of "only a myth" as a deprecatory phrase; the Biblical creation story, for example, is *"only* a myth."** This use of the word "only" as a deprecation of myth began with the Christian Fathers in the third century A.D. as their way of fighting against the common people's faith in Greek and Roman myths. The Fathers argued that only the Christian message was true and the Greek and Roman stories were "only" myths. But if the Church Fathers could have had more confidence in the great wealth of mythology which came with Christianity—from the celebration of Christmas with the Wise Men following the star in the east to the indescribably charming gift giving, or the impressive experience of Easter with its celebration of spring

---

*Clyde Z. Nunn, *The Rising Credibility of the Devil in America.* (See also Chapter 15.)

†*Listening: Journal of Religion and Culture* 9, no. 3 (Autumn 1974): 94.

**Isaac Asimov, "The Threat of Creationism," *New York Times Magazine* (June 14, 1981). (Italics mine.)

and the birth of plants and flowers and grain as well as the myth of the resurrection—they would have had less need to attack the great myths of classical Greece and Rome.

But there is another reason in our day for the mistaken definition of myths as falsehood. Most of us have been taught to think only in rationalistic terms. We seem to be victims of the prejudice that the more rationalistic our statements, the more true they are, as we saw in Hannah Green's substitute psychiatrist. This monopoly on the part of left brain activity expresses not real science but pseudo-science. Gregory Bateson rightly reminds us that "mere purposive rationality unaided by such phenomena as art, religion, dream, and the like, is necessarily pathogenic and destructive of life."* As we have said earlier, our first reaction when the myths have not sufficed is mythoclasm; we attack the very concept of myth. The denial of myths, as we shall see later, is itself part of *our refusal to confront our own reality and that of our society.*

"Depend upon it," Max Muller wrote. "There is mythology now as there was in the time of Homer, only we do not perceive it, because we ourselves live in the very shadow of it, and because we all shrink from the full meridian light of truth."†

There is surely no conflict between science rightly defined and myth also rightly understood. Heisenberg, Einstein, Niels Bohr, and countless other great modern scientists have made that clear. It is interesting to note how many of the great scientific discoveries begin as myths. We do not have Einstein's answer to Freud's defense of myth in his letter on the question, "Why war?," but there is no reason to doubt that it was affirmative. The relation between science and myth is put succinctly by W. B. Yeats, "Science is the critique of myth."**

Our problem is not merely one of definition. It is one of inner commitment, a problem of psychology and the spiritual

*John Brockman, *About Bateson* (New York: Dutton, 1977), p. 92.
†Max Muller, "The Philosophy of Mythology," *The Science of Religion* (London, 1873), pp. 353–355.
**Henry Murray, *Myth and Mythmaking,* 1960, p. 114.

effort to garner up the courage to gaze at "the full meridian of truth."

MYTH AS OUR GLIMPSE
OF INFINITY

It is through myths that men are lifted above their captivity in the ordinary, attain powerful visions of the future, and realize such visions.

                    Peter Berger, *Pyramids of Sacrifice*

There are, broadly speaking, two ways human beings have communicated through their long and fitful history. One is rationalistic language. This is specific and empirical, and eventuates in logic. In this kind of communication the *persons who are speaking the words are irrelevant to the truth or falsehood of what they say.*

A second way is myth. The myth is a drama which begins as a historical event and takes on its special character as a way of orienting people to reality. The myth, or story, carries the values of the society: by the myth the individual finds his sense of identity, as we shall see in Chapter 2. The narration always points toward totality rather than specificity; it is chiefly a right brain function. By their myths, we could say, we shall know them. The myth unites the antinomies of life: conscious and unconscious, historical and present, individual and social. These are formed into a narration which is passed down from age to age. Whereas empirical language refers to objective facts, *myth refers to the quintessence of human experience, the meaning and significance of human life.* The whole person speaks to *us,* not just to our brain.*

In mythic films one can leap over centuries and find oneself in ancient Rome or walking with Socrates in the streets of

---

*Those who wish to read more on this topic are referred to Ernst Cassirer, *An Essay on Man* (New Haven: Yale University Press, 1944).

ancient Athens. Or one can leap ahead into the future in space-ships. This is why films, the "movies," are a special art of the twentieth century. Or the moods can change instantaneously as the film artist indicates. Mythic films like *Platoon* can make horrible, unbelievable experiences come to life. The deafening noise, the unending jungle, the drugs, the snakes, the rape, the blood and the profanity, the cruelty of the otherwise nice young men just out of college, and withal the human qualities of the soldiers caring for each other or shooting each other—that was the myth. Nor is myth just these symbols: they must be arranged as a narration which speaks to our conscious and subconscious. This and other films communicate a picture which is put together into the essence of the myth. The result is a soul-shaking narration in which "we are not fighting the enemy but fighting ourselves," as one of the characters in *Platoon* remarks near the end. With these films many veterans heaved a great sigh of relief and murmured, "That was Vietnam!" The film *Platoon* presents what Jung would call the "shadow" and I have called in *Love and Will* the "daimonic."

Millions of words were used to describe in 1987 the falls from grace of James Bakker and Jimmy Swaggart, two of the leaders of the wing of fundamentalist religion; but when one name, "Elmer Gantry," was used, people immediately understood. Elmer Gantry is the myth of a clergyman who gets involved in illicit sex and the misappropriation of funds, created by Sinclair Lewis and presented by him in the novel by that name in 1926, half a century before Bakker and Swaggert.

Thus the myth, as Thomas Mann put it, is an eternal truth in contrast to an empirical truth. The latter can change with every morning newspaper when we read of the latest discoveries in our laboratories. But the myth transcends time. It does not matter in the slightest whether a man named Adam and a woman named Eve ever actually existed or not; the myth about them in Genesis still presents a picture of the birth and development of human consciousness which is applicable to all people of all ages and religions.

Myth is not art, though it is used in all the arts; it promises more; its methods and functions are different. Myth is a form of expression which reveals a process of thought and feeling—man's awareness of and response to the universe, his fellow men, and his separate being. It is a projection in concrete and dramatic form of fears and desires undiscoverable and inexpressible in any other way.*

Oedipus was an archaic Greek tale, which in Homer's narration took on the proportions of a myth and through the pen of Sophocles became the myth of the hero who seeks his own reality, a pursuit which in our day is known as the search for identity. The man who cries, "I must find out who I am!" as does Oedipus, and then revolts against his own reality, stands not only for the Greeks but for all of us in our ambivalent struggle to find our identity. Hence Freud used the myth of Oedipus as central in his contemporaneous psychology. Like most of the ancient Hebrew and Greek myths, this narration of the triangular struggle in the family becomes true in different ways for people of all cultures, since everyone is born of a father and mother and must in some way revolt against them—which is the definition of a classic like Oedipus.

Psychoanalyst Bruno Bettelheim faced the same problem of overemphasis on rationality in his charming book on fairy tales, *The Uses of Enchantment.* He called on the ancient philosophers, Plato and Aristotle, to support him:

Plato—who may have understood better what forms the mind of man than some of our contemporaries who want their children exposed only to "real" people and everyday events—knew what intellectual experiences make for true humanity. He suggested that the future citizens of his ideal republic begin their literary education with the telling of myths, rather than with mere facts or so-called rational teachings. Even Aristotle, master of pure reason, said: *"The friend of wisdom is also a friend of myth."*†

---

*Lillian Feder, *Ancient Myth in Modern Poetry* (Princeton: Princeton University Press, 1971), p. 28.

†Bruno Bettelheim, *The Uses of Enchantment* (New York: Vintage, 1977), p. 35. (Italics mine.)

Thus the authorities on the teaching of virtue and courage to the youth—what the Greeks called *arête*—realized that myth is the foundation of values and ethics.

Every individual seeks—indeed *must* seek if he or she is to remain sane—to bring some order and coherence into the stream of sensations, emotions, and ideas entering his or her consciousness from within or without. Each one of us is forced to do deliberately for oneself what in previous ages was done by family, custom, church, and state, namely, form the myths in terms of which we can make some sense of experience.

TWO

Our Personal Crises in Myths

Myth . . . expresses, enhances, and codifies belief; it
safeguards and enforces morality; it vouches for the
efficiency of ritual and contains practical rules for the
guidance of man. Myth is thus a vital ingredient of human
civilization; it is not an idle tale, but a hard-worked active
force.

Bronislaw Malinowski,
Magic, Science and Religion

THE MANY CONTRIBUTIONS of myths to our lives can be
listed under four headings. First, myths give us our *sense
of personal identity*, answering the question, Who am I? When
Oedipus cried, "I must find out who I am and where I came
from!" and when Alex Haley searches for his *Roots*, they are
both illustrating this function of myth.

Second, myths make possible our *sense of community*. The
fact that we think mythically is shown in our loyalty to our
town and nation and even our loyalty to our college and its
various teams which produce such mythic phenomena as Tro-
jans and 49ers. These would be absurd except that they illustrate the important bonding of social interest and patriotism

and other such deeply rooted attitudes toward one's society and nation.

Third, *myths undergird our moral values.* This is crucially important to members of our age, when morality has deteriorated and seems to have vanished altogether in some distraught places.

Fourth, mythology is our way of dealing with the inscrutable *mystery of creation.* This refers not only to the creation of our universe but creation in science, the mysterious "dawning" in art and poetry and other new ideas in our minds. "Myth is the garment of mystery," writes Thomas Mann insightfully in the preface to his great book on ancient myths, *Joseph and His Brothers.*

SATAN AND CHARLES

An art critic severely handicapped by writer's block illustrates the myth of personal identity. Charles, as we shall call him, had lived in and out of severe despair for a number of years. Though not formally religious he had during World War II briefly become a Roman Catholic with the desperate hope of getting help in pulling himself together. He had tried various other ways, including classical psychoanalysis, but the experiences remained at the "talking" level and never touched him in his depths. He continued struggling by himself for some months and then, in despair, came to me for psychoanalysis again.

In the course of his free associations after several months of analysis, he said, "I am the writer who does not write. . . . I am the man who doesn't pay his bills, I am the needy one. That's the way I recognize myself on the street, not 'O yes, there's Charles,' but 'O yes, there's the needy man!' " On hearing this I was struck by the fact that it seemed more than words; he really did get his identity through seeing himself as the myth of the needy man.

In a later hour he stated, "My neurosis protects my soul.

... It is the most precious thing for me.... If I could get well, it would be a defeat for me." He heartily disliked the popularly stated goals of therapy, e.g., to make one productive, happy, well adjusted, and though he knew neither he nor I held such goals, the culture did; and he heartily disliked our contemporary secular culture.

The critical point in the analysis came when there surfaced in his free associations, "Satan was a rebel for God." He mused with pleasure over the phrases, "Satan the savior! Satan the rebel!"

In his therapy we then focused specifically on the myth of Satan, with which he identified. He emphasized that Satan, in the form of Lucifer, had been thrown out of heaven and existed by virtue of what he rebelled against. Thus he was saying that he himself existed by virtue of the myth of being a rebel. No wonder his neurosis protected his soul; indeed it constituted his soul! His belief in Satan, he emphasized, was not a form of Manichaeanism, for Satan really did believe in God. When we accepted in his therapy the myth of Satan, we found that it brought together a number of strands of his previously elusive character structure: his rebellion, his negativity, and along with these his considerable creative possibilities as a writer.

The reason Charles' previous therapy had proved ineffectual seems to have been that it was too rationalistic. It had consisted mainly of conscious talking—which Charles could do end-lessly—and it never touched the deeper levels of his emotions. The myth of being a "rebel for God" relieved his neurotic guilt and he could then accept the normal guilt of every human being, which turned out to be a stimulus for the therapy. He could now respect himself while at the same time being a constructive rebel; he was freed from the need to destroy himself in the process. There is so much pretense and falsehood in our society that it is not surprising that negation, as in Satan, has to come out in therapy. The myth of Satan was a shorthand way of getting to the basis of his defiance and negativity, and it was essential to our achieving a successful outcome of the therapy.

As Charles structured his life by clinging subconsciously to the myth of Satan,* so each of us has his or her myth around which we pattern our lives. This myth holds us together and gives us our capacity to live in the past and future without neglecting each instant of the present. The myth bridges the gap between conscious and unconscious: we then can speak out of some unity of the tremendous variety in each of our selves. The forms that this myth may take, of course, are infinite. The myths each of us brings to therapy are unique, just as each human being is different from every other one. But the individual myths will generally be a variation on some central theme of the classical myths, in this case Satan, which refer to the dynamic, existential crises in all persons' lives.

The problem of identity, as Erik Erikson has emphasized, is present in our clients and in all of us, and we can approach a solution through listening to the various myths the client may bring up. For we all think of ourselves not in moral or rational categories but rather as central characters in the drama of life. Each of us may be hero or heroine, or criminal or rogue or onlooker, or any other character in the drama, and the emotions we experience will fit these characters.

Indeed, our consciousness is more profound when it takes into itself the so-called destructive myths like Satan. As Paul Tillich wrote in the fly-leaf of the copy of *The Courage To Be* which he gave to me, "The self-affirmation of a being is the stronger the more non-being it can take into itself."† Satan in our day has of course received a bad press, and those therapists who follow the motto of "accent on the positive" will tend to cover up such negations. But when we do this we have omitted the fact that every conscious myth is balanced in our unconsciousness by the contrary picture. To leave out Satan means, for all practical purposes, to leave out our positive ultimate concerns as well.

---

*See Chapter 14 for further description of the origin of the myth of Satan.
†Tillich, *The Courage To Be* (New Haven: Yale University Press, 1952).

Satan has turned out to be an amazingly powerful myth, and has many pseudonyms with forms of satanic power, such as "Lucifer" and "Mephistopheles." Satan was on speaking terms with God in the prologue to the Book of Job, and also in the similar prologue to Goethe's *Faust.* In this drama Faust asks Mephistopheles who he is, and the devil responds,

> I am the spirit that seeks to do evil
> But always turns out to be good.*

Milton's *Paradise Lost* would be without its power except for the myth of Satan; *Moby Dick* would lose its very heart if Satan in Captain Ahab were omitted. Among the modern psychiatrists, Harry Stack Sullivan speaks well of Satan, for very good reason, since Satan emphasizes exactly what we are concerned with in psychotherapy. The late psychologist at Harvard, Henry Murray, has written at length about Satan and has described how he developed from Lucifer, the "morning star" and "the shining One, first and highest of the angels," to the creature we mistakenly scorn as the Devil.†

Charles then began to make progress in his clarification of himself when he hit upon the myth of Satan. If any psychotherapy is to be successful in any deep, lasting way, it must help the patients to relate to such evil and experience again the myth by which human beings make the perilous journey into and through their hell. It is that tortuous path which we will explore later in this book in Chapter 9, "The Therapist and the Journey Into Hell."

---

*Faust (New York: Norton, 1976), 1. 1335.

†Murray, "The Personality and Career of Satan," in *Endeavors in Psychology* (New York: Harper & Row, 1981), p. 531. Murray continues his fascinating description:

Originally the Devil was "full of wisdom and perfect in beauty," . . . St. Thomas Acquinas taught that Satan was one of the pure angels of God probably "superior to all."

But Lucifer was jealous of his elder brother, Christ, and this sibling rivalry made him evil. Thus resentment was "engendered by envy of God's supreme position of power and glory." Satan proclaimed, "I will be like unto the Most High." Thus envy, or hubris, was present in original sin.

A PATIENT'S DREAM
OF ATHENA

Another use of myth as a way of revealing oneself is in the experience of Ursula, a woman in her early forties who had studied in Hollywood and been an actress in several films. She had previously been in therapy twice for extended periods of time, but though she had had a good relationship with the respective therapists, her psychological disturbances had continued unabated. She was unable to go out of her house alone (she was brought to my office for her sessions by a hired driver), and the fact that she was unable to go to dances or parties or the openings of dramas on Broadway in which her husband starred troubled her deeply. She also suffered under the conviction that she was lesbian (which turned out not to be so), but she had never in her whole life had any gratifying sexual experience with a man.

During the first month of therapy she had often asked at the end of the hour, "Do you think I can get over these problems?" I found myself responding with some variant of, "You can if you really want to." This response would always lead to a momentary flare-up of anger on her part. Did I not realize that she would not be making these difficult trips to my office if she did not really want to get over these blockages?

Near the end of her first month of psychotherapy, she had the following dream:

I was cut in the forehead. I searched around for a bandage. All I could find was a Kotex. I put that on the cut. It's all right if you don't mind.

Her associations to the dream were that the cut referred to her coming to see me; we are "cutting" into her head. Since it was a cut in the forehead, it could also tell us that she had a tendency to intellectualize, which we knew anyway but it did not interfere with our doing productive work. The Kotex seemed to refer partially to her sexual seductiveness toward me, although it was not in a degree as to be troublesome. Other associations with the Kotex were procreation: since Kotex is used for menstrual periods she could have a baby (which could refer to her expecting a positive outcome in our therapy, though I thought it was too early in the treatment to verbalize that). The "if-you-don't-mind" remark seemed to be simply the statement of a middle-class person of "good" upbringing.

But is this all?

By no means. There is in this dream an ancient myth which is more important, in my judgment, than all of the things we have said so far. It is the narrative of the birth of Athena, who leapt out of a slit in Zeus' forehead fully armed. It is the famous birth of Athena who was androgynous; she had had no mother, and this was believed to give her the ability to be the impartial judge in the last play of Aeschylus' great trilogy, *The Oresteia*, which marks the beginnings of human civilization.

At first glance this myth in the dream might seem to be making me, the therapist, into Zeus, and thus flattering me for the moment. But wait: the cut is in *her* forehead, not mine. So *she* will be the king of the gods and the maker of miracles! I can expect some competitiveness since I had a budding Zeus in my consulting room.

The myth in this dream told me two other things that were important for the therapy. First, there was a sense of power and forthrightness as well in the reference to having a baby, all of which suggested to me that her prognosis was good: she would in all probability get her neurosis under control (which she did). Second, it told me that my adding the words "if-you-really-want-to" after each question about her prognosis was fortunate, and her momentary flare of anger after each such response from me was understandable if her secret (and probably unconscious) aim was to play king of the gods and defeat me as she assumedly had defeated the other two therapists before me. Probably the mistake of the first two therapists, I hypothesized to myself, was that they got drawn into assuming the responsibility for her success in therapy and she therefore did not have to go through her own "hell."

The reader may well ask, Suppose the patients are unsophisticated and have never read the Greeks or any other classics? While it is true that this woman was eminently interesting and a pleasure to work with, it is not true that she consciously knew about this myth. So far as I can surmise, she had not read it and did not consciously know it. This illustrates that myths do not require that one have read them specifically. *Myths are archetypal patterns in human consciousness,* as Joseph Campbell and others have pointed out. We are all born of a mother and we die: we all confront sex or its absence; we work or we avoid it; and so on. The great dramas like Hamlet are mythic in the sense that they present the existential crises in everyone's life. We cannot escape believing in the assumption that myth and self-consciousness are to some degree synonymous. Where there is consciousness, there will be myth. One will have dreams of the myth of Oedipus out of the vicissitudes of living in a triangular family (father, mother, child) whether he or she has actually read this classic drama or not.

Jung writes, "A negro of the Southern States of America dreams in motifs of Grecian mythology and a Swiss grocer's apprentice repeats, in his psychosis, the vision of an Egyptian Gnostic."*

Myths are original revelations, states Jung, of the preconscious psyche. They are involuntary statements about unconscious psychic happenings. "They are the psychic life of the primitive tribe, which immediately falls to pieces and decays when it loses its mythological heritage, like a man who has lost his soul." The Swiss psychologist agrees with many other authorities that the alarming poverty of symbols is now the condition of our life.†

Jung believes that poets are in touch with a reality beyond

---

*Archetypes of the Collective Unconscious (Princeton: Bollinger Press, 1959), p. 50.

†Ibid., p. 512.

that which the rational mind can perceive; they know that they have discovered the "spirits, demons and gods." The deepest level of the unconscious, writes Jung, can be discovered only through myth and ritual. He sees myths as necessary interlinks between the human spirit and the natural man. Out of this theory come the archetypes, the expression of the collective unconscious.

Each of us, by virtue of our pattern of myths, participates in these archetypes; they are the structure of human existence. It is not necessary to be a scholar in order to be influenced by them; it is only necessary that one existentially participate in human life. "I have written that myths get thought in man unbeknownst to him," Lévi-Strauss states. "For me it [the myth] describes a lived experience."* Dreams are a *private* application to one's life of *public* myths in which we are all participants.

The first of these existential crises is of course *birth*. Each of us was born with fanfare or lack of it, though we were not self-aware at the time, and each of us later gives to his or her birth some meaning far more significant than the mere fact. Heroes regularly are seen as having a special birth, as Otto Rank pictures in his *Myth of the Birth of the Hero*. Moses was found by Pharaoh's daughter in a crib floating in the bullrushes of the Nile; Jesus was born of a virgin with a star in the east; Oedipus was exiled to die in the wilderness as soon as he was born. We all look back and prize our birth, or hate it, or are baffled by it, or have a million and one other reactions which can only be encompassed in a myth.

Another crisis occurs around the ages of five and six, the Oedipal longing which makes itself felt as an expression of the yearning for the parent of the opposite sex; here *Oedipus Rex* is the fitting myth. In the stage of puberty around twelve or later, we find myths expressed by the cluster of rituals when the

*Claude Lévi-Strauss, *Myth and Meaning* (New York: Schocken Books, 1979), p. 3.

boy child becomes a man and the girl child becomes a woman. The myths are expressed in rituals of *confirmation* in the Christian church, or as *bar mitzvah* in Jewish synagogues, or in the tribal rituals of the American Indian boy joining the braves and the girl becoming an adult woman who can have children of her own.

Another existential crisis in growth is the adolescent's assertion of independence, which is shown in the great Greek classic, the *Oresteia*. Whether interpreted by Aeschylus in ancient times, or Sartre or Jeffers in modern life, the myth of Orestes is central in the crises which mark the adolescent's path. It is renowned as the hero's struggle in becoming freed from the biological tie to mother and father.

Then come the crises of love and marriage with their neverending proliferation of myths about Aphrodite, Eros, Psyche, ad infinitum. The existential crisis of *work* is expressed in the myth of Sisyphus, which we will discuss in greater depth in *The Great Gatsby*. Finally, when we anticipate death, we are overwhelmed with the abundance of myths attending this existential crisis, not least of which is the grandeur and fascination in Dante's meeting with his dead acquaintances and friends in the Inferno (see Chapter 9). It seems impossible to let go of our loved—or hated—ones, and so we devise never-ending future lives of punishment for our enemies and beatitude for our friends.

As Gilbert Highet, the late professor of classics at Columbia University, wrote so charmingly:

The central answer is that myths are permanent. They deal with the greatest of all problems, the problems which do not change because men and women do not change. They deal with love; with war; with sin; with tyranny; with courage; with fate: and all in some way or other deal with the relation of man to those divine powers which are sometimes to be cruel, and sometimes, alas, to be just.*

*Highet, *The Classical Tradition: Greek and Roman Influences on Western Literature* (New York: Oxford University Press/Galaxy Books, 1957), p. 540.

It is not true that old myths either die or wither away. The fact that these crises have to be met in some fashion by every creature with consciousness is one aspect of the element of infinity in which myths participate. The myths are reinterpreted by each succeeding generation to fit the new aspects and the needs of the culture. The great *Oresteia* had its source in the dim origins of Greek poetry before Homer; it was then reinterpreted by Aeschylus as the myth of the youth enduring the struggles required to become a man and identify with his father. Orestes' great guilt at killing his mother, his being pursued and driven into temporary psychosis by the Furies until he is finally forgiven at the famous trial at Athens in which human justice is supported by divine power—all these fall into place.

The whole of civilization hangs on the outcome of this trial in the *Oresteia.* For in this symbolic act of the trial the jury is made up of men, *not* gods; men and women must now take responsibility for their own civilization. The myth tells us it is *our* responsibility in this day of "greenhouse effect" and the other threats to our lives on earth.

SARTRE AND *THE FLIES*

Let us look at Sartre's use of the ancient drama of Orestes, surely a historical treasure, among the most magnificent of all human creations. In our post-Freudian day, when the psychology of adolescence is researched and discussed endlessly, one might think the drama of Orestes would be interesting only as a classical replica. But one would be wrong. When Jean-Paul Sartre needed a modern drama to communicate to the despairing French people while Paris was occupied by the Germans in World War II, he chose the ancient drama of Orestes.

Paris was then suffering literally under the Nazi heel; German officers marched up and down in front of the theater. Sartre rewrote the old drama of Aeschylus and entitled his version *The Flies.* The drama opens with a bronze statue of Zeus dominating the stage while the people in Argos* are engaged in their yearly orgy of morbid guilt. Sartre's Orestes, a youth of seventeen who comes on the stage with his friend Pylos, is so far a copy of Aeschylus' drama.

But from here on Sartre puts his own interpretation on the ancient myth. He has Orestes engage in an argument with Zeus, who had been till that time in the play a bronze statue at the back of the stage. Zeus now steps down from his pedestal and tries to persuade the youth not to go ahead with his planned matricide, which will cure Argos of its guilt-infested doldrums. Zeus stands for the power of the Nazis, the generals who might be marching past the theater at that very moment. How do you stand against authoritarian orders when you are a conquered people under the heel of the Nazis in 1944?

Zeus cries out in the drama that he created Orestes and all other human beings, and therefore Orestes has to obey his orders. Orestes' resounding answer to Zeus must have invigorated the French audience, "But you blundered—you made me free!"

Angry, Zeus causes the stars and planets to whirl through the skies to exhibit his great power in the creation of the heavens. Then he challenges the youth, "Do you realize what despair lies in wait for you if you follow the path you are on?"

Orestes answers with a sentence which inspires us with some of the power it had in Paris in 1944, *"Human life begins on the far side of despair!"*

The universe may not be just or rational in Sartre's view, but men and women can affirm the freedom of human beings in the face of tyrants. "Orestes is the Resistance hero," as Hazel Barnes puts it, "who will work for freedom without remorse even though he must commit acts which will inevitably bring death to some of his people."†

---

*For these purposes, the ancient cities of Argos and Mycenae are synonymous.
†Barnes, *The Key Reporter* 41, no. 4 (Summer 1986): 3.

DRAMAS EXPRESSING MYTHS

Great dramas, like *Hamlet* and *Macbeth,* speak to the hearts of
all of us. By the same token they remain in our memories as
myths, year in and year out, giving us an increasingly profound
appreciation of our humanness. Beckett's *Waiting for Godot* is
such a drama. It is a tender and profound myth which grips us
in its depths of contradiction; it possesses the same poignancy
as Nietzsche's parable, "God is dead." The characters of the
drama wait for a myth which says we are in the absence of the
gripping character of the drama.

This search for meaning in life, this quest in an age when
one waits forever for God, is suffused with tenderness in our
common perplexity at being human. When Estragon says to
Vladimir, "Well, shall we go?" and Vladimir answers, "Yes,
let's go," but the stage directions state, "They do not move."
This profound myth shows the depth of our human uncertainty; we live as in a sleepwalk. Norman Mailer wrote of this
drama that the doubt concerns the "moral . . . basis of Christianity which was lost with Christ." And the London *Times*
speaks of this drama as "suffused with tenderness for the whole
human perplexity . . . [with] stabs of beauty and pain."*

Though the myths of Orestes and Oedipus were written in
that brilliant burst of civilization in ancient Greece, there are
similarly powerful myths from the Hebrew tradition—Adam
and Eve awakening to consciousness, Jacob wrestling with the
angel, Isaiah and the Suffering Servant, ad infinitum. These
two sources of ancient myths, the Greek and the Hebrew, are
the "mother" and "father" of Western civilization, and we will
forever be indebted to them.

In his *Death of a Salesman,* Arthur Miller shows us again the
mythic drama and the playwright's concern for the issues of

---

*Beckett, *Waiting for Godot* (New York: Grove Press, 1954).

right and wrong. Miller asserts that the great bulk of contemporaneous theater on Broadway *trivializes* drama: it produces gross entertainment without confronting the great issues of life and death which cry out of the Greek dramas and Biblical tales. What I have called existential crises Miller describes as psychic situations:

What we take away from the Bible may seem like characters—Abraham and Isaac, Bathsheba and David—but really, they're psychic situations. That kind of storytelling was always fantastic to me. And it's the same thing with the Greeks. Look at Oedipus—we don't know much about him, apart from his situation, but his story bears in itself the deepest paradoxes in the most adept shorthand.*

Arthur Miller's *Death of a Salesman* presents a powerful myth for millions of Americans and for this reason is played time and again over television and on stages throughout America. At the end of the drama, after Willy's suicide, a little group stands around his grave. His widow reminds the lifeless Willy that the last payment on the house was to be made that day, and cries out, "Willy, why did you do it?"

But the older son sadly comments that Willy "never knew who he was." Charley the neighbor tries to reassure them:

Nobody dast blame this man. . . . Willy was a salesman. And for a salesman, there is no rock bottom to the life. He don't put a bolt to a nut, he don't tell you the law or give you medicine. He's a man way out there in the blue, riding on a smile and a shoeshine. And when they start not smiling back—that's an earthquake. . . . Nobody dast blame this man. A salesman is got to dream. . . . It comes with the territory.

BIFF: Charley, the man didn't know who he was.

HAPPY, *infuriated:* Don't say that! . . . I'm gonna show you and everybody else that Willy Loman did not die in vain. *He had a good dream. It's the only dream you can have—to come out number-one man.* He fought it out here, and this is where I'm gonna win it for him.

New York Times, May 8, 1984.

BIFF, *with a hopeless glance at Happy, bends toward his mother:* Let's go, Mom.

When they leave Linda stays behind a moment,

LINDA: I'll be with you in a minute. Go on, Charley. *He hesitates.* I want to, just for a minute. I never had a chance to say good-by. . . . Forgive me, dear. I can't cry. I don't know what it is, but I can't cry. I don't understand it. Why did you ever do that? I made the last payment on the house today. Today, dear. And there'll be nobody home. *A sob rises in her throat.* We're free and clear. *Sobbing more fully, released:* We're free.

Here we see a powerful presentation of a contemporary American myth, a myth which engulfs us all to some extent. For Miller is saying that we "don't know who we are," whether we are traveling salesmen, or selling our knowledge in universities, or selling new inventions, or selling junk bonds. We like to believe we have a "good dream . . . to come out number-one." This drama, coming chronologically between the myth of Horatio Alger and the myth of the investments and junk bond salesman, paints a picture via the stage of the myth of millions of us, all of us wondering at some level "who we are." As our question is mythic, so must our answer be mythic, which gives us some opportunity to feel that it will be a "good dream—to come out number-one."

The endeavor to find the myth of our identity is shown in the way we, like Willy, sell ourselves—our work, our ideas, our efforts, even as it involves, as with Willy, a shine on our shoes and a smile on our face. And we may find one way or another when our myths let us down, that "we never knew who we were." But if our drama is like Orestes, or Willy, or any other, we still to some extent are waiting for Godot; we find nonetheless that we have lived our years, for better or for worse. We are salesmen, in search of our personal myths. Arthur Miller's myth takes us all in and is a myth of the workaday world in the great crowd of ourselves and our countrymen.

THREE

In Search of Our Roots

> What does our great historical hunger signify, our
> clutching about us of countless other cultures, our
> consuming desire for knowledge, if not the loss of myth, of
> a mythic home, the mythic womb?
>
> > Friedrich Nietzsche,
> > "The Birth of Tragedy
> > from the Spirit of Music"

S URELY NIETZSCHE IS RIGHT: our powerful hunger for myth
is a hunger for community. The person without a myth is a
person without a home, and one would indeed clutch for other
cultures to find some place at some time a *"mythic womb."* To
be a member of one's community is to share in its myths, to
feel the same pride that glows within us when we recall the
Pilgrims at Plymouth Rock, or Washington crossing the Dela-
ware, or Daniel Boone and Kit Carson riding into the West.
The outsider, the foreigner, the stranger is the one who does
not share our myths, the one who steers by different stars,
worships different gods.

At a World Series game sixty thousand people join in singing
the "bombs bursting in air," and "our flag was still there," the

flag which waves "o'er the land of the free and the home of the brave!" All these are part of the myths which make America a community. When the San Francisco 49ers won the football Super Bowl, there was such wild ecstasy in the city for two days and nights that a visitor from Mars would have thought the citizens had been engulfed by a mass psychosis. And the visitor would be right—it is a "normal psychosis." The 49ers were not born in San Francisco: the players are "bought" from all over the country and have no loyalty except to their own job. But they do carry the powerful myth of San Francisco, a city in which 750,000 people dwell and to which there is established a mythic loyalty. All these behaviors illustrate the myths which hold us all together. In his perceptive book, *American Myth/ American Reality,* the historian James Oliver Robertson specifically defines myth as "that which holds us all together."*

In Hannah Green's narration (see Chapter 1) we saw Deborah unable to participate in the common myths of her society, so she is forced to invent her own private community made up of such figures in the Kingdom of Yr as the Collect, Idat, Anterrabae, Lactamae. And we saw how effective Deborah's mythic community was, for she fell into a deep sleep, protected by these mythic creatures, which assuaged her loneliness even though she was isolated from the society around her.

In ancient Athens, Pericles proclaimed in his oration to the widows and children of the warriors who died in the Peloponnesian War, "These slain soldiers were proud to die for Athens." The same holds true for other cities and countries which do not share the greatness of Athens. The city in which we grew up still wears a halo in our memory because there, for good or evil, we were born, we went through the experiences of youth, we fell in love, we identified with the workaday world, and so on. This myth goes far back to the time when we did owe our lives to the city behind whose walls, say of Mycenae or

*New York: Hill and Wang, 1980.

of Troy, there was a measure of peace and protection. In the medieval and ancient walled cities, one's myths went as far as the wall but no farther.

Indeed, in one influential school of psychoanalysis, the William Alanson White Institute, such famous psychoanalysts as Harry Stack Sullivan, Erich Fromm, and Frieda Fromm-Reichmann held that psychological problems have their sources in people's relation to the psychologically significant persons in their culture. Thus the myths which come up in therapy are crucially linked with home and culture.

THE PASSION TO FIND
OUR HOME

One member of our mainly mythless century, Alex Haley, set out to find his own myth and reported his search in his book, *Roots.* Whether consciously or unconsciously, Haley took Nietzsche's advice literally, "man stripped of myth . . . must dig frantically for roots, be it among the most remote antiquities." In the spiritual maelstrom of slavery, with its unimaginably humiliating injustices, two of which were forced breeding and requiring slaves to take the names of their owners, the psychological identity of the slaves was routinely crushed. In the Old Testament the cruelest punishment Yahweh could wield against human beings was to "blot out their names from the book of the living," like the communist countries where history was rewritten to make it say certain individuals never existed and create the phenomenon of the nonperson. This robbing a person of identity, this destruction of his or her myth, is a spiritual punishment which threatened the human character of the slaves, even though their humanity persisted under the most brutal conditions, as in their folk songs.

In his yearning to find his own roots, Alex Haley writes, "I had to find out who I was. . . . *I needed to find meaning in my life.* "* All Haley knew was that his ancestor in Africa, Kunta Kinte, then a stripling, went down to the river to make a drum. The boy was ambushed, knocked unconscious, and, when he came to, herded with other blacks like cattle onto a ship by slave-runners to be sold on the block in cities of the American South. How can one believe he is human if he has no roots? As Haley looked back, the refrain kept running through his mind, I-must-find-out-who-I-am!

It is fascinating to see that these are almost exactly the words of Oedipus in *Oedipus Rex* written twenty-three hundred years ago, *"I must find out who I am and where I came from."* In both figures, Haley and Oedipus, having a myth of their past was crucial to having a present identity and, if the truth were known, crucial to having a future as well.

How does one explain the fact that more American people turned their television sets on to see this drama of *Roots* than any other program in history? Is not the reason that *in America so many of us are rootless?* The ancestors of most of us, for example, came as immigrants in the nineteenth century to escape starvation in the potato famine in Ireland, or the foreclosure of mortgages in Sweden, or the pogroms of Eastern Europe. They courageously chose to leave their myths behind. Congratulating themselves on being free and without roots, these Americans nevertheless suffered an endemic feeling of loneliness, a prodding of restlessness which de Tocqueville mentions time and again as he points out that this causes us to move from city to city following a wanderlust that imprisons our souls. Our clinging to cults and our narcotic passion to make money is a flight from our anxiety, which comes in part from our mythlessness.

---

*Italics mine. The carryover of the theme is shown toward the end of the book: "Grandma would get on that subject sometimes . . . and Mama would abruptly snap . . . 'Oh Maw, I *wish* you'd stop all that old-time slavery stuff.' . . . Grandma would snap right back, 'If *you* don't care who and where you come from, well, *I* does!' " *Roots* (New York: Dell, 1980), p. 704.

On the ship, Alex Haley chose to sleep each night in the hold of the boat to relive as closely as possible what his distant ancestor had been forced to do. Suddenly in his imagination the whole story "broke," as such creative ideas do, and he knew how he would present the book. The myth came to life. Later he held in his hands the bill of sale transferring the slave, Kunta Kinte, from one master to another, and he could only stare at it and mutter, "My God!"

This book and the television program it fathered, this example of the search for one's myth, set loose an active movement, even if short-lived, among all sorts of people in America to find their own special roots. Children of immigrants from Holland and Poland and all of Europe, in trips to the lands that had once been the homeland of their ancestors, pored over death certificates and the engraving—hoary, weather-beaten, and mostly illegible—on gravestones in foreign cemeteries. All of this was in the hope, sometimes rewarded and sometimes not, of finding some roots, "be it among the most remote antiquities," as Nietzsche asserts. In Haley's case, it is the poignancy of the ancestors, such as Kunta Kinte, which makes its core something to cherish and to love no matter how painful the process of discovery. Typical for a myth, cruel facts are welded together with beneficent facts into a pattern which we can cherish and call our own. We could define psychoanalysis as the search for one's own myth. How healing is such a myth to the person who can find and live with it!

This myth of our past, this source, is a point of reference which we can revere. Unlike the Flying Dutchman, the mythic ship which could never take refuge in a port, we have found our past; and this itself is a guarantee of some port in a possible future.

MYTHS AS CELEBRATIONS

"Life in the myth is a celebration," wrote Thomas Mann. The myths of community are generally happy, joyful myths which enliven us; they mark the holidays, or holy days. We salute each other with *"Merry* Christmas," or *"Happy* New Year." The holy days which draw us together in carnivals, such as Mardi Gras in New Orleans and in Mediterranean and South American cities preceding Lent, are times of overflowing color and mythic mystery. Then it is permissible to love everyone and to abandon oneself to the spontaneity of the senses. Good Friday and Easter are the celebration of the eternally amazing myth of the crucifixion of Jesus and the resurrection of the Christ, Passover as the original Last Supper, all blended with the celebration of the newborn beauty in the blooming of lilies, the tender time of newly grown grass and plants and other loveliness which breaks through the crust of the earth in spring.

These holy days gather around them through the ages the mythic character of eternity. We get from them a sense of union with the distant past and the far off future. Christmas—literally, a mass for Christ—has become blended with the myth of the Germanic and Nordic tribes of Northern Europe, and hence we have such symbols as the Christmas tree with all its glitter and with the presents emblazoned around it. The gradual process of accretion, of absorption and merging of local myths with the myths from the religious past, gives the holy day this aura of eternity. The myth of Christmas is a prototype of the birth of the hero, as Otto Rank writes, describing the baby Jesus in the crib in a stable with the Wise Men following the star in the east and bringing gifts. The myth implies that we are wise if we too participate in the spirit of giving.

Rituals are physical expressions of the myths, as in holidays and the sacraments of religion. The myth is the narration, and the ritual—such as giving presents or being baptized—expresses the myth in bodily action. Rituals and myths supply fixed points in a world of bewildering change and disappointment.* The myth may be prior to the ritual, as it is in the celebration of Holy Communion; or the ritual may come first, as with the Super Bowl triumph of the 49ers. Either way, one gives birth to the other. No self can exist as a self apart from a society with its myths, whether that society is a concrete reality or a subjective construct like Deborah's Kingdom of Yr.†

In Europe the community's myth is symbolically emblazoned by the churches in the towns and cities. High over the collection of houses, which are built close together for protection, there rises the Cathedral of Chartres or the great spires of Cologne, bolstered from outside by flying buttresses and informed inside by mythic Bible stories. These Biblical myths led the person gazing upon them to the adoration of the Most High God and other Christian myths which everyone in the village knew by heart. The church was there for all to see, the custodian of the heart and spirit of the community, the central symbol around which its myths were woven. In the villages of New England there is a similar overarching symbol of the myth of the community. When driving through Vermont or New Hampshire, one comes to the center of the village and sees the "common ground," a large square of green grass with the village church towering at one end as though its simple beauty in Puritan white gives an eternal blessing to the town.

Hence for the citizens of the city-state, exile was a powerful threat in ancient and medieval days. One had to surrender his

---

*Clyde Kluckhohn, "Myths and Rituals: A General Theory," *Harvard Theological Review* 35 (January 1942): 45–79. Kluckhohn goes on to say, "Myths, likewise, give men 'something to hold to.' The Christian can better face the seemingly capricious reverses of his plans when he hears the joyous words 'lift up your hearts' " (New York: Norton, 1975, pp. 77–79).

†See my *Meaning of Anxiety* (New York: Norton, 1975, pp. 77–79) for a description of "voodoo death" in primitive tribes. When the whole community believes the victim of voodoo will die, the man lies down and, in two or three hours, expires. He has been "cut dead" by his community, as William James explained it, and by this power exerted on him, he himself believes he will die. It is an illustration of the function of the myth held by the community to take over the mind and will of the victim.

mythic center when he was exiled from his city, where he was immersed in the language and the ethics which were the veins and arteries of myths and hence the society. Exile generally destroyed the psychic life of the person exiled; he was broken literally by being without a country. But exile might in rare cases force the exiled person into a greater surge of creativity, a sublimation one could call it, as it did with Dante and Machiavelli. Dante was forced by his exile from Florence to re-experience his myths in solitude, out of which there came his magnificent poem, *The Divine Comedy.* And without Machiavelli's exile, *The Prince* may never have been written.

The presence of constructive myths is a product of the cultivation in citizens of the need for compassion, especially for the stranger. It was a great step in the ancient history of the Israelites when, in their Book of Leviticus, they placed the law, "Thou shalt judge the stranger [read: person of different myths] by the same laws as thou judgest the children of Israel."

The presence of a home, a place where one is listened to, where one can feel "at home," is essential to healthy myth. Many of our patients in therapy find that their neurotic problems are related to their never having had a home where they were listened to. Ronald Laing tells of his session with a little five-year-old girl who never talked. Brought to his office by her parents, she came into the inner consulting room and sat down on the floor like a "miniature Buddha," so Dr. Laing described her. He sat down opposite her in the same way. She moved her hands this way and that, and Laing followed, moving his hands in the same way. The whole hour passed without a word being uttered but with their merely going silently through this tiny replica of a tribal dance. At the end of the hour they got up and the little girl left. But she then began talking with her parents. He learned later that the parents had asked her what had happened in that room, and she had retorted, "None of your business."*

*Personal communication from Dr. Laing.

Children who do not talk may be showing, like the above child, that the milieu into which they are born is hostile, cold, inhospitable. One response to this is not to become part of it by refusing to talk. Others suck their thumbs for interminable periods or in other ways show they have to have something to be close to, if not a home at least a pet or a doll which carries some mythic meaning.

Such is the necessity of having a community, a home where we can feel we belong, a family where we will be protected and in which we can feel some intimacy. Without a myth that makes a child part of a community, a home which gives warmth and protection, the child does not develop in true human fashion. As Dr. Rene Spitz demonstrated several decades ago, orphans who are never mothered tend to withdraw into silent corners of the crib, and ultimately some of them literally die from lack of love.

To have friends and a family you can call your own, whether in reality or fantasy, is not only a desideratum; it is a necessity for psychological and spiritual as well as physical survival. We all cry for a collective myth which gives us a fixed spot in an otherwise chaotic universe.

WHERE HAVE ALL OUR HEROES GONE?

The myth of the homeland is symbolized by the hero, upon whom are projected the highest aims of the community. Without the hero the community lacks a crucial dimension, for the hero is typically the soul of the community. Heroes are necessary in order to enable the citizens to find their own ideals, courage, and wisdom in the society. "Society has to contrive some way to allow its citizens to feel heroic," said Ernest Becker. "This is one of the great challenges of the twentieth century."* We hunger for heroes as role models, as standards of action, as ethics in flesh and bones like our own. *A hero is a myth in action.*

Through our projection we become more like our hero, as Hawthorne illustrates in his story, "The Great Stone Face." The main character in this tale lives in view of the mountain, the top rocks of which form a heroic face. It had been predicted that someday a noble man would arrive whose face would bear an undeniable likeness to the great stone face. Hawthorne's hero spends his life doing good for his fellow villagers, looking up at the great stone face and waiting for its likeness to come. When he is an old man, the people suddenly recognize that *his* face is the likeness of the great stone face on the mountain top.

The hero carries our aspirations, our ideals, our beliefs. In the deepest sense the hero is created by us; he or she is born collectively as our own myth. This is what makes heroism so important: it reflects our own sense of identity, and from this our own heroism is molded. When my book, *Paulus: Reminiscences of a Friendship,* was published, one reviewer attacked it on the grounds that I seemed to make a hero of Paul Tillich. This was dangerous in our twentieth century, continued the critic, because it left the way open for hero worship, as was shown in the followers of Adolf Hitler, who used heroism demonically. One can sympathize with this argument, since the heroism which was cultivated by Hitler surely led to the greatest acts of destruction in our world's history. But we must not throw the baby out with the bath water. Lacking heroes in the 1990s, we are unable to live out our myth of communal aims and ideals in society.

Time was when Charles Lindbergh was a hero to all America and to the literate world as well. In 1927 he embodied the

---

*Personal communication. Ernest Becker himself, after having written several excellent books, died a premature death from cancer. He was a hero himself to many readers.

simple but in those days great human courage that was required to fly his flimsy biplane across the Atlantic Ocean all alone. Lindbergh was welcomed by tens of thousands of cheering Parisians awaiting him at the Paris airport. This event proved that the America of the Jazz Age had a soul as well as saxophones. Lindbergh was welcomed in New York by a tumultuous tickertape parade without previous parallel. He took it all with his all-American shy smile, a young Midwesterner representing the quiet courage of the heartland of America. His plane—which hangs in the Air and Space Museum in Washington—was called the *Spirit of St. Louis,* but it represented the spirit of all of us, whether from Missouri or not. We emulated the hero, and a multitude of likewise shy men and women, young and old, felt the strengthening of their own self-esteem in their identification with Lindbergh. Amelia Earhart represented a similar phenomenon for women in her pioneering spirit and willingness to take risks. Lindbergh and Earhart were carriers of the lonely myth we all sought in our own hearts, to be centered in ourselves as heroic Americans, capable of setting and achieving our goals by our own self-assertion and courage. We all felt secretly that we had, or could aspire to have, the same kind and degree of courage which Lindbergh and Eleanor Roosevelt and a few others exhibited.*

One problem is that we have confused celebrities with heroes. The definition is still valid, "A celebrity is someone who is known for being known." From the Nielsen ratings on down, from the society pages to the shining advertisements we get in every mail begging us to accept ten million dollars from some gentleman's hands, there are "celebrities" with phony invitations. But rare indeed is the genuine hero.

Often in America we confuse heroism, following the move-

---

*The sad postlude to this heroic act was, of course, the kidnapping of the Lindbergh baby and Lindbergh's seeming to side with the Nazis in World War II. This illustrates that heroism does not reside in the flesh and blood of one person, but in a spiritual quality we confer upon him or her.

ment called yuppies, with the making of the most money. In a
lecture at the University of California at Berkeley, Ivan Boesky,
the billionaire Wall Street trader and role model of many yuppies during the 1980s, stated, "There is nothing wrong with
greed." The enthusiastic cheering of the audience filled the
hall, how much of it curiosity rather than hero worship it is
impossible to say. But at the very moment this book is being
written, Ivan Boesky is in prison serving time for illegal trading
on the stock market and for criminal activity on Wall Street.
He not only went to prison himself but implicated a number of
his colleagues along with him. One wonders what Boesky now
feels, as he looks out from prison, when he remembers his
statement about greed, "After making a successful deal you can
feel good about yourself!"

It is our fake heroes who give heroism such a bad name.
Oliver North apparently was considered a hero by President
Reagan and a number of his countrymen. North clearly broke
laws, the full extent of which is not yet known. Is it any wonder
that we have few heroes today?

Studies of students also reveal the collapse of heroism. Arthur Levine made such a study in *When Dreams and Heroes
Died,* and came to some sobering conclusions:

[This] information reveals, among other things, that students today
are overwhelmingly materialistic, cynical about society and its institu-
tions (including higher education)—and so competitive about grades
that they condone cheating. More significantly, their aspirations are
inward, personal, and individualistic rather than social or humanitar-
ian, reflecting the "me first" philosophy that has pervaded the nation
in the past decade.*

Our task, as part of the discovery of contemporary myths, is
to rediscover the fundamentals of heroism. It is refreshing to
find a college president stating, "I think students need heroes,
period. When I meet with students again and again and ask

*San Francisco: Jossey-Bass, 1980. This is a quotation from the summary by the
publishers.

who their heroes are, the question strikes them as being odd."*

Friedrich Nietzsche states our aim strongly:

That the Great Man should be able to appear and dwell among you again, again, and again, *that* is the sense of all your efforts here on earth. That there should ever and again be men among you able to elevate you to *your* heights: that is the prize for which you strive. For it is only through the occasional coming to light of such human beings that your own existence can be justified. . . . And if you are not yourself a great exception, well then be a small one at least! and so you will foster on earth that holy fire from which genius may arise.†

I am deeply troubled by the decline of the humanities in the United States, for it is there that students come into contact with the best of Western literature. A graduate professor of English literature in a western university states that in his class there are five students, while in the graduate classes of computer science across the hall there are three hundred. We seem to have forgotten Max Frisch's statement, "Technology is the knack of so arranging the world that we do not experience it." It is the *what* of human existence rather than the *how* for which we are famished. These cry out from our unread classics and the riches of history and the untouched literature of all centuries. But the cry for the study of myths is heard as a still small voice on many campuses. Martin Luther King, one of the few authentic twentieth-century heroes, dared to dream, and he risked life and limb in his consecration to bringing that dream into reality.

When I was in college, I recall a verse, though it is not deathless poetry, nevertheless was an inspiration to me as I walked across the campus many a night:

> Hold fast your dreams!
>
> Within your heart
> Keep a place apart

*James O. Freedman, quoted in the *New York Times,* August 23, 1987.
†Friedrich Nietzsche, *Werke* (Leipzig: Alfred Kröner, 1919), vol. 6, pp. 496–497.

Where dreams may go
And sheltered so
May thrive and grow
        Where doubt and
        Fear are not.

Hold fast,
Hold fast your dreams!

Whether one's hopes succeed or fail is not the hero's or
heroine's main concern. We emulate the hero, and a multitude
of women and men, old and young, modest and shy, feel a
triumph on their own pulse, a strengthening of their own self-
esteem, as they experience their identification with Martin Luther King, for example. Albert Schweitzer and Mother Teresa,
I suggest, are heroes to us as Mahatma Gandhi was a half
century ago. Although Mother Teresa will not succeed in re-
lieving the major part of Calcutta's suffering, and although
Schweitzer failed to reduce the plagues in Africa, these heroes
still glow like stars in our mythic firmament. For they give us
the greatest gift possible, an assurance that there are persons in
our universe with whose characteristics we hope to identify.

Our heroes carry our aspirations, our ideals, our hopes, our
beliefs, for they are made of our myths. In the profound sense
the hero is created by us as we identify with the deeds he or she
performs. The hero is thus born collectively as our own myth.
This is what makes heroism so important: it reflects our own
sense of identity, our combined emotions, our myths.

The rediscovery of heroism is central in the regaining of our
myths and the arising of new myths that will suffice to inspire
us to go beyond the cocaine, the heroin, the depressions, and
the suicides, through the inspiration of myths that lift us above
a purely mundane existence. George Eliot, in the nineteenth
century, imaged her picture of heroes, the "choir invisible,"
inspiring future generations:

Oh, may I join the choir invisible
Of those immortal dead who live again

In minds made better by their presence; live
In pulses stirred to generosity,
In deeds of daring rectitude, in scorn
For miserable aims that end with self,
In thoughts sublime that pierce the night
                              like stars,
And with their mild persistence urge men's
                              search
To vaster issues.
               So to live is heaven:
To make undying music in the world. . . .*

MYTHS AND MORALS:
MURDER IN CENTRAL PARK

The barrenness of our culture with respect to ethical values rests upon our barrenness of myths, which means many of us have no faith to live by. Since myths are passed on chiefly by the family, and since this is where we get our first acquaintance with the myths of our society, it behooves us to examine carefully the strangling in Central Park of eighteen-year-old Jennifer Dawn Levin in the summer of 1986 by nineteen-year-old Robert Chambers, Jr.†

Both of these young people were from affluent families, both had attended superior preparatory schools and had access to the vast culture of New York City. Both came from homes which had been split by divorce, and both had been given everything except what really matters, a dependable family life. Neither Jennifer nor Robert had strong parental ties. Neither had the socializing effect of religion or the ethical bonds that lend mythic power to human resolutions. The night of the

*Eliot, "The Choir Invisible," in *One Hundred and One Famous Poems* (Chicago: Cable, 1926), p. 137.
†The quotations concerning this murder are taken from the *New York Times*, September 11, 1986.

murder they had come from their group in a bar. They were sexually free and apparently jaded; they had walked in Central Park to make love. He claimed she tried to bite off his penis and he then strangled her with her own brassiere.

Joan Farrell, a private investigator in Manhattan whose daughter graduated from the same school as Robert and Jennifer, stated with reference to this crime,

I blame the parents more than the bar owners for the attitudes of these kids. . . . A lot of these kids are given a great deal without being taught to respect it. . . . It's very easy to just hand them twenty dollars and say have a good week-end. I think that's the biggest downfall of the generation that came up with my daughter.

Dr. Roy Grinker, a Chicago psychiatrist, said in connection with the murder, "Money isn't the root of all evil, but it is the root of a parent's ability not to be available to their children— physically or psychologically." Commenting also on this strange killing, Dr. Bernice Berg, a psychologist at Bank School in Manhattan, said,

When parents spend 90 percent of their time making more money than they could possibly spend and 5 percent of their time with the family, these values are passed on to the kids. It tells them families are not important. Making money, having money, and spending money is.

The owner of the bar which these two had frequented and had left together that evening of the killing tells of the great need of these young people and their friends for hugging, touching, and just being around someone who cared for them and showed it.

These two young people were, in a mythic sense, homeless. "Myth safeguards and enforces morality," as Malinowski proclaimed, and if there are no myths there will be no morality. Robert and Jennifer had no pattern of myths and ethics even to rebel against. They were homeless obviously not in a physical or financial sense but rather psychologically and spiritually. *It is a truism to state that they grew up in a mythic vacuum and therefore in an ethical rootlessness.* When Robert Chambers reenacted the murder scene, there was a profound pathos in his repetition of the phrase, "I wanted to go home, I wanted to go home." But he had no home in a mythic sense. Among the "explanations" of this murder can be heard a shrill protest against the mythlessness and spiritual barrenness, indeed the *homelessness,* in our society.*

In *Love and Will*† I pointed out that behind will lies wish. This does not mean that whatever one wishes will then become the goal of one's resolution, but it does mean that the deeper levels of human motivation must include wishing, whether one calls it yearning, longing, passionate desiring, or something else. Otherwise the willing is merely applied from the outside and is never transformed into action. We must have a conviction before an act of will can be effective. "Wish" is part of the area in human consciousness which includes hoping, yearning, imagination, believing—all of which have to do with the innate dimension of feelings that give birth to motivation. This is expressed in the conviction which is required of all aspirants for membership in Alcoholics Anonymous, for example; they must *want* with their total being to break the habit.

Wishing, longing, yearning, myth making—all these activities of human consciousness are as central as they have ever been, and any teaching of resolutions or guiding rules that does not include these activities is doomed to failure. *Wishing and hoping come directly out of the functions of dreaming and making myths.* "In dreams begin responsibilities,"** as the poet Delmore Schwartz so rightly reminded us, and we could say

*Our section on the myth of Horatio Alger in Chapter 7 also discusses the relation between myths and morals in our day.

†New York: Norton, 1969.

**Delmore Schwartz, *In Dreams Begin Responsibility and Other Stories* (New York: New Directions, 1978).

with even more cogency, if less poetically, in myths begin ethics and aspirations. It was a wise person who stated, "I don't care who makes a society's laws as long as I can make their myths."

FOUR

Myth and Memory

Hardly had I finished the manuscript when it struck me
what it means to live with a myth, and what it means to
live without one. . . . [The] man who thinks he can live
without myth, or outside it, like one uprooted, has no true
link either with the past, or with the ancestral life which
continues within him, or yet with contemporary human
society. This plaything of his reason never grips his vitals.

C. G. Jung

ADRIENNE, A WOMAN in her late twenties, stated a number
of times in the early sessions of therapy that she clung to
the idea of suicide. She continually thought of jumping into
the river or stepping in front of a truck. When I reminded her
that if she really wanted to do one of those things she obviously
could, she dropped that tack. But she continued with her manner of coming into each session upset by everything, repeating
almost each time, "I am in the worst crisis I've ever been in!"

The phrase "I can't" came up dozens of times in each session; almost always when I offered some interpretation, she
would greet it with an irritated "No." She seemed to live off
anger. I silently mused that she probably had been able to get

away with this behavior in her life so far because she was a strikingly beautiful woman. Her neurotic pattern was obviously breaking down. But how to find a niche where we might get at it?

In an early session, she began by saying, "I don't know whether this hour will be therapy or not. I'm in a state of shock." She cried a little and then continued in a whining voice that her man friend had taken a lease on an apartment in which there was not enough room for her. He had rejected her and she was devastated. Then she said, "You have to say something. . . . Somebody has to drop a bomb."

I agreed. I asked whether she was aware of the tone of voice in which she was saying these things? "No." And did she recall that she had said the previous session that she had had enough of this man and was considering throwing him out? "No." I also pointed out that she went through every session with the same story, only different characters. I wondered why she came for therapy at all; was it merely to find a wailing wall?

This cleared the air, but we were still unable to get anyplace therapeutically. Then I asked her to tell me her earliest childhood memories. She gave two. The first was of her grandfather who was sick and dying; he vomited up yellow stuff. "I was filled with the awareness that I was powerless to do anything about it."

The second was relevant to our immediate point here:

I was playing baby with my mother. I would play a hurt baby and she would comfort me, diaper me, and so on. Part of the game was that each time she did something, I was to say, "No, that doesn't help."—I liked to play this.

It was certainly clear that she liked to play this game for she had spent her life playing it and was now doing so with me. The first "memory" fits in a subsidiary way: she was helpless to do anything about her grandfather, which suggests that she saw herself going through life helplessly, unable to affect the people around her.

But the second was more pertinent: "I am the hurt baby, and *I must demonstrate that no one can help me.*" That pattern was the myth which had guided her behavior during her whole life up till now and was an excellent opening for her therapy. When I pointed this out, she at last got her feet on the ground, and we were able to tackle her therapy with some promise of success.

As we see in this passive, angry woman who plays the endless game of proving that the world cannot help her, the myths of a given person can often be discerned with a particular clarity in such earliest childhood memories. It is not that the particular memory actually *happened*—we can never know whether it did or not, and furthermore it does not matter in the slightest whether it is a real event or a phantasied* one. The patient herself generally cannot be certain whether it actually occurred or was a dream or a phantasy. This is the same problem that Freud faced when he developed his theories of infant sexuality on the basis of the "memories" his Victorian women revealed to him about having been raped by their fathers. At first Freud accepted these revelations as factual, only to be chagrined when he began to suspect that many of them were myths and not empirical happenings. But the stories were equally significant as myths of a child dominated by an arrogant, Victorian father who expected the child to meet his every desire. The narration is of real importance as a myth, and from our point of view this creation of the myth around an event—real or imagined—is the significant issue.†

---

*I spell the term "fantasy" when the subject refers to a conscious event, "phantasy" when it is an unconscious event.

†I am aware of the various interpretations of this issue, but do not wish to go into them here.

MEMORY NEEDS MYTH

Memory depends mainly upon myth. Some event occurs in our minds, in actuality or in fantasy; we form it in memory, molding it like clay day after day—and soon we have made out of that event a myth. We then keep the myth in memory as a guide to future similar situations. The myth does not tell us much about the possessive patient's literal history, but it does tell us a great deal about the person who does the remembering. For the person re-forms the event, shapes it, adds color here and a few details there; and then we have a revelation of this person and his or her attitude toward life. As Sartre would say, "The myth is a behavior of transcendence."

The myth is formed by the child's endeavor to make sense of strange experiences. The myth organizes experience, putting this and that together and brooding about the result. In the creative processes of memory and the need of the human mind for unity, the myth is born and nurtured. The formation of the myth is a relief, great or small, for the child. Often the myth is the only thing the child's mind can hang on to, and whether it is painful or not, it will be less painful than the actual historical event. Myths have a soothing effect, even though—or we may say *especially* though—they may be about cruel things. The poet Susan Musgrave wrote,

> You are locked
> in a life
> you have chosen
> to remember.*

The choice is generally unconscious, but it is nonetheless effective.

---

*Quoted by Elizabeth Simpson, in *Nothingness: Journal of Humanistic Psychology* 19, no. 3 (Summer 1979).

What the person remembers from his or her childhood, for example, from the second or third year, is at the most one or two events, and he forgets the thousand and one other things that happened to him during those years. The infant is fed three meals a day, is put to bed 365 times a year, but he forgets all these other things and remembers only this one. Thus the remembering has nothing whatever to do with the frequency of the event—indeed, we are most apt to forget the things we do most frequently, like getting up in the morning. The memory must possess some special significance, some important meaning for the little girl or boy.

In our example above, Adrienne's memory dwells upon two events. Time adds its color, and the myth is then empowered by the "unhappy childhood" motif. Soon she has the "memory" in the form of a myth which she relates twenty-five years later to me, her therapist. Adrienne lived by the secondary myth of her grandfather's death ("I am powerless to do anything about problems in life"), but her primary myth is her satisfaction in not letting the world help her. Thus the game she played with mother she continues playing all her life: *"I am terribly needy and the world is powerless to do anything for me."*

At some point the myth has become subconscious: then it becomes, "What a satisfying sense of power I get out of demonstrating that the world cannot do anything to help me, in fact I will arrange my life so no one *can* help me!" She learns to get pleasure out of telling other people, in this case her therapist, "No, that doesn't help." This denial of her own power gave her, paradoxically, a real sense of power over her environment and her world, even though it was objectively destructive.

Memory is a strange phenomenon, and it is even more strange when we consider its relation to myth. Students are generally taught in psychology classes in American colleges and universities that memory is a kind of file on the model of the computer, a bank in which we record our day-to-day experiences. Then we file away our memories to be called forth when we need them. In college we are taught that the "laws" of memory are *recency, vividness,* and *frequency.* * That is, we are supposed to recall something from memory to the extent that it had happened frequently and vividly and had occurred recently.

Nothing could be farther from the truth. All these tests in psychology classes are for remembering *nonsense* syllables— you have a good memory if you could remember by rote what nonsense the teacher has written on the board. The bookworm, the intellectual robot, obviously finds these "laws" made to order. But creative students are often offended by such tests because they know (or at least suspect) that the whole project is just what it is called, namely, nonsense.

How absurd is that approach to memory! What a misconception that the human memory has nothing to do with the *significance* or with the *meaning* of the remembered event for the person. Ernest Schachtel proclaimed in his classic essay, in his book *On Memory and Childhood Amnesia,* "Memory is never impersonal [e.g. never 'nonsense'], but operates on the basis of the significance for the given person."

ADLER AND EARLY MEMORIES

Alfred Adler was the first among the early leaders in psychotherapy to see the significance of early childhood memories. A perceptive and humble man, he was gifted with unusual sensitivity for children. One of the early bellwethers in psychother-

---

*Ernest Schachtel, *Metamorphosis* (New York: Basic Books, 1959), p. 309. The above mechanical view of memory led Oscar Wilde to make his satirical remark, "The great enemy of creativity is a good memory." Yes, indeed—when memory works on the basis of nonsense syllables. But this obviously is not genuine creativity. Wilde is referring to the person who reflects back to the professor his exact syllable; the student who strains to recall the assignment as literally as possible; the idiot savant; the antiquarian who omits whatever is original, new, fresh—and delightful. Such students may get high grades but they are never inspired, never catch fire with a new idea.

apy, he influenced Harry Stack Sullivan through Adolph Meyer, who had translated one of Adler's first books and was Sullivan's teacher in psychiatry. An associate of Freud in the early decades of this century, in 1913 Adler broke off to start his own school, in which he made the social aspect of myths his central concern. He believed that the cause of neurosis is the lack of "social interest," i.e., neurotics are persons who are isolated from their fellow human beings. Psychological problems are not solved until the patient develops an adequate concern with society, an acceptance of his responsibility toward the community. Thus Adler radically opposed the gospel of exclusive self-love; he preferred to speak of self-esteem or integrity, or, to use his special term, "social interest." He was radically opposed also to the kind of therapy which overemphasized independence and egocentricity. He would have been as critical of the "all-for-me," narcissistic view of the self as Bellah* or MacIntyre.† Perhaps the reason he has been so often overlooked in the evolution of therapy in America is that he does not fit our intoxication with narcissism and the ego-centered self. Adler was an active socialist, and like Wilhelm Reich and unlike Freud, he was heart and soul concerned with politics.

Out of his great skill in treating children, Adler developed his central concern with the "guiding fiction," which is a synonym for "myth." It refers to a significant event in one's early childhood that the person remembers; the event is turned into a myth which the person keeps as a guide for one's way of life, whether it is fictitious or not. *The person refers to this guiding fiction down through the subsequent years as the secret myth of oneself.* One knows oneself through this myth, as Charles knew himself as "Satan," or the actress knew herself as Athena

*Robert N. Bellah et al., *Habits of the Heart* (Berkeley: University of California Press, 1985).

†Alasdair MacIntyre, *After Virtue: A Study in Moral Therapy* (Notre Dame: University of Notre Dame Press, 1981).

(see Chapter 2). Thus Adler always asked the client in the second or third session in therapy, "What is your earliest childhood memory?" He believed that there "can be no accidental or indifferent memories, and the process of memory cannot be compared in any way to a photographic record."*

Looking into literature—the written home of memory—we find some exciting poets describing the function of this capacity. "This is the use of memory," said T. S. Eliot toward the ending of "Little Gidding,"

> For liberation—not less of love but expanding,
> Of love beyond desire . . . and so liberation
> From the future as well as the past.†

Memory can liberate us from attachment, from desire or attachment to the wrong things. Memory is our internal studio, where we let our imaginations roam, where we get our new and sometimes splendid ideas, where we see a glorious future that makes us tremble. Memory and myth are inseparable, a point I have never heard in any psychology courses. Memory can, according to Dante, form the past into any myth, any story, any hope (see Chapter 9). Dante believed that memory can lead us to God via myth.

Memory is the mother of creativity. This is a myth worth pondering. For it is in memory that one saves and savors the significant experiences, the dazzling sights, the critical events. In memory these precious experiences form themselves together into a myth which tells us a story. We say we "sleep on an idea," and when we wake up we may feel we have arrived at a new insight, as though it were a gift from the gods. And who

---

*Lewis Way, *Adler's Place in Psychology* (London: Macmillan, 1950), p. 73.
†Stephen Sicari, "Dante's Wake: T. S. Eliot's 'Art of Memory,'" *Cross Currents* (Winter 1988–89).

is to say it is not? Mnemosyne, or "Memory," is the goddess who puts together our materials with which new discoveries are made and poems are written and great books and enduring paintings are inspired.

FIVE

Freud and the Mystery of Myths

The theory of the instincts is so to say our mythology.
Instincts are mythical entities, magnificent in their
indefiniteness. In our work we cannot for a moment
disregard them, yet we are never sure that we are seeing
them clearly.

Sigmund Freud,
letter to Fleiss, 1897

THE ABOVE STATEMENT is remarkable indeed. First, Freud
frankly and specifically admits the mythic base of his theories in psychoanalysis. And the phrase, "magnificent in their
indefiniteness," is doubly remarkable since it suggests that in
their very lack of definiteness lies the value of myths. Their
magnificence keeps myths open, growing, productive of new
insights, which the observer would never have had if he were
limited to empirical statements. This is what makes myths inspiring, for their drama perpetually suggests surprising interpretations, new mysteries, novel possibilities. The very things
for which rationalists have criticized myths turn out to be their
greatest advantage. The Oedipus myth, for example, is forever
suggesting new interpretations of the meaning of this triangu-

lar father-mother-child form and, as in *Oedipus in Colonus*, new interpretations of responsibility. The contemporary concern with sexual exploitation of children by parents in families is yet another interpretation of the Oedipus myth.

Freud's next statement—"we cannot for a moment disregard them"—is likewise the statement of a true scientist. We must keep contradictory assumptions in mind, as Alfred North Whitehead stated, without permitting damage to either conclusion until we know differently. Life consists of living in contradictions; and the person who forgets that is doomed to live in a make-believe world. Living in contradiction takes courage, but it is thrilling at the same moment. The final clause, "yet we are never sure that we are seeing them clearly," is a revelation of Freud's honesty and will be understood by every therapist who has experienced the many meanings of a myth. "Myth is the garment of mystery," writes Thomas Mann in his epic book, *Joseph and His Brothers.* *

OEDIPUS—
MYTH OF SELF-DISCOVERY

Freud wrote to Ferenczi about his "unsparing effort to understand himself"; his own self-analysis, he stated, was "harder than any other." He adds, very much like the original Oedipus, "But it will have to be carried through!"† Jones tells us that Freud's self-analysis gave him a flood of light on all human destiny. It was the adumbration on a great theme, so great that it can be considered the simplest of all things, the triangular situation of mother-father-child.

Freud elsewhere stated significantly, "The myth, then, is the step by which the individual emerges from group psychology."

*Mann, *Joseph and His Brothers* (New York: Knopf, 1935), p. 33.
†Ernest Jones, *The Life and Work of Sigmund Freud* (New York: Basic Books, 1953), p. 325.

That is to say, we owe the emergence of our self-consciousness to our capacity to think in terms of myth. We may speak of paradigm, or hypothesis, or some other such concept; but these equal some kind of mythology, as Freud well says. Far from being a handicap, myth is essential for progress in our understanding of science and of culture. Freud discovered that when we get to the basic level of the human mind, we are surprised to find myths.

It is important to note that these discoveries were made by Freud in 1897, several years before his great book, *The Interpretation of Dreams,* was published. Freud is thus to be seen as a central cultural figure, in the line of Schopenhauer, Kierkegaard, and Nietzsche; and like these other great contributors, he had a profound influence on the radical changes taking place in the transition from the nineteenth to the twentieth century. Whatever one may think of the technique of psychoanalysis, Freud's importance as a cultural figure cannot be denied. He had the mind of an explorer and an archeologist, as shown also by his great collection of statues and artifacts from cultures of long ago. Surely one of the most influential and original thinkers of our time, he recognized the significance of the irrational dynamics and daimonic side of human nature. Like Nietzsche and Schopenhauer, he was emphatic in exposing the futility of the Victorian/Puritanical notion of willpower. He devoted himself to the chief problem of the transition from the nineteenth to twentieth century—how to live in an age of repression.

Freud's experience in discovering myths is shown in a catastrophic experience in his own self-analysis. He had originally believed that the seduction and rape stories his patients told him were true in fact. But it dawned on him when "memories had come back of sexual wishes about his mother on the occasion of seeing her naked," writes Jones,

and his awareness that his father was innocent and that he had projected on his father rivalry of the Oedipal kind which he later came to see was not true in fact. Hence the breakdown of this theory of parental seduction was part of the dawning of the truth of the Oedipus complex. His own personal phantasies forced him to this new conclusion. It was then that he wrote to Fliess, in 1897, to give him "the fateful news" that the seduction stories he had believed in were not literally true.*

The merging of all these elements tells us again about how memory is related to myth. The drama of father and mother and child is kept alive in a self-generating way, not just a memory of a factual phenomenon but as a dynamic, growing, active drama. The myth is always being reinterpreted, growing, changing, even adding to itself. Then when memories do come alive, they are more than memories; they have assumed the character of myth. Indeed, the cruelty of Laius in putting the infant Oedipus out to die, Jocasta hanging herself, Oedipus wrenching the secrets from old Tiresias and then gouging out his own eyes—all are part of this great myth. In this sense psychoanalysis is a reflection of the basic interpersonal patterns which have been present since the dawn of human history.

That triangular form of the perdurable relationship, hung with a thousand different shades and colors, is the ladder the child must climb as he or she grows in the world. To us it is tremendously interesting that Freud regretted this conclusion forced upon him; he regarded it as a radical loss. "In the collapse of all values only the psychological theory has remained unimpaired,"† he wrote to Fliess. He then turned to the writing of his first and most influential book, *The Interpretation of Dreams*. His new psychology and his new understanding of mythic truth were the essential bases of this work.

By employing the language of myth, Freud, like Einstein, creates a symbolic structure—a comprehensive psychological equation—

*Ibid., I: 325, 326.
†Ibid., p. 356.

which opens up the possibilities of further scientific knowledge and avoids any suggestion that he is setting down eternal truth.*

Feder adds these comforting words: "If we live in this paradox, we can enjoy our existence on this planet."†

Freud came to the conclusion that myths show a "conscious ignorance and an unconscious wisdom." Those who believe our modern culture has gone "beyond myth" had best ask themselves: Are we not showing precisely this "conscious ignorance and an unconscious wisdom"?

MYTHS OF LOVE AND DEATH

Most impressive of all in Freud's mythology is his description of the eternal conflict between Eros, the myth of love, and Thanatos, the myth of death. The former draws people together, leads to friendship, interdependence, and all the constructive aspects which make for unity with our fellow men and women. The fact that we can live with some joy and pleasure, some sense of intimacy with our fellows, is an expression of the myth of Eros, as Freud put it. This is the positive, the up-building, the warmth of life—which we will see cropping up in many ways, like the cultural creativity of Faust in Goethe's last section, and in the experiences of Peer Gynt as he struggles over oceans and mountains till he at last comes to terms with his love for Solveig. Freud uses Eros as a catchall for the powers in us to rise to a struggle the likes of which are not found as the product of any other force. Out of this conflict of Eros against Thanatos comes the civilizing force which seeks to tame the primitive destructive tendencies of the human creature.

This struggle of Eros, we have said, takes place against its antagonist Thanatos, the myth of death. Just as there are many gradations of Eros, so Thanatos includes many phases, includ-

*Feder, *Ancient Myth in Modern Poetry,* p. 44.
†Ibid., p. 46.

ing illness, fatigue, and all of what Paul Tillich called non-being. The forces that tear us apart, the dread of finitude, all that which fights against Eros, is included in the myth of Thanatos. This conflict between love and death, said Freud, is the "battle of the giants which nursemaids try to appease with their lullaby about heaven."*

Out of this continuous struggle civilization is wrought. Works of art are produced, great poetry is written, ideas spring up, all from the conflict of Eros and Thanatos. There is no creativity without this struggle. Eros by itself would be insipid, childish, uninteresting, indeed, as irrelevant as the little boy "Cupid" as he appears in so many paintings of the Italian Renaissance.

The great things in civilizations come from Eros struggling against Thanatos. Thanatos without Eros would be an emptiness beyond even cruelty. But as these two great forces struggle against each other, we see the paradox of normal life; we see, for an example which contains both myths, the beauty and the magnificence of cathedrals at the same time as their gargoyles mock the human viewers down below.

Freud's positing of the war between Eros and Thanatos was stark, dramatic, tragic. . . . Human beings are caught in the endless conflict between these two poles. The eternal warfare within us creates the sense of guilt which continually torments us: it is the price we pay for civilization, which results only when man's deepest aggressive instincts are curbed.†

---

*Lillian Feder, to whom I owe the above quotation, understandably writes, "Freud is never so heroic, never so admirable, than when he is, in his mind, creating the myths." Ibid.
†Ibid.

THE TRAGEDY OF
TRUTH ABOUT ONESELF

When we read the actual drama of Oedipus, as it came to Freud and comes to us from the pen of Sophocles, we are surprised to see that the myth has nothing to do with conflicts about sexual desire or killing one's father as such. These are all done long in the past before the drama begins. Oedipus is a good king ("the mightiest head among us all," he is called) who has reigned wisely and strongly in Thebes and has been for a number of years happily married to Queen Jocasta. The only issue in the drama is whether he will recognize and admit what he has done. The tragic issue is that of seeking the truth about oneself; it is the tragic drama of a person's passionate relation to truth. *Oedipus' tragic flaw is his wrath against his own reality.* *

Thebes is suffering under another plague as the curtain rises

*When Oedipus is born it is predicted that he will kill his father, King Laius of Thebes. To forestall this prophecy, Laius gives the baby to a shepherd with instructions to expose it on the mountainside so it will die. But the kindhearted shepherd takes the baby home. As a boy he goes to Corinth, where he is brought up in the household of the King of Corinth. When he is a young man, he hears the prophecy that he will kill his father so he leaves Corinth to avoid this prediction. On the road he meets a coach. He has an argument with the driver, and the passenger, who is King Laius, gets out of the coach to help the driver, is struck by Oedipus, and falls dead. Oedipus then continues to Thebes, where he solves the riddle of the Sphinx and as a reward is given the kingship and weds Queen Jocasta.

This Oedipus myth is particularly cogent in our day because it is central both in psychoanalysis and in literature. We find it, for one example, in the much admired drama by Shakespeare, *Hamlet.* The hero is charged by his father's ghost to avenge his death at the hands of the uncle, who has then married Hamlet's mother. Hamlet, however, is a hero at the beginning of the modern period, and hence in his self-consciousness he always postpones action. When by accident he is killed in the conclusion, he cries out to his friend Horatio,

> If thou didst ever hold me in thy heart,
> Absent thee from felicity awhile,
> And in this harsh world draw thy breath
>   in pain
> To tell my story. . . .

on the actual drama. Word has been brought from the oracle
that the plague will be lifted only when the murderer of the
previous King Laius is discovered. Oedipus calls the old blind
prophet, Tiresias, and thereupon proceeds a gripping and powerful unfolding step by step of Oedipus' self-knowledge, an
unfolding replete with rage at the truth and those who are its
bearers, and all other aspects of our human struggle against
recognition of our own reality. It is interesting that Freud, after
watching the drama on the stage, cried out, "Ach, it is a psychoanalysis!"

Tiresias' blindness symbolizes the fact that one can more
insightfully grasp *inner* reality about human beings—gain *insight*—if one is not distracted by the impingement of external
details.

Tiresias at first refuses to answer Oedipus' questioning as to
who is guilty with the words:

> How terrible it is to know . . .
> Where no good comes from knowing! Of these matters
> I was full well aware, but let them slip. . . .*

In response to Oedipus' new demands and threats, he continues,

> . . . Let me go home;
> . . . So shalt thou bear thy load most easily.
> 　　　　　　. . . Ye
> Are all unknowing; my say, in any sort,
> I will not say, lest I display my sorrow.

The drama then unfolds as the progressive revelation of
Oedipus to himself, the source from which the truth proceeds
being not Oedipus himself but Tiresias. *Thus Tiresias is the
psychoanalyst.* The whole gamut of reactions like "resistance"
and "projection" is exhibited by Oedipus as he fights the more

---

*Quotations from Sophocles, *Oedipus Tyrannus*, in *Dramas*, trans. Sir George
Young (New York: Everyman's Library, 1947).

violently against the truth the closer he gets to it. He accuses Tiresias of planning to betray the city; is this why he will not speak? The old seer replies,

> I will not bring remorse upon myself
> And upon you. Why do you search these matters?

Then in a burst of angry projection Oedipus accuses Tiresias of having killed Laius himself. And when the king is finally told the truth by the goaded prophet that he, Oedipus himself, is the murderer of his father, Oedipus turns upon Tiresias and his wife's brother, Creon, with the charge that these words are part of their strategy to take over the state.

Jocasta, Oedipus' wife, tries to persuade him not to place any weight on the seer's accusation and bursts out in a very human tirade,

> Listen and learn, nothing in human life
> Turns on the soothsayer's art.

Jocasta, the mother whom he has married, now herself becomes aware of the terrible knowledge that awaits Oedipus. She tries desperately to dissuade him:

> . . . But why should men be fearful,
> O'er whom Fortune is mistress, and foreknowledge
> Of nothing sure? Best take life easily,
> As a man may. For that maternal wedding,
> Have no fear; for many men ere now
> Have dreamed as much; but he who by such dreams
> Sets nothing, has the easiest time of it.

When Oedipus still proclaims his resolve to face the truth, wherever it may lead, whatever it may be, she cries,

> Don't seek it! I am sick, and that's enough. . . .
> Wretch, what thou art O mightst thou never know!

Oedipus is not dissuaded but insists that he must know who he is and where he came from. *He must know and accept his own reality, his own myth, and his fate.*

> I will not hearken—not to know the whole,
> Break out what will, I shall not hesitate. . . .

The old shepherd who rescued the infant Oedipus from death on the mountainside is finally brought, the one man who can provide the final link in the fateful story.

"O, I am in horror, now, to speak!" the shepherd cries. And Oedipus answers, "And I to hear. But I must hear—no less."

When Oedipus does learn the final, tragic truth, that he has killed his father and married his mother, he pulls out his eyes, the organ of *seeing.* His punishment is first *exile,* imposed by himself but later, as in *Oedipus in Colonus,* the second drama, imposed by Creon and the state. The tragedy has now come full circle. He was originally exiled when he was a few days old on his father's order, and now, an old man, he will be again in exile.

This exile is a fascinating symbolic act from our modern psychoanalytic viewpoint, for we have held in earlier chapters that the greatest threat and greatest cause of anxiety for an American near the end of the twentieth century is not castration but *ostracism,* the terrible fate of being exiled by one's group. Many a contemporary man castrates himself or permits himself to be castrated because of fear of being exiled if he doesn't. He renounces his power and conforms under the great threat and peril of ostracism.

RESPONSIBILITY NOT GUILT

We now turn to the drama which reveals the healing, integrative aspects of the Oedipus myth, namely *Oedipus in Colonus.* The old blind Oedipus is led by the hand of his daughter Ismene to Colonus, which is a grove of trees a few miles from Athens. There the old man pauses to contemplate his problems and to find some meaning in these horrible experiences he has endured.

There is very little "action" in this drama. It is almost entirely a man meditating on his tragic suffering and what he has learned from it. So far as I know, this drama is never mentioned in psychoanalytic literature in America, an amazing fact in itself. One reason for its neglect is that discussion of the integrative functions of myths in general tend to be omitted in psychoanalytic discussions. But, more specifically, a consequence of the literalistic interpretation of the myth as having to do with sex and killing the father requires that we stop when these are worked through, punishment meted out, and the situation accepted, as at the conclusion of *Oedipus Rex.*

But viewing the myth as the presentation of the human struggle, the truth about oneself, we must indeed go on, as Sophocles does, to see how a person comes to terms with the *meaning* of these acts which Oedipus has committed. This subsequent drama is Oedipus' stage of reconciliation with himself and his fellow men in the persons of Theseus and the Athenians, and it is a reconciliation with the ultimate meaning in his life. "For the gods who threw you down sustain you now," as his daughter Ismene phrases it.

Since it was written by Sophocles when he was an old man of eighty-nine, this drama can be supposed to contain the wisdom of his old age as well.

The first theme we find in Oedipus' meditation at Colonus is *guilt*—the difficult problem of the relation of ethical responsibility to self-consciousness. Is a man guilty if the act was unpremeditated, done unknowingly? In the course of his probing old Oedipus comes to terms with this; the answer is responsibility but not guilt.

Creon has come from Thebes, having heard the prophecy that the city which has Oedipus' body will always have peace, to persuade old Oedipus to return. But the old man defends himself indignantly against the brash accusations of guilt with which Creon attacks him:

> If then I came into the world—as I did come—
> In wretchedness, and met my father in a fight,

And knocked him down, not knowing that I killed him
Nor whom I killed—again, how could you find
Guilt in that unmeditated act? . . .
As for my mother—damn you, you have no shame,
Though you are her own brother—

. . . .

But neither of us knew the truth; and she
Bore my children also— . . .
While I would not have married her willingly
Nor willingly would I ever speak of it.*

Again, about his father he cries out that he has

A just extenuation. This:
I did not know him; and he wished to murder me.
Before the law—before God—I am innocent!

It is clear that Oedipus accepts and bears his responsibility.
But he insists that the delicate and subtle interplay of conscious
and unconscious factors (as we could call them) makes any
legalistic or pharisaic imputation of guilt inaccurate and wrong.
It is a truism since Freud that the *problem of guilt is not within
the act but within the heart,* as indeed Jesus said four centuries
after Sophocles wrote this drama. The drama holds that the
sins of meanness, avarice, and irreverence of Creon and Poly-
nices are "no less grave than those sins of passion for which
Oedipus was punished, that in condemning them to the merci-
less justice soon to descend, Oedipus acts thoroughly in accord
with a moral order which his own experience has enabled him
to understand."†

In angry, vehement words, Oedipus refuses the tricky proposal of Creon, the present dictator of Thebes, who tries to get
the exiled king to return by capturing Antigone as a hostage.
Fortunately Theseus, ruler of Athens, comes out in time to

*Quotations from Sophocles, *Oedipus at Colonus,* in *The Oedipus Cycle,* trans.
Robert Fitzgerald (Chicago: University of Chicago Press, 1949).
†Note by Fitzgerald, ibid., p. 176.

send his troops to overtake Creon and bring Antigone back again to the grove at Colonus.

The myth does point toward a conclusion emphasized by modern existential psychotherapists, that because of this interplay of conscious and unconscious factors in guilt and the impossibility of legalistic blame, we are forced into an acceptance of the universal human situation. *We then recognize the participation of every one of us in man's inhumanity to man.* The words to Oedipus from the hero, King Theseus, who exhibits no inner conflict at all, are therefore poignant and eternally important:

> . . . for I
> Too was an exile. . . .
> I know I am only a man; I have no more
> To hope for in the end than you have.

Another theme in this integrative drama is the power of Oedipus to impart *grace*—now that he has suffered through his terrible experiences and come to terms with them. As he himself says to the Athenians who have come out to see him and his daughter in the grove at Colonus:

> For I come here as one endowed with grace,
> By those who are over Nature; and I bring
> Advantage to this race. . . .

Theseus accepts this: "Your presence, as you say, is a great blessing." This capacity to impart grace is connected with the maturity and other emotional and spiritual qualities which result from the courageous confronting of his Oedipus' experiences. He cries,

> One soul, I think, can often make atonement
> For many others, if it be devoted. . . .

But there is also a clear symbolic element to make the point of his grace unmistakable: the oracle has revealed that his body after death will ensure victory to the land and the ruler which possesses him. The mere *presence* of his body is enough.*

The last emphasis in the outworking of this myth is *love*. At the end of the drama old Oedipus takes his daughters with him back to a great rock to die. A messenger, who then came back to the group to report the marvelous manner of Oedipus' death, states that his last words to his daughters were:

> . . . And yet one word
> Frees us of all the weight and pain of life:
> That word is love.

Oedipus does not at all mean love as the absence of aggression or the strong affects of anger. Old Oedipus will love only those he chooses to love. His son, who has betrayed him, asks for mercy and states, "Compassion limits even the power of God," but Oedipus will have none of it. The love, rather, he bears his daughters, Antigone and Ismene, and the love they have shown him during his exiled, blind wanderings is the kind of love he chooses to bless.

His sharp and violent temper, present at the crossroads where he killed his father years ago and exhibited in his sharp thrusts with Tiresias in *Oedipus Rex,* is still much in evidence in this last drama, unsubdued by suffering or maturity. The fact that Sophocles does not see fit to remove or even soften Oedipus' aggression and anger—the fact, that is, that the "aggression" and the "angry affects" are not the "flaws" he has old Oedipus get over—all this illustrates our thesis that the aggression involved in killing his father is not the central issue of these myths. Oedipus' maturity is not a renouncing of passion to come to terms with society, not a learning to live "in accord with the reality requirements of civilization." It is Oedipus' reconciliation with himself, with the special people he loves, and with the transcendent meaning of his life.

Finally, the messenger comes back and reports, describing Oedipus' miraculous death and burial,

---

*This "presence" will come up in a number of myths we will discuss: Solveig's presence for Peer Gynt, Briar Rose's presence for the Prince, and so on.

> But some attendant from the train of Heaven
> Came for him; or else the underworld
> Opened in love the unlit door of earth.
> For he was taken without lamentation,
> Illness or suffering; indeed his end
> Was wonderful if mortal's ever was.

This touching and beautiful death of a great character is magnificent as Sophocles presents it dramatically. As *Oedipus Rex* is the myth of the "unconscious," the struggle to confront the reality of the dark, destructive forces in man, *Oedipus in Colonus* is the myth of consciousness, the aspect of the myth which is concerned with the search for meaning and reconciliation. Both together comprise the myth of human beings confronting their own reality.

THE HEALING POWER
OF MYTH

From our concern with these dramas of Oedipus, we can see the healing power of myths. First, the myth brings into awareness the repressed, unconscious, archaic urges, longings, dreads, and other psychic content. This is the *regressive* function of myths. But also, the myth reveals *new* goals, *new* ethical insights and possibilities. Myths are a breaking through of greater meaning which was not present before. The myth in this respect is the way of working out the problem on a higher level of integration. This is the *progressive* function of myths.

The tendency has been almost universal in classical psychoanalysis to reduce the latter to the former, and to treat myths as regressive phenomena, which are then "projected" into ethical and other forms of meaning in the outside world. The upshot of this is that the integrative side of myths is lost. This is shown in the great emphasis on *Oedipus Tyrannus* in psychoanalytic circles while *Oedipus in Colonus* is forgotten.

But *myths are means of discovery.* They are a progressive revealing of structure in our relation to nature and to our own existence. Myths are *educative*—"e-ducatio." By drawing out inner reality they enable the person to experience greater reality in the outside world.

We now emphasize the side that is generally overlooked, *that these myths discover for us a new reality as well.* They are roads to universals beyond one's concrete experience. It is only on the basis of such a faith that the individual can genuinely accept and overcome earlier infantile deprivations without continuing to harbor resentment all through one's life. In this sense myth helps us accept our past, and we then find it opens before us our future.

There are infinite subtleties in this "casting out of remorse." Every individual, certainly every patient, needs to make the journey in his and her own unique way. An accompanying process all along the way will be the transforming of one's neurotic guilt into normal, existential guilt. And both forms of anxiety can be used constructively as a broadening of consciousness and sensitivity. This journey is made through understanding and confronting myths which have not only an archaic, regressive side but an integrative, normative, and progressive aspect as well.

PART II

MYTHS IN AMERICA

SIX

The Great Myth of the New Land

> The discovery of America galvanized and inebriated the
> Western world. It did more than anything else—even
> Copernicus and Galileo—to overturn the world view of the
> Middle Ages. It revolutionized the thought of Western
> man. He was now convinced that human society was
> getting off to *an entirely new start.*
>
> Thomas Merton

WE FIRST ARE SURPRISED to note the curious phenomenon
that *myths precede discovery.* Medieval Europe did not
"want" a new world in the centuries before Columbus set forth
in his three tiny ships in 1492. The Vikings under Leif Ericson
had come to America in the eleventh century, and the Irish
had made several trips to North America before them. But
these discoveries were largely ignored. Medieval people were
concerned with their own inner world and with heaven, the
world above, not a new world like their present one. It took an
inner change in Europe before the people could let themselves
see and experience a new world. A new mythic world had first
to be born; it was then time to discover a new outer world as
well. We note that people's myth is decisive, rather than bare

historical fact, in what they let themselves see and not see. It is not by its history that the mythology of a nation is determined, but, conversely, its history is determined by its mythology.* This reminds one of Virgil's saying, "We make our destiny by our choice of the gods."

To be able to discover and populate the New World required the Renaissance, with its great surge of humanistic change in Europe. The new burst of love for nature which is shown in Italian art, for example, supplanted the stiff mosaics of the Middle Ages. There was a new confidence in human possibilities, a new sense of adventure, a challenge on all sides to push beyond previous boundaries of geography and science. These new myths set the stage for Columbus to make his voyage. As is often the case, *myth leads to fact rather than the reverse.* The myth leads people to give their attention to one possibility rather than another, and hence to change the direction of their intentions and their dreams. Columbus proposed his expedition at the right time—the *Kairos†*—when people were ready to accept the discovery of the new world.

In people's minds this discovery of America was due to God's favor. It was part of His plan for a fresh beginning for mankind, in an age when almost everything was starting anew. The New World myth did not ignore older myths. The myths which filled the minds and souls of the people on the *Mayflower* were myths of Paradise, the Garden of Eden, the Golden Age. The people transformed these ancient myths into what was to become the great myth of America.** Since myths are beyond time, they could all be formed into one glorious narrative. Stephen Vincent Benet wrote in 1943, in "Western Star," that the myth was filled:

> With something of the wonder and the awe
> Those mutinous sailors saw . . .

*Ernst Cassirer has pointed this out in *The Myth of the State* (New Haven: Yale University Press, 1946).

†*Kairos* is a Greek word used by Tillich and others meaning the "destined time."

**Robertson, *American Myth/American Reality,* p. 33.

Sleepy and cursing, damning drink and bread,
To see before them there, . . .

But thin with distance, thin but dead ahead,
The line of unimaginable coasts.*

THE MYTH
OF THE FRONTIER

In his keen insights into the influence of the frontier on American society, Frederick Jackson Turner set the important myth for understanding the frontier. He saw the significance of what people were getting away *from* as well as what they were getting *to*. The free land on the frontier, drawing people away from Europe, enabled Americans to build a new frontier and a new culture, partially dependent upon Europe but with its own special characteristics. The frontier was thus the crucial myth; its special characteristics became distinctively American.

Turner pointed out that the restless energy in our new settlements and cities was combined with the individualism, the self-reliance, "the bounteousness and exhuberance which comes with freedom."† The new country had distinctive characteristics which Turner believed were largely due to our leaving Europe behind and striking out for ourselves. He emphasized the impact of the wilderness on this transplanted existence. Although his penetrating analysis did not come until 1890, he described a new western spirit and a new way of thinking about American history. Within the United States, this viewpoint lifted local history from the confines of antiquarianism into *mythic meaning*.

America was to become for the West a myth of the rebirth of humanity, without the sin or evil or poverty or injustice or

---

*Quoted in ibid.
†Frederick Jackson Turner, *Encyclopedia Brittanica*, vol. 22 (Chicago: William Benton, 1983), p. 625.

persecution which had characterized the Old World. Our
Statue of Liberty is emblazoned with an inscription, erected in
the nineteenth century but expressive of these earlier centuries
as well,

> Give me your tired, your poor,
> Your huddled masses
>   yearning to breathe free,
> The wretched refuse of your teeming
>   shore,
> Send these, the homeless,
>   tempest-tossed, to me:
> I lift my lamp beside
>   the golden door.

This myth of the New World has continued down to the present. In his orations during World War II, Churchill proclaimed that "England will hold on until the New World
comes to the rescue of the Old."

In the settling of this land the pilgrims and pioneers and
explorers, even the forebears of the Hollywood gunmen like
Clint Eastwood who took the law into their own hands, were
pictured as believing in divine righteousness or its synonym,
manifest destiny. The myth of the lone pioneer borrowed
power from the classical myth of Odysseus, whose own heart
had become the battleground for the strife of the gods, as the
frontiersmen portrayed in this country are the expression of the
destiny of America. Lord Byron interrupted *Childe Harold* to
rhapsodize about Daniel Boone and the American wilderness,
in which Boone is pictured as innocent, happy, benevolent, not
savage but simple, in his old age still a child of nature "whose
virtues showed the corruptions of civilization."*

There was a sense of destiny in the western desert, or if you
were religious, a sense of the presence of God wherever the
desert might be. Hence Jesus went into the desert for forty days

---

*Henry Nash Smith, *Virgin Land* (Cambridge: Harvard University Press, 1975),
p. 55.

and nights; Buddha did the same, and many a hermit has gone into the solitary desert to commune with himself and God. The desert of the West is what Paul Tillich called the "holy void." It is a myth into which one sinks, and whether or not it is holy or anxiety-producing depends upon you, the individual viewer.

The fact that Satan (or Mephistopheles or Lucifer) was originally God's co-worker casts light on the strange identification of people in America with the evil figures, say Jesse James or Bonnie and Clyde or the train robber called the Grey Fox, whom all the townspeople including the school band turned out to cheer as he was taken off to the penitentiary. Even now when children sing the western song, "He robbed from the rich/And gave to the poor," it is part of their identification with the myth of Robin Hood, a mythical medieval outlaw who robbed for the sake of the poor.

One of the curious things about the myth of the Wild West is that the west was reputed to have a healing power. Theodore Roosevelt, a sickly teen-ager, went west to develop his physique, to find himself psychologically, and to build himself into a courageous man. In the Horatio Alger myth, as we shall see in "Luke Larkin's Luck" (see Chapter 7), the "evil" family, the members of the aristocratic Duncans, were sentenced by the judge to go west to rebuild their honesty and integrity.

Daniel Boone, Kit Carson, Mike Fink, Calamity Jane, even Custer and Buffalo Bill, not only were our personal heroes but also stood for the myth of the healing power of the new land. These mythic heroes were quite conscious of their function as God's agents appointed to civilize the west—Buffalo Bill believed that he stood between civilization and savagery.

The myths of American freedom can also be used for very different effects. A young man in therapy described how his family had come from the Old World as homesteaders and moved as immigrants to a farm in South Dakota. Nobody would speak to this homestead family for the first four years. As a child he and his siblings took the bus to school, where they were also ostracized. His family was Catholic, and when he harmlessly asked another child which church the latter attended, the other child's mother drove a horse and buggy later that afternoon four miles to his house to rebuke his parents noisily for their son's prying into others' religion. His older brother got into fights because he was mocked in school; his older sister dropped out of the unhappy environment in her eleventh year and went to another school, but she seems not to have gotten over the neurotic difficulties the previous ostracism left.

The Statue of Liberty does not "lift her lamp beside the golden door" for all immigrants. The fear of ostracism is often present in the crowds of immigrants who moved into Minnesota and northern Wisconsin and Michigan. As children most of us—to our profound later regret—spoke of immigrants as Bohunks and Polocks, and in the cities they were Dagoes and Kikes. The romantic air with which we surround our Statue of Liberty covers up the fact that we generally hear of the successful immigrants like Andrew Carnegie and Edward Bok and other immigrants who became great.

LONELINESS IN AMERICA

Our most powerful and pervasive myth, which has had an amazingly widespread influence in this country and wherever radio is heard throughout the world, is that of the lone cowboy and the west.* We recall the *Lone Ranger,* introduced by the overture to *William Tell* (the hero of a similar myth in his own

---

*When my children were young, I used to take them occasionally to "westerns" for their own interest and amusement—or so at least I told myself. I knew the plot was always the same: when the Indians are galloping around the wagon train, now drawn up in a circle to protect those still alive among the pioneers and their families, just before the wagons are completely overrun, the sounds of a bugle are heard and over the hill we suddenly see the Stars and Stripes and the U.S. Cavalry galloping to the rescue, with a handsome lieutenant at their head. I tell myself I won't feel anything each time. But when the bugle does blow and the flag and galloping soldiers do come over the hill, I am thrilled as I always was. Such is the power of myth!

country of Switzerland). The program went into its nightly adventure, in which the Lone Ranger wore camouflage to show that he would continue to be unknown. With Tonto, his faithful helper, the Lone Ranger galloped ahead to redress some wrong. At the end of the program, his identity still unknown, the Lone Ranger galloped away into the lonely evening again. This myth merges loneliness and the myth of the west. The loneliness seems a kind of cultural inheritance, with our lone ancestors, the hunters, the trappers, the frontiersmen, all of whom lived a life of relative isolation and bragged about it.

Chronicled by an endless number of films, the myth of the lonely cowboy was made to order for Hollywood and the American mood. The background was the western mountains in their scarlet and purple against the endless ochre of the desert sand. In the films the courage of American frontier men and women dared all. The women who were saved—or saved themselves—from villains were delicate southern beauties or rugged frontier women who could chop wood and shoot with the best of the men. And there was the final lone shootout between the hero and the villain. Westerns illustrate the love for repetition that Freud mentions; we seemed to have an endless appetite for seeing the same theme over and over again as an authentic myth.*

When Henry Kissinger, then secretary of state, was asked by Oriani Fallaci how he explained "the incredible movie star status" he enjoyed, Kissinger replied that it came from "the fact that he had always acted alone." Kissinger was referring to his role as a "lonely cowboy" in flying from Lebanon to Jerusalem to Cairo, not by horseback but by diplomatic jet. "Americans like that immensely," he said.

Americans like the cowboy who leads the wagon train by riding ahead alone on his horse, the cowboy who rides all alone into town . . . with

---

*This surprising phenomenon of loneliness in the midst of gay and happy Americans was pictured in the deservedly popular book, *The Lonely Crowd*, ed. David Reissman et al. (New Haven: Yale University Press, 1973).

his horse and nothing else. Maybe even without a pistol. . . . This cowboy doesn't have to be courageous. All he needs is to be alone to show others that he rides into town and does everything by himself. Americans like that.*

This early loneliness would seem to be connected, as a kind of cultural inheritance, with our lone ancestors, the hunters, the trappers, the frontiersmen, all of whom lived a life of relative isolation and bragged about it. But now it is not physical loneliness that we in the twentieth century are troubled with. In this age of radio and television no one is far from another person's voice at every moment. We noted the loneliness of Deborah in *I Never Promised You a Rose Garden;* even though people were around her all the time she felt completely alone and had to construct her own gods. We are often considered a country of joiners; we join everything from Rotarians to Kiwanas clubs to fraternities and sororities and women's societies of all sorts. This perpetual joining, I propose, is *a reaction-formation, a device for covering up the competitiveness and the loneliness underneath.*

Some people come for therapy simply because they are unbearably lonely. We therapists are now seeing more and more patients who seek help because they are driven to find someone who will listen to them with no stake in it except to wish them well. Again like Deborah in Chapter 1, in our day of instantaneous communication by electronics and satellites, more patients than ever have never experienced anyone who would genuinely listen with only his or her welfare in mind. One joins Lennon and McCartney in their Beatles' song: "All the lonely people—where do they all come from?"

The loneliness goes deeply into our American mythology. On the turnpikes in New York or Houston or Los Angeles, many drivers look as though pursued by an inner loneliness hurrying some place but never knowing where that place is. Their expressions have a forlorn quality as though they had lost

*Oriani Fallaci, *Interview with History* (New York: Liveright, 1976), p. 41.

something—or rather as though *they* were lost. Or they act as though they were pursued by guilt, or by what memories of violence, or by what frantic hope? What is lacking in people's attitude in our day is a sense of peace—quiet, deep, relaxed peace.

The loneliness is one expression of our rootlessness.* Many people in our day, separated from tradition and often cast out by society, are alone with no myths to guide them, no unquestioned rites to welcome them into community, no sacraments to initiate them into the holy—and so there is rarely anything holy. *The loneliness of mythlessness is the deepest and least assuageable of all.* Unrelated to the past, unconnected with the future, we hang as if in mid-air. We are like the shades Odysseus meets in the underworld, crying for news about the people up in the world but unable themselves to feel anything.

Part of the cause of this loneliness is our lack of historical roots in America and our continual moving, so that we rarely give ourselves time to put down roots. When we are pressed, we pack up and take the plane or car or train to some other place. De Tocqueville records his surprise that the American, on building a house in which one naturally expects him to live and to enjoy, no sooner gets the roof on it than he puts it up for sale and is off to some new place.

We lack the sense of history that Europeans feel. On walking out of doors, a French villager immediately sees a cathedral which connects him with history of centuries ago; his rootedness is obvious in his eyes and mood, and it is a real assuagement of loneliness. Whether he ever goes to the church or

---

*On returning from Europe, Philip Slater remarks in his *Pursuit of Loneliness* that everyone looks lonely in America. "These perceptions are heightened by the contrast between the sullen faces of real people and the vision of happiness television offers: men and women ecstatically engaged in stereotyped symbols of fun—running through fields, strolling on beaches, dancing and singing. Americans know from an early age how they are supposed to look when happy and what they are supposed to do or buy to be happy. But for some reason their fantasies are unrealizable and leave them disappointed and embittered." Philip Slater, *The Pursuit of Loneliness* (Boston: Beacon, 1976).

believes what its representatives teach is irrelevant, the great edifice stands there connecting him with myths of centuries of the past. But in America we pride ourselves on building skyscrapers to tear down in a hundred years or less. While the European moves mostly in *time,* the American moves mainly in *space.*

VIOLENCE
AND LONELINESS

The loneliness is expressed in our being a violent people at the same time as we are very democratic. The violence in America, even in our twentieth century, is easy to see but hard to admit and explain. With our "Saturday night specials" we murder fifty times as many of our fellow countrymen as the Swedes or the British; indeed, our homicide rate is much greater than any civilized nation outside of Central America. We "nice" Americans regularly identify with the pioneers who massacred Indians according to the will of God under a new name, manifest destiny.

We make heroes out of gangsters. In the movies we identify with the criminal; during Prohibition, Dillinger, public enemy number one, was a kind of hero, and other gangsters are heroic now as they are played by Clint Eastwood. The overwhelming violence on the television screen has become hackneyed, but whether or not it breeds violence in young viewers, it certainly ministers to the feeling that we can depend upon no one but ourselves. We are surrounded by potential enemies, which makes us feel we ought to consider wearing bulletproof vests and must never relax our guard. Indeed, one reads in the newspaper that a contemporary minister in Texas wears a bulletproof vest during his sermons since he, standing alone in the pulpit, makes an easy target for an assassin's bullet.

Hence loneliness and the denial of it, or the escape from it, are such important myths in America. Children can escape it by watching TV, adolescents cover it up by constant partying and episodic sex, middle-aged people repress it by the marriage-divorce merry-go-round. Hence encounter groups are so important in America; anybody can announce a new "growth" group and persons will flock to it to be taught the new techniques of living and loving spontaneously, unaware of the contradiction in the very phrase "techniques of spontaneity." For we were all brought up, so goes the myth, on the subconscious equivalents of Paradise at Plymouth Rock and tales of the magic success on the frontier, and we find nothing to take their place except repeating the old shibboleths.

THE SEDUCTION
OF THE NEW

From the beginning we early Americans pushed westward, always discovering something new. We named our states *New* York, *New* Mexico. The myth of the new was always beckoning to us. God must favor us, we believed, for every day new discoveries greeted our hunters and frontiersmen, our trappers and our miners; a lush countryside invited us in every direction. Ore was later to be discovered in the mountains, the forests on the hills kept a steady stream of the riches of lumber pouring upon us—all climaxed by the literal discovery of gold in California in 1849. No wonder in America we love any *new* technique; one kind of computer is pushed off the market by the invention of a *new* one; any new brand of aspirin or vitamin is grabbed up with insatiable appetite. The proliferation of cults and gurus, which occurs especially in our west, is the expression of new religions, new ways of life, new heavens, and new techniques for reaching these heavens, all summed up in the phrase "New Age."

This helps explain why the different kinds of psychotherapy

took off like rockets in this New World in contrast to the merely studied interest they received in Europe, although every early form of therapy—Freudian, Adlerian, Jungian, Rankian, Reichian—had been discovered in Europe. The representatives of new forms of therapy developed by Horney, Fromm, Alexander, Fromm-Reichmann, and others also came literally to these shores as emissaries from Europe. How we lapped up these new approaches to therapy! On all sides, we wanted the *new*.

In the field of therapy this became the myth of the changing self: we in America want to find a new self, a new set of expectations. The most important moral implication of this myth is that the typical American does not come to therapy to be "cured" but rather to find a *new* life, to *change* into a different way of living.

Change is a great word in America; we not only believe in it, we worship it. We see it all about us, and we shall see it emblazoned in Gatsby's complete faith in his capacity to change his accent, his name, indeed to *invent* himself. De Tocqueville saw this clearly:

The American has no time to tie himself to anything, he grows accustomed only to change, and ends by regarding it as the natural state of man. He feels the need of it, more, he loves it; for the instability, instead of meaning disaster to him, seems to give birth only to miracles all about him.

Such change, whether it is judged as Providence or Progress, is always assumed to be good in America. In politics, which is a pattern of myths par excellence, the myth of the new is of great importance—*vide* the New Deal, the New Frontier, new blood, new visions. No one in this country runs on the platform of preserving the old frontiers. We recall that Kennedy's charm in his election was partly that he represented new ideas, a youth leaving the old behind. The real question, namely, the *quality* of the new, is rarely asked. It is assumed in this New World to be better because it is new. This is the myth of change, where we put on the new self, where we follow the belief in Cuéism, "Every day in every way I'm getting better and better."

This mood is allied to the fact that we assume that history, even the little of it that we have in this country, is not significant; we cast off European history with a sense of relief. Many Americans secretly believe Henry Ford was right when he said, "History is bunk!" For him history began with the invention of the Ford flivver. Concerned only with the present and the future, our myth omits the actual richness of American history; for the very love of the new, the expectation of all kinds of change in psychotherapy, works against real progress. The patient in therapy, in his expectancy for a new life, misses the greater values of deep inner poise and serenity.

But all the while—to follow this myth to our present state— we have the underlying suspicion that we are simply running away by our New Age methods. When we talk about changing personalities, we need a more mystical term. The term that was born was "transforming": we say we are engaged in "transforming persons." In the 1970s Werner Erhard in California founded the EST seminars, and the movement spread like a prairie fire across the country.

About half a million mostly young, mostly affluent, mostly white persons, . . . paid Erhard and his fellow trainers between $300 and $500 to be transformed in a weekend from confused underachievers into self-assured, take-charge types who "got it"—accepted responsibility for their own lives.*

But it was a short-lived myth. Half a decade later this fountain of transformation began to dry up and soon nobody heard anything about EST, as it was called. Not surprisingly, however, Erhard himself had been transformed. He had now developed a system of "breakthrough" for transforming businesses

*Mark Dowie, "The Transformation Game," *Image* (San Francisco) (October 12, 1986): 22–26.

called Transformational Technologies. Money was now to be made in the corporations. As the reporter of this new form of change puts it,

In our born-again, discard and replace culture, where conversation has replaced correction, fast transformation has become as easy for a self as fast food. It no longer seems to matter what you become in the process of transformation, *just so long as you are transformed.* And if you're still the same imperfect animal despite your funny new vocabulary, simply transform yourself again.*

THE MYTH OF PROTEUS

The Greek god Proteus represents the myth of change. Whenever Proteus was in any dangerous or difficult situation, he could change himself into some new form which promised security, whether animal or tree or insect. The American psychiatrist Robert Lifton has brilliantly described this personality which is always in the process of change, *Protean.* To a considerable extent in America the myth of change, the unending quest for the new, the yearning for transformation, is for us a fleeing from anxiety as it was for Proteus. Homer describes Proteus when, in the *Odyssey,* Odysseus and his men encounter the wily one and must ring from him the directions home, and it was absolutely necessary:

> When Proteus at last slept
> We gave a battle cry and plunged
> for him,
> locking our hands behind him.
> But the old one's
> tricks were not knocked out of
> him; far from it.
> First he took on a whiskered
> lion's shape,

*Ibid., p. 16.

a serpent then; a leopard; a
great boar;
Then sausing water; then a tall
green tree.
Still we clung on, by hook
or crook, through every
thing.
Until the Ancient saw defeat,
and grimly
opened his lips to ask me.*

But this addiction to change can lead to superficiality and psychological emptiness, and like Peer Gynt, we never pause long enough to listen to our own deeper insights. Lifton uses the myth of Proteus to describe the chameleon tendencies, the ease with which many modern Americans play any role the situation requires of them. Consequently, we not only do not speak from our inner integrity, but often have a conviction of never having lived as our "true selves."

In such a situation, the myth of change can be a synonym for superficiality. We live according to others' expectations. When a celebrated film actor in therapy was asked his ideas, he answered, "I have no ideas. If you want me to say anything, you must write it down on a card, start the cameras rolling, and I'll say it." This man was no different from many of his colleagues, though he had become affluent and a celebrity. But he was also deeply depressed and felt he had missed the meaning of his life—as indeed he had. He described his perpetual mood as "the salt which has lost its savor."

Whether we dress it up by such terms as "new age," "transformation," "new possibilities," or something else, the myth of Proteus, of continuous change, does temporarily protect us from anxiety. We Americans are always on the move to escape the anxiety of the human paradox and the anxiety of death. *But*

*Homer, *The Odyssey*, trans. Robert Fitzgerald (Garden City, NY: Anchor Books, 1963) p 66.

the price for this evasion is a deep loneliness and sense of isolation. With these go depression and the conviction that we have never really lived, that we have been exiled from life.

One of our contemporary poets, W. S. Merwin, discusses the expression of the myth of Proteus in modern Americans. First he states, "Myth is the most important and powerful vehicle in defining the role of the poet in the present." He sees us in our day as acting out our Protean myth. In his interpretation of the myth of seizing Proteus as a quest for the gifts of wisdom and prophecy, which man projects on the gods, Merwin states,

We run from danger by emulating Proteus, a characteristic not only of the neurotic personality of our time but of all of us. So our passion for change in America harbors within itself our endeavor to escape the spectre of death, to escape any danger which we see threatening us.*

"The head he turned toward me wore a face like mine," Merwin continues, thus confessing that he too has fallen from time to time for the seduction of Proteus. The myth of Proteus is shown by Wordsworth to capture us by our commercialism.

> The World is too much with us; late and soon,
> Getting and spending, we lay waste our powers;
> Little we see in Nature that is ours;
> We have given our hearts away, a sordid boon!

But like all myths, the myth of Proteus is not in itself only evil. It is that our error is our absorption in commercialism and our letting our love for money overcome our capacity to appreciate the nature around us:

> . . . Great God! I'd rather be
> A Pagan suckled in a creed outworn,

---

*Lillian Feder, "Myth in the Poetry of W. S. Merwin," in *Poets in Progress*, ed. Edward Hungerford (Evanston, Ill.: Edward Hungerford, 1962), pp. 412–413.

So might I, standing on this pleasant lea,
Have glimpses that would make me less forlorn;
Have sight of Proteus rising from the sea,
Or hear old Triton blow his wreathed horn.*

*Wordsworth, "The World Is Too Much with Us".

SEVEN

Individualism and Our Age
of Narcissism

In America . . . I have seen the freest and best educated of
men in the circumstances the happiest to be found in the
world; yet it seemed to me that a cloud habitually hung on
their brow, and they seemed serious and almost sad in their
pleasure . . . because they never stop thinking of the good
things they have not got.

de Tocqueville

AMERICANS CLING to the myth of individualism as though it
were the only normal way to live, unaware that it was
unknown in the Middle Ages (except for hermits) and would
have been considered psychotic in classical Greece. We feel as
Americans that every person must be ready to stand alone, each
of us following the powerful myth of the lone cabin on the
prairie. Each individual must learn to take care of himself or
herself and thus be beholden to no one else. James Fenimore
Cooper put these words in the mouth of his eighteenth-century
hero, Leatherstocking, when a friend was being rebuked for his
solitary life,

No, no judges. I have lived in the woods for forty long years, and have
spent five years at a time without seeing the light of a clearing, bigger

than a wind-row in the trees; and I should like to know where you'll find a man, in his sixty-eighth year, who can get an easier living, for all your betterments, and your deer-laws; and, as for honesty, or doing what's right between man and man, I'll not turn my back to the longest winded deacon on your Patent.*

Called "rugged individualism" in political circles, and "fierce individualism" by some historians, this myth has obviously great advantages for a democracy. But it exhibits the basic flaw of leaving us no solid community to call our own. No one doubts the important role played by the tough, weather-beaten scouts, dressed more like Indians than Europeans, in the founding and exploring of this nation, and especially the hunters, trappers, and scouts from the Alleghenies all the way through the far west—all individuals to the core. They contributed a myth of lonesome individualism that makes our own loneliness a strange and noble kind of moral achievement.

Walt Whitman, whom many students regard as the greatest poet of America, writes in "Song of Myself,"

> One's self I sing . . .
> Of life immense in passion, pulse,
>   and power,
> Cheerful, for freest action formed
>   under the laws divine,
> The Modern Man I sing.

and,

> I celebrate myself, and sing myself, . . .
>
> I loafe and invite my soul,
> I learn and loafe at my ease observing
>   a spear of summer grass.†

Even in religion, which is supposed to work for community, this individualism is shown in the revivalism that swept the

---

*Henry Nash Smith, *Virgin Land* (Cambridge: Harvard University Press, 1975), p. 63.

†Walt Whitman, *Leaves of Grass* (New York: Heritage Press), p. 25.

middle west and far west like a prairie fire in the middle of the nineteenth century. The emphasis was on the individual as a figure standing alone. When huge crowds gathered to be "saved," the songs they sang took no account of any other persons in the hundreds of people around each individual:

> I come to the garden alone,
> When the dew is still on the roses;
>   And a voice I hear, falling on my ear,
> The Son of man discloses.

> And he walks with me and he talks with me,
>   And he tells me I am his own,
>   And the joy we share as we tarry there
>   None other has ever known.

Robert Bellah has emphasized that in America our morality, stated originally by Benjamin Franklin, is focused so "exclusively on individual self-improvement that the larger social context hardly comes into view."* This myth of individualism goes way back to a story in ancient times, though it has a different name.

THE MYTH AND NEUROSIS
OF NARCISSUS

The lovely and talkative nymph Echo lived free from care and whole of heart until she met Narcissus, hunting in the forest. She no sooner beheld the youth than she fell deeply in love with him.

*Bellah, *Habits of the Heart* (Berkeley: University of California Press, 1985), p. 33. This book is a strong indictment of our overemphasized individualism in America.

A speech of mine to a psychiatric convention was picked up by several newspapers around the country, and while the editors agreed with most of my points, they took radical exception to my proposal that individualism in this country needs to be mitigated. Without exception they could not conceive of becoming less individualistic. It seemed so central to their moral system that it could have become their eleventh commandment.

But all her blandishments were unavailing, and in her despair at his hard-heartedness, she implored Aphrodite to punish him by making him suffer the pangs of unrequited love.

Aphrodite did not forget poor Echo's last passionate prayer and was biding her time to punish the disdainful Narcissus. One day, after a prolonged chase, he hurried to a lonely pool to slake his thirst.

Quickly he knelt upon the grass and bent over the pellucid waters to take a draught; but he suddenly paused, surprised. Down near the pebbly bottom he saw a face so fair that he immediately lost his heart, for he thought it belonged to some water nymph gazing up at him through the transparent water.

With sudden passion he caught at the beautiful apparition; but the moment his arms touched the water, the nymph vanished. Astonished and dismayed, he slowly withdrew to a short distance and breathlessly awaited the nymph's return.

The agitated waters soon resumed their mirror-like smoothness; and Narcissus, approaching noiselessly on tiptoe and cautiously peeping into the pool, became aware of first curly, tumbled locks and then a pair of beautiful, watchful, anxious eyes. It seemed to him that the nymph was about to emerge from her hiding place to reconnoiter.

Time and again the same pantomime was enacted, and time and again the nymph eluded his touch; but the enamored youth could not tear himself away from the spot haunted by this sweet image, whose sensitive face reflected his every emotion and who grew as pale and wan as he—evidently, like him, a victim to love and despair.

There Narcissus lingered day and night, without eating or drinking, until he died, little suspecting that the fancied nymph was but his own image reflected in the clear waters. Echo was avenged; but the gods of Olympus gazed compassionately down upon the beautiful corpse and changed it into a flower bearing the youth's name, which has ever since flourished beside quiet pools, wherein its pale image is clearly reflected.

THE NEUROSIS
OF OUR TIME

Out of this lonely and isolated individual there has come a new psychotherapeutic category fittingly called the "narcissistic personality." Freud and his immediate followers obviously cited and described narcissism, however, in Freud's day, this neurosis had not become prominent. But especially in America the narcissistic personality has become the dominant type of patient in the decades since the 1960s.*

The narcissistic patient in therapy is the modern myth of lonely individualism.† This person has few if any deep relationships and lacks the capacity for satisfaction or pleasure in the contacts he does have. He is, par excellence, the depressed "man in the gray flannel suit," as the novel phrased the description of this kind. Christopher Lasch well describes this type of person in *The Culture of Narcissism:*

Liberated from the superstitions of the past, he doubts even his own anxiety. . . . Even though his sexual attitudes are permissive rather than puritanical, he gets no lasting pleasure from them. Acquisitive in the sense that his cravings have no limits . . . he demands immediate gratification and lives in a state of restless, perpetually unsatisfied desire.

"In a narcissistic society—a society that gives increasing prominence and encouragement to narcissistic traits," he peers as though into the well at his own image. Lasch believes that "the prevailing attitude, so cheerful and forward looking on the surface, derives from a narcissistic impoverishment of the psyche."**

---

*Christopher Lasch, *The Culture of Narcissism* (New York: Norton, 1979).
†Two psychiatrists have been central in describing the narcissistic type of personality, Hans Kohut and Otto Kernberg.
**Lasch, *The Culture of Narcissism*, pp. xvi–xvii.

These patients are difficult to work with in therapy, since their narcissism prevents their establishing any deep relationship with the therapist. They seem cooperative on the surface, for they know how one *should* act in therapy, and they follow the rules without ever being deeply committed to any relationship: They remain isolated, deeply lonely individuals. So therapy with them (which often goes on for an excessive number of years) becomes a situation in which the therapist is a "retainer," a perpetual source of moral advice on all decisions, one whom you visit at every new need for guidance. That this is a mockery of good psychotherapy goes without saying; the *sine qua non* of interpersonal relationship is not there. Instead, the patient gets advice on this or that specific decision, which results in the confirmation of his original problem, i.e., he cannot make personal decisions on his own. *Narcissism destroys individuality, contradictory though that seems.*

Our society is on two levels, the one optimistic, always smiling, shown particularly in the ads on television for ocean cruises with entertainment all provided, or running in the fields, dancing, and driving Cadillacs, in a period of almost universal happiness. This is on the surface. But just below the surface there is the reality of depression—indeed, fear of nuclear disaster, much sexual activity without lasting relationships. "People then complain of an inability to feel. They cultivate mere void experiences, seek to beat sluggish flesh to life, attempt to revive jaded appetites."* Therapists, not priests, are popular preachers of self-help. Even when therapists speak of the need for "meaning" and "love," they define love and meaning simply as the fulfillment of the patient's emotional requirements, not as a relationship of caring. Narcissism is an emerging dilemma which gives people the tormenting experience of inner contradiction, blocking their spontaneity and sending them into therapy.

These narcissistic persons have many acquaintances but no

*Ibid., p. 11.

close friends. They are sexually liberated but they experience no passion. They generally are well educated, but they gave up most of their intellectual interests when they graduated from college. The narcissistic type is often skilled at stocks and bonds, but sooner or later this seems a purposeless game. They usually make very good salaries—sometimes in the millions—but it gives them little satisfaction. In short, they have everything that is promised in the TV ads to bring happiness—travel and shiny cars and beautiful women—but happiness eludes them. They are often celebrities, but they find this also to be exasperatingly empty. They are modern and sophisticated and they come in increasing numbers to psychoanalysis, but therapy is difficult and slow.

Most of all, such persons are exceedingly lonely. It seems the only emotions they feel are a mild but permeating depression and a sense of having missed out on the joys of life even though, paradoxically, they have had everything. As de Tocqueville tells us, "They never stop thinking of the good things they have not got."

The narcissistic personality can be considered in America as a further development of American individualism. But this also brings new difficulties in that the development of the technique of psychoanalysis seems increasingly to support the narcissism rather than to analyze it away. Therapy, for a number of reasons—some financial, some theoretical, and some simply an outgrowth of the behavioristic trends in our traditional American psychology—moves toward narcissism and excessive individualism, each empowering the other. Our psychotherapy then tends to be problem-centered rather than person-centered.

THE HORATIO ALGER MYTH

De Tocqueville's insights agree with William James', who called the pressure to succeed a "bitch goddess." How did we develop this bastardized marriage between individualism and success? That we did wed these two attitudes is clear enough. As R. W. White puts it: "[American] culture stresses an individualism tied to competition, aggressively directed toward fellow human beings, as the basis for personal and collective security. Each person should stand on his own feet in order to fight for what he gets—such is the philosophy of this culture."*

After the Civil War, we needed a new myth to sustain people in the great drive to succeed, which was measured chiefly financially, but in status and prestige as well. We needed a myth to console and inspire us in our worship of "the bitch goddess of success." The drive toward success inebriated people and soon became identified with individualism in the famous American Dream.

The statement of an early leader of the Massachusetts Bay Colony, Governor John Winthrop, that God sends the wealth, became wedded to the Calvinistic doctrine that the man of wealth was therefore the good man, for his wealth showed that God approved of him. This new myth, probably the most important in American history in the last century, was handed to us in the many stories written by Horatio Alger. It provides a mythical paradigm "for the organization man." I owe to James Oliver Robertson and his book *American Myth/American Reality* the following outline of one of these stories, "Struggling Upward or Luke Larkins' Luck."†

First presented in a serial in a magazine aptly entitled *Ways to Success*, this story sold 50 million copies in paperback and

*R. W. White, *Lives in Progress* (New York: Dryden, 1954).
†Robertson, *American Myth/American Reality*, pp. 165–168.

was read by millions more. The story begins with a typical American competition, namely an ice-skating race. Randolph Duncan, whose father was Prince Duncan, a banker, having all the characteristics of European aristocracy including the name of his father, Prince, is matched against Luke, a poor boy, the son of a carpenter's widow. Luke makes his way by being janitor of the school. He is presented as "eager to work, reliable, generous," and his face has a "pleasant expression, a warm-hearted, resolute look."

Luke is tripped up by an accomplice of Duncan and so loses the race and the Waterbury watch, which was the prize. When Luke comes up to congratulate him, Duncan remarks patronizingly about the watch, "You are a poor boy. It doesn't matter to you." And Luke replies, "I don't know about that, Randolph. Time is likely to be of as much importance to a poor boy as a rich boy." The implication here is that time is money to the corporations and their offices; everything runs on the exact time, whereas to the farmer or janitor a watch is a luxury.

Luke is then saved from conviction for a crime he did not commit by a "tall, dark-complexioned stranger" who takes him to New York City, where he meets Mr. Armstrong. The latter remarks that Luke is "a thoroughly good boy, and a smart boy too. I must see if I can give him a chance to rise. He seems absolutely reliable." One notes that important word "rise"— success meant rising indefinitely.

The upshot of the story is that Luke discovers that the banker, the father of Randolph, has stolen some bonds from Mr. Armstrong, and the tale concludes with Luke's discovering the theft and achieving success in New York, while Randolph and the Duncan family are required to move to the west to recuperate their integrity. What is fascinating here is that the west is "healing," as we have pointed out; it is the place where people get their strength and their integrity. Then this power from the west—which I take to be the power from absorbing the American myths—is absorbed by the individual and he is transferred back to the east, where the myth is used for the climb to success in the great corporations.

This dark-complexioned, tall stranger mentioned above is a curious figure. He brings to mind the "strange traveler" in Ibsen's play *Peer Gynt,* a man who is crucial to Peer Gynt at last finding *his* own integrity. The "tall stranger" is parallel furthermore to Mr. Cody, the rich man who gives Gatsby his first job and a yachtsman's costume. There is also the omnipresent element in the story of being taken care of by someone who *likes* you; it reminds us of the myth presented in *Death of a Salesman,* where Willy Loman puts so much stake on being the "best liked."

These Alger stories gave a powerful sanction to the individual and sustained each person working in the great corporations. It helped persons to accept their station, meet their anxiety, and quench their guilt and gave a structure to their sense of morality and their identity. We have our great examples of such success: the chief hero of the Horatio Alger myths was Andrew Carnegie, who came to this country as an immigrant boy, worked his way up to president of American Steel, and sold his interest in it for four hundred million dollars. He wrote a book called *Road to Success* and made lecture tours around the country on how to succeed.

The myth of success consoled us in the difficulties of struggling to "rise" to higher and higher positions. When we were anxious with such questions as, Did I reach too far? Or too high? we could console ourselves: only a bold person would reach the top. When we had a pang of guilt at exploiting our fellow men, we could whisper to ourselves that we need not take the responsibility for others, that they must learn on their own, and this expression of individualism then relieved us of our guilt.

Luck, in "Luke Larkin's Luck," is unpredictable, something over which we have no control. How is one to be certain that his endeavors will yield the vaunted "success"? No wonder physicians researching ulcers and heart trouble in contemporary people state that the "pervasive Horatio Alger myth is a

prime cause of type A behavior."* This describes the syndrome
of the person in our day who is driven, always in a hurry, tense,
lean, competitive, and prone to stress-related diseases. This,
rightly say the researchers, is "fed by the Horatio Alger
Myth."†

That word "luck" in this story of Luke Larkin is a repetition
of the myth of the Renaissance goddess Fortuna, which in turn
comes down from the Greek mythic figure Tyche, who traveled everywhere at the side of Zeus. She is pictured on a constantly revolving wheel, and in her journeys around the world
she "scattered with careless hands her numerous gifts, lavishing
with indifference her choicest smiles." In our culture it is still a
matter to a great extent of "luck"; Fortuna is unpredictable,
dependent on the vagaries of the stock market and other things
over which we have little or no control.

CONTEMPORARY EVIL IN PARADISE

Most dramatically of all, ex-President Reagan was the spokes-
man for the Horatio Alger myth. He affected the rags-to-riches
style: he made a point in his news conferences of telling how he
had to eat "oatmeal-meat" as a boy. He now has become a
millionaire, an ideal he holds for every American. When
pushed in one of his news conferences to state his bottom-line
position on the question of whether he was for the rich or the
poor, he stated firmly, "What I want to see above all is that this
country remains *a country where someone can always get
rich.*"** Here is the Horatio Alger myth to a syllable—the plea
that this country continue to strive for the myth of Horatio
Alger. President Reagan also took pride in the fact that in his
judgment—and possibly also in reality—the great rise of the

New York Times, February 14, 1984.
    †That this emphasis is still active is shown by a "sign-off" of a TV program every
night with the words, "Americans don't want to survive—they want to succeed."
    **New York Times*, June 29, 1983.

Dow-Jones average and the spending spree led to what he called the "greatest example of entrepreneurial success in history."*

The stock market boomed to a height never dreamt of before. Money flowed freely, and armed with credit cards the nation seemed to be on a gigantic spending spree. We were inundated on television and radio by those living out an adage of Coolidge half a century earlier, "Advertising is the method by which the desire is created for better things." Our new inventions in computer techniques and VCRs and travels by ship or plane presented new possibilities at every moment. Young people filled the business schools to overflowing, and the newspapers idealized the numerous millionaires in their twenties who were making it "big." Reagan took partial credit for this "miracle of prosperity," as he called it. It was the heyday of individualism in the business world.

As one writer on the takeovers put it: "It is the American dream: for a kid from the Bronx or a boy from rural Wisconsin to sit at the very center of the turbulent takeover wars that are transforming Wall Street and corporate America, and make millions by the age of thirty-five."†

Parallel to the financial boom was the rapid growth of gambling. "In Pennsylvania the lottery prize reached the giddy height of $115 million.... Once upon a time, mass irrationality was considered a menace to democratic government. But in this age of lotteries ... mass hysteria is an important ingredient of public finance." It is well known that gambling fleeces the poor more than the rich. Gambling capitalizes on the myth of Fortuna—that we can get rich through "luck." And we can then live the life which those laughing rich people on television screens present so vividly to us.

Twenty-six states at this writing have state-sponsored lotter-

---

*I am told by an authority that this great gain in the Dow-Jones average was due to the pouring of Japanese money into the stock market rather than actual gains in American industry.

†Moira Johnston, *Takeover* (New York: Arbor House, 1986), p. 1.

ies, and the number is increasing. *Newsweek* reports, "America's gambling fever . . . is part of the weekly, even daily routine of tens of millions of Americans." Lottery earnings have been growing an average of 17.5 percent annually. George Will points out rightly, "Gambling is debased speculation, craving for sudden wealth. . . . This age of lotteries" is a mass hysteria.*

In gambling and lotteries several powerful myths are expressed. The first is the *mother's breast:* one needs only to open one's sucking mouth and, magically, the breast falls in. Another is being fed by some great goddess who takes care of him or her in her hidden ways. In this sense the stated aim of this nation— to increase production—is powerfully undermined by gambling. The stronger the hope to win big on the stock market or lottery or betting on a football game, the less effort one will put forth in honest work. Then work becomes irrelevant: one will live, so goes the myth, by manna dropping from heaven, or more fittingly one lives by the effluence from the world of demons.

This is George Will's statement on gambling:

Gambling fever reflects and exacerbates what has been called the "fatalism of the multitude." The more people believe in the importance of luck, chance, randomness, fate, the less they believe in the importance of stern virtues such as industriousness, thrift, deferral of gratification, diligence, studiousness. It is drearily understandable why lotteries—skill-less gambling; gambling for the lazy—are booming at a time when the nation's productivity, competitiveness, savings rate and academic performance are poor.

THE AGE OF MELANCHOLY

Underneath and covered over by the gleeful noises of the lotteries and the shopping sprees in America is a widespread psychological depression. This was uncovered by two far-reaching

*All George F. Will quotations are from *Newsweek,* May 8, 1989.

studies extending over two years by the National Institutes for Mental Health. Something has happened since World War II. Psychological depression is now going on at a rate ten times as high as before World War II.* Martin Seligman, one of the psychologists who performed the study, sums up its results: "If you were born in the last fifty years, you have ten times as much chance of being seriously depressed as you would if you were born in the fifty years before that time."†

The inquiries in this study went on over two years; 9,500 persons were interviewed. The questions studied were whether the person had prolonged low moods, suicidal thoughts or actions, loss of interest in usually enjoyable activities, lack of motivation for extended periods, loss of appetite, and the psychological depressions for which lithium or similar drugs are prescribed.

This widespread epidemic of depression, Dr. Seligman indicates, has gone hand in hand during the past fifty years with a loss of psychological and spiritual guidance. The family influence has evaporated in a culture which has little belief in God.

There has occurred a bankruptcy of sources to which one, particularly the youth, could turn for solace or direction when he or she has had a personal failure. The person has only him or herself as the court of last appeal, and that, says Seligman, is a frail court indeed. We have already cited the rise in suicide in youth in the 1970s, and these studies put that dismal figure into its context.

As a scientific check against their own prejudices, Seligman and his colleagues studied two primitive cultures. One was the

*From James Buie, " 'Me' Decades Generate Depression," *Monitor* (American Psychological Association) 19, no. 10 (October 1988), summary of the research of Dr. Martin Seligman.

†These summaries are from a report, "Why Is There So Much Depression Today?" given by Martin E. P. Seligman to the American Psychological Association, 1988. These investigations were supported in part by NIMH grant 19604, NIMH grant 40142, NIA grant AG05590, and a grant to Seligman from the MacArthur Foundation Research Network on Determinants and Consequences of Health-Promoting and Health-Damaging Behavior.

Amish of Lancaster County in Pennsylvania, who have no automobiles and have preserved an island of early nineteenth-century community with no influence from what we could call modern American society. The other was the Kaluli of New Guinea. The investigators found that in these societies a person goes through well-established social structures, consisting of myths and rituals when he or she has a failure or some personal loss. The breakdown in myths is made good so that the individual can pick himself up without inner loss.

The individual in our culture, however, when picking himself or herself up after a failure, has nowhere to turn except "to a very small and frail unit indeed: the self." This again is one reason the profession of psychotherapy has grown so rapidly, though obviously this profession cannot be considered a sufficient answer to the epidemic of depression. American people, by and large, have few societal guides, as we have pointed out in earlier chapters—no rituals, no myths to give them solace in time of need.*

The sheer size of individual buying power, "the decline of the power of religion and the family and of commitment to the nation has weakened the buffering effect of faith against depression."

Martin Seligman proposes the tentative solutions from himself and his colleagues. One "frightening possibility is that we will rashly surrender the sweet freedom that individualism brings, giving up personal control and concern for the self in order to shed depression and attain meaning. The twentieth century is riddled with disastrous examples of societies that have done just this to cure their ills. The current yearning for fundamentalist religion both in America and throughout the world appears to be such a temptation." The flight into cults, which was so prominent, particularly on the west coast, is another example.

---

*See Chapter 3, in which the relation between crime and the weakening of family influence is discussed.

But Seligman proposes a "more hopeful possibility: a balance between individualism, with its perilous freedoms, and commitment to the common good, which should lower depressions as well as make life more meaningful."

We are here emphasizing that one symptom of the whole-sale condition that Seligman describes is our lack of viable myths and rituals. *It is imperative that we rediscover myths which can give us the psychological structure necessary to confront this widespread depression.* Otherwise we will never be able to control the devastating use of drugs.

NARCISSISM, DRUGS,
AND MONEY

Bill Moyers went into a section of New York City where one can at any time buy drugs, especially crack and cocaine, from boys on the street corner. There were no policemen around; the people told him that when one "cop" was shot several months earlier, there were a number of police force there for a few days, but they had left. Moyers was told by the boys themselves that they start selling cocaine and crack when they are about twelve years old. When there is a vacancy in their ranks, there is always someone waiting to take the missing seller's place. This was the only job in the area. There were also several college students in the group gathered around Moyers. Later in the interview Moyers asked these boys point-blank why they sold drugs. Their answer was simple, "Money, money, money."

They had learned that this was the aim of a considerable part of our society. On television they had seen Ivan Boesky, the in-trader, who was then in prison for embezzling many millions. Also they noted that those who get a million dollars are lionized and their pictures are saluted in the newspapers. These boys had noted that young people get their MBAs and make a million dollars before they are thirty; it does not seem to matter how they got it. Moyers tried to learn whether they had any role models. In denying any such persons, the boys mentioned the Watergate affair, Boesky, North, and other such persons around the country. These boys were aware that the lottery prize in Pennsylvania had risen to $115 million, that half the states in the union now have this form of gambling, and that the number is growing.

By happenstance, just after the report of Moyers' interview, photos in the TV news were shown of ex-President Reagan and his wife landing in the airport in Japan. It was announced that on the next day Reagan was to receive $2 million for two twenty-minute speeches. One wonders whether the young people had been right when they repeated their goals of "Money, money, money!"*

We have traced the original myth of individualism, which was so central for the early settlers of America, through Whitman's poetry and the myth of Horatio Alger. These influences have surely formed and molded the myths and the way of life of our present decades. We will seek to clarify the forming and reforming of life in America which, in our consciousness, can re-form these myths in ways that will form the basis for our living constructively in the twenty-first century.

*The great sums of money, such as Michael Milken being fined for $600 million, add to the idea that the attraction in contemporary life lies in making these great sums. See *New York Times,* April 25, 1990.

EIGHT

~

Gatsby and the American Dream

His life had been confused and disordered . . . but if he
could once return to a certain starting place and go over it
all slowly, he could find out what that thing was.
F. Scott Fitzgerald,
The Great Gatsby

AFTER THE ENDING of World War I in 1918, there was in
America a great deal of unleashed energy with no place to
go. Everyone seemed full of free-floating passion to participate
in the war effort, most of which energy was then left hanging in
the air by the Versailles treaty. How was our energy to be
expressed? A great deal of it was channeled into the amazing
twelve-year phenomenon known as the Jazz Age.

THE JAZZ AGE

This age of the nostalgic whining of saxophones was a time of
rebellion against almost everything. It was the time when Prohibition and the Volstead Act made organized crime pay richly
and sired a contempt for all laws and ethics in general. "Puri-

tanism" was a dirty word. The rebellion was most obvious in
women's styles: long hair went out and the French bob came
in, and it is hard for us nowadays to recall the horror that first
greeted this shearing of feminine hair. Women rebelled against
ankle-length gowns, and suddenly dresses were above the
knees, as in the John Held, Jr., cartoons. Along with the
Charleston and ragtime, the flapper was in with necking and
petting, the automobile furnishing a movable form of cover for
this truncated sex.

Money flowed freely in the 1920s. In politics it was the age
of Warren Gamaliel Harding's presidency, which ended in
utter disgrace, and the Teapot Dome scandal, which dwarfed
the scandals to come until our present days. Blessed with President Coolidge's proclamation "The business of America is
business," there was mad gambling on the stock market, the
great extent of which was not recognized until that historic
day, October 29, 1929, when the stock market crashed, the
banks were closed, and the intense suffering of the Great Depression began.

In this Jazz Age we experienced a great surge of interest in
"selling" everything, including ourselves. Books were published
on how to sell your personality to employers and how to sell
yourself to your lover and prospective mother-in-law. The distinction was never clear as to why selling *yourself* was good but
selling your *body* on the street corner was not. Bruce Barton, a
successful New York advertising man, wrote a book portraying
Jesus as the Great Salesman, *The Man Nobody Knows,* which
was read from coast to coast. Get-rich-quick schemes were
spawned by the moment; almost everyone got burned purchas-
ing Florida real estate which turned out to be soggy marshland.
There were the cults: Aimie Semple McPherson, Father
Coughlin, and so on.

I propose that the Jazz Age was the first throes of collapse of
the American dream. *The structure of myths on which America
had existed for four centuries was now thrown into radical transition.*

Such enlightened intellectual leaders as Frederick Jackson Turner, whose "frontier hypothesis" had been the chief formula for the myth of the frontier, seemed not to be aware of the import of the times. Turner believed that the midwestern state universities would save democracy by producing trained leaders.

I prefer to believe . . . that education and science are powerful forces to change these tendencies and to produce a rational solution of the problems of life. . . . I place my trust in the mind of man seeking solutions by intellectual toil . . . bold to find ways of adjustment . . . committed to peace on earth.*

Turner wrote these idealistic words in 1924, in the middle of the Jazz Age, with no foreshadowing of the imminence of the Great Depression and the radical shifting of the structure of myths on which America had been based.

In this Jazz Age was produced a work of art which chronicled the deterioration of the underlying myths and predicted the results of their collapse. This was the classic novel, *The Great Gatsby*, by F. Scott Fitzgerald. Fitzgerald is recognized as the voice par excellence of the Jazz Age. He carried the soul of this distraught period in his own handsome, lithe body and fantastically rich imagination. He had been named after a distant relative, Francis Scott Key, who wrote the American national anthem. In a house in St. Paul, Minnesota, which had been in his mother's family for generations, Scott was brought up by an overdirective mother, his father being, in the eyes of his mother's family, a failure in the business world. His mother lavished affection on Scott rather than on her unsuccessful husband.

We see Scott experiencing puppy love with his partners at dancing school but already as a boy writing. We see him later at Princeton, writing a brilliant college musical, but then being dropped from school because he flunked math and chemistry.

*Smith, *Virgin Land*, p. 259. But Turner is obviously anxious about the future; his remark smacks of reassurance.

We see him drunk in New York, fighting with bouncers and getting badly beaten up, but recovering and still writing. We see him going back for his fraternity reunion at Princeton, getting into another fight in which both his eyes were blackened, being expelled forthwith by his fraternity for unseemly conduct, and then trying to crawl back in through the window.

Fitzgerald wrote directly out of the center of the Jazz Age with all its turmoil and all its romance. He produced, along with a great number of mediocre stories in a mad struggle to get out of debt, several good books and one work of genius, *The Great Gatsby*. This novel gave readers a "touch of infinity," so said its editor, Maxwell Perkins. It is the most poignant account of the conflicted, self-pitying, but tragic soul of the Jazz Age. This novel presents the tragedy of the American myth which had so successfully guided America since the landing on Plymouth Rock.

At a certain point in his career, Fitzgerald withdrew from his alcoholism and his playboy activities, withdrew his splendid imagination—which Edna St. Vincent Millay was later to describe as a great diamond possessed by an old woman—and sought, in solitude, to write a book that would do justice to his great talent. Such had been his promise to Maxwell Perkins, his editor. Like Gatsby in his book, he sought now to find out what had caused the chaos in his life. The "thing" for Gatsby was what had happened in his falling in love with Daisy. The blocks of Gatsby's (and Fitzgerald's) life,

formed a ladder to a secret place above the trees—he could climb to it, if he climbed alone, and once there he could suck on the pap of life, gulp down the incomparable milk of wonder . . . listening for a moment to the tuning fork that had been struck upon a star.*

The Great Gatsby is Fitzgerald's spiritual autobiography. He uses the word "forever" often in this book; Maxwell Perkins wrote him, "You are able with an occasional glance at the sky

---

*The Great Gatsby (New York: Scribners, 1925), pp. 111–112.

to impart a sense of eternity." It is a book which deals with the myths of the day; it has "the symbolic truth of a global vision."

TRAGIC SUCCESS

The son of shiftless and unsuccessful farm people of North Dakota, Jim Gatz reflected the American myth of Proteus, in one form. He believed he could recreate himself, deny his parentage and his roots and build a new identity. In his imagination he had never really accepted them as his parents at all.

Already as a boy Gatsby had written in the back of a comic book the self-improving rules to make himself a great success, his own Horatio Alger story. "The truth was," Fitzgerald writes, "that Jay Gatsby of West Egg, Long Island, sprang from his . . . Platonic conception of himself. . . . So he invented just the sort of Jay Gatsby that a seventeen-year-old boy would be likely to invent, and to this conception he was faithful to the end."* As his biographer, Andre Le Vot writes, Fitzgerald in this book "reflects better than all his autobiographical writing the heart of the problems he and his generation faced. . . . In *Gatsby,* haunted as it is by a sense of Sin and Fall, Fitzgerald assumed to himself all the weakness and depravity of human nature."†

Like Luke Larkin in the Horatio Alger myth, Gatsby is first befriended by the rich owner of a yacht, Mr. Dan Cody, when he swims out to warn Cody of an unseen rock on which the anchored yacht would founder.** Cody hires him and gives him a blue yachtsman's uniform, the first of Gatsby's line of uniforms—the army uniform in which he courts Daisy, the white suit when he later entertains lavishly in his mansion

---

*Ibid., p. 99.

†Andre Le Vot, *F. Scott Fitzgerald, A Biography* (New York: Doubleday, 1983), p. 142.

**Cody, we remember, is the true name of Buffalo Bill. In this Fitzgerald also shows his tie to American mythology.

("You always look so cool," Daisy was later to remark).

Sent to Louisville for his military training, Gatsby falls in love with the heiress, Daisy. They consummate their love beneath the blossoming lilacs of spring. They promise to wait for each other till the war is over. But he does not count on her conformist nature, her lack of character, her devotion to "the dancing feet, the fortunes behind everything." When in Europe hearing that she has married Tom Buchanan, a monied society man from Chicago, Gatsby vows he will regain her. Committing his whole self to this dream, he changes his name, his manner of dress, attends Oxford for five months, where he acquires a new accent, and comes back to America to become rich, to buy the new mansion with the "blue lawn" on Long Island Sound. All is concentrated on one purpose, to win back Daisy, who with Tom now summers across Long Island Sound.

He has complete faith, in typical American fashion, that he can transform his dreams into action. Nick, the interlocutor who has rented the ordinary house next door for the summer, has his own views about life—conformist, moralistic, Puritanical, coming as he did from the midwest followed by Yale—which are exactly opposite to Gatsby's views. But Nick is forced to admit about Gatsby, "there was something gorgeous about him, some heightened sensitivity to the promises of life." Gatsby had an "extraordinary gift for hope, a romantic readiness such as I have never found in any other person and which it is not likely I shall ever find again."[*]

Gatsby believed unconditionally in the powerful American myth of the "Green Light," a symbol which comes up often in this novel. The green light was on the end of Daisy's dock, as though enticing Gatsby. The first glimpse Nick got of his neighbor was one evening when Gatsby stood out on his lawn looking across the sound at this green light, raising his arms in a yearning gesture, "and I swear I saw him tremble," says Nick.

This eternal Green Light is a revealing myth of America, for

[*]Fitzgerald, *The Great Gatsby*, p. 2.

it means new potentialities, new frontiers, new life around the corner. There is no destiny, or if there is we construct it ourselves. Everything is ahead; we make anything we choose of life. The Green Light beckons us onward and upward with a promise of bigger and better things in higher and higher skyscrapers, interminably rising into infinity. The Green Light turns into our greatest illusion, covering over our difficulties, permitting us to take evil steps with no guilt, hiding our daimonic capacities and our problems by its profligate promises, and destroying our values en route. The Green Light is the Promised Land myth siring Horatio Alger.

Gatsby certainly was a success in the Horatio Alger sense; he had become literally rich, and though probably unconscious of it, he was completely committed to that myth we inherited from the nineteenth century. His half-literate father, who has, we will see later, come from North Dakota when he read his son's death notice in the Chicago paper, overcomes his grief at seeing his son in the coffin by his elation at the proofs all about the house of Gatsby's great success: "He had a big future before him. . . . If he'd of lived, he'd of been a great man. A man like James J. Hill. He'd of helped build up the country."*

Obviously Gatsby had money galore—even though the money was gotten illicitly, the way many people in the Jazz Age got theirs. There has been in America no clear-cut differentiation between right and wrong ways to get rich. Playing the stock market? Finding oil under your shack in Texas? Deforesting vast areas of Douglas fir in the state of Washington? Amassing piles of money for lectures after getting out of prison as a Watergate crook? The important thing in the American dream has been to *get* rich, and then *those very riches give a sanction to your situation.* The fact of your being successful is proof that God smiles on you and that you are among the saved. It is not hard to see how this, in true Calvinistic tradition, drifted into getting rich as the eleventh commandment.

*Ibid., p. 169.

If money could buy everything, Gatsby would have been the most fortunate of men. But the success and the money all went to flesh out the vast dream which held Gatsby in its thrall and which he took as the reality of his life. Money could buy the vast parties, the great glitter of the mansion, the freely flowing liquor, the jazz music which floated from the orchestras as the hundreds of people flocked to the lights like moths at night. But all were important only because sooner or later these accoutrements of Babylon would draw in Daisy. True to his myth, Gatsby was successful at this also—Daisy came out and they gradually rehearsed the lines so dear to Gatsby's heart.

Gatsby's tragic flaw was that he took his dream—the American dream—for reality. He had complete faith in it and never doubted that his transformation and his ultimate success were assured. Nick speaks of "the colossal vitality of his illusion." If Kierkegaard is right that "purity of heart is to will one thing," Gatsby was indeed pure of heart. Strangely, he is the one person in the book who possesses complete integrity. When he tells Nick of his goal to have Daisy confess that she loved and loves only him, and to marry him in the great house in Louisville just as they had originally planned, Nick remonstrates, "You can't re-live the past." Gatsby responds, "Can't re-live the past? Of course you can."*

Nick overcomes his abhorrence of Gatsby's way of life—his having made his money through his connections with bootleggers and his serving as the front for gangsters. The corrupt means Gatsby uses to achieve his ends have not altered his fundamental integrity, his spiritual intactness, writes Le Vot. His means reflect the corruption of the times, they are the only ones available to an indigent cavalier seeking his fortune. True corruption, Nick discovered, lies in the hearts of those who despise Gatsby, especially in Tom's. Gatsby's integrity consisted of his daring to dream and to be faithful to his dream; it never even occurred to him to tell that it was Daisy, not he,

*Ibid., p. 111.

who was driving his car when it killed Myrtle Wilson. It was not Gatsby who was to go wrong, says Nick, "it was the foul dust that floated in the wake of his dreams that temporarily closed out my interest in the abortive sorrows and short-winded elations of men." In the same sense, it is not the American myth in itself that leads us astray; it is the "foul dust that floats in the wake" of this dream. It is hanging onto the Horatio Alger myth when it no longer applies; it is using the past myths to rationalize the poverty and hunger in the world; it is the increasing of paranoia out of recourse to a past long since dead.

But Gatsby's dream was too insistent. "You demand too much," Daisy was to whimper in the grand showdown in the Plaza Hotel, when Gatsby insists she say to Tom that she never loved him. Fitzgerald goes on, "Only the dead dream fought on as the afternoon slipped away, trying to touch what was no longer tangible, struggling unhappily, undespairingly."* We note that Fitzgerald writes *un* despairingly. *True despair is a constructive emotion capable of eliciting creative solutions to a situation.* This was just what the Jazz Age was incapable of feeling. Nick mused, as Gatsby lay in his coffin and not a word came from Daisy, that perhaps Gatsby "no longer cared. If that was true he must have felt that he had lost the old warm world, paid a high price for living too long with a single dream."†

THE INABILITY TO CARE

In the Jazz Age, writes Fitzgerald, and behind our loneliness was the lack of authentic caring. His compatriots felt that caring threatens our independence and our freedom to pull up stakes on a whim and move to some other place. Gatsby's dream founders, speaking concretely, on the rocks of the inability of people to care. This is specifically presented by Fitzgerald

*Ibid., p. 135.
†Ibid., p. 162.

as the carelessness of Tom and Daisy. "They were careless people, Tom and Daisy—they smash up things and creatures and then retreat back into their money or their vast carelessness, or whatever it was that kept them together, and let other people clean up the mess they made."*

Fitzgerald uses the word "careless" on almost every page. Near the end, after Gatsby has been killed, Nick tells us of a fantastic repetitive dream he has.

> I see it as a night scene by El Greco: a hundred houses, at once conventional and grotesque, crouching under a sullen, overhanging sky and a lustreless moon. In the foreground four solemn men in dress suits are walking along the sidewalk with a stretcher on which lies a drunken woman in a white evening dress. Her hand, which dangles over the side, sparkles cold with jewels. Gravely the men turn in at a house—the wrong house. But no one knows the woman's name, and no one cares.†

This recurring dream—which can be taken as his own dream since it emerges from his fantasy—casts light on Fitzgerald's own compulsive, and hence anxious, drunken brawls. He has no house of himself, the dream is saying; he will be homeless and lonely forever. But more than that, he is being carried by men who do not care, and perhaps under the surface, we don't care either. This is why this book is haunted by a sense of the myth of sin and fall.

The word "care" should be taken in its literal meaning: the ability of people to have compassion, to communicate on deeper levels and to love each other. It has some relation to Freud's myth of Eros. Tom and Daisy had no sense of mercy, which expresses care and usually can be counted on to mitigate human cruelty.

Heidegger made care *(sorge)* the basis of being: without care our selves shrink up, we lose our capacity to will as well as our

*Ibid., pp. 180–181.
†Ibid., p. 178.

own selfhood.* Sometimes there is a hint in Fitzgerald that the lack of care represents original sin, one's incapacity to sense and to communicate with the heart of another; and he even implies that it is impossible to escape doing violence to another person's deepest feelings and needs. Fitzgerald often uses the terms "unutterable," "inexpressible," "incommunicable," as though he is struggling hard to communicate something which in fact cannot be spoken, struggling to explain that we were set upon this tiny whirling planet with a passionate need to love each other, but we can do it only partially. The last day at that weird breakfast just an hour before Gatsby is shot in his own swimming pool, Nick and Gatsby are trying to get some perspective on the tragic events of the previous day. Gatsby tries to persuade himself that Daisy may have loved Tom "just for a minute, when they were married—and she loved me more even then, do you see?"† He was in reality waiting with one ear to the phone—would Daisy call or send some token? None came.

When Nick left he turned to shout across the lawn to Gatsby, "They're a rotten crowd. . . . You're worth the whole damn bunch put together."** Nick adds that he always was "glad I said that. It was the only compliment I ever gave him." All this despite the fact, as Nick puts it, that Gatsby "represented everything for which I have an unaffected scorn."‡

These are the two sides of Fitzgerald in a Laocoön conflict, and he presents them in juxtaposition throughout the book. The struggle is between the ethos of the Jazz Age and Fitzgerald's own integrity, his sensitive imagination which on one level saw with amazing clarity the sin and hell motif of the 1920s and on another level was seduced by the very things he hated. This is what makes the book so poignant.

A central theme in Fitzgerald's novel is loneliness. At

---

*See Rollo May, *Love and Will* (New York: Norton, 1969), p. 290.
†Fitzgerald, *The Great Gatsby*, p. 152.
**Ibid., p. 154.
‡Ibid., p. 2.

Gatsby's parties, amid the richest, most abandoned forms of music and dancing and drinking, there was no communication at all, only "enthusiastic meetings between people who never knew each other's names." And when Gatsby stood on his porch, "his hand up in formal gesture of farewell" to the departing guests, "a sudden emptiness seemed to flow now from the windows and the great doors, endowing with complete isolation the figure of the host."*

Nick himself is sensitive to the lonely atmosphere as he wanders about New York. "I felt a haunting loneliness sometimes, and felt it in others—poor young clerks in the dusk, wasting the most poignant moments of night and life."† After the showdown in the Plaza, Nick suddenly remembers that this day was his birthday. "Thirty—the promise of a decade of loneliness, a thinning list of single men to know, a thinning brief-case of enthusiasm, thinning hair."**

But the most lonely figure of all in the book is Jay Gatsby, the host of these fantastic parties which he himself did not like. From the moment we first see him in the dusk standing alone on his front lawn yearning across Long Island Sound toward the green light on Daisy's wharf, from that moment to his funeral, he is the prototype of loneliness. *The fact that Gatsby would not have recognized it as such makes it all the more telling; it was not for him an emotion which comes and goes but a character state, a state of being.* Nobody else in the world reached behind his driving purpose; he was in actuality a self-made person, and, like all self-made persons, he was cut off inwardly from any deep relationship. Everybody flowed in and out of his great house for a purpose which was completely separate from the parties—to bring Daisy to him.

As Gatsby's body lay in his coffin in the house, Nick kept hearing as though Gatsby were imploring him, "Look here, old sport, you've got to get somebody for me. . . . I can't go through

*Ibid., p. 56.
†Ibid., p. 57.
**Ibid., p. 136.

this alone." Nick reassures the dead Gatsby, "I'll get somebody for you, Gatsby. Don't worry. Just trust me and I'll get somebody for you—"*

But in spite of all Nick's phoning, and though the funeral cortege of three cars waited an extra half hour, Gatsby's final loneliness at his funeral is summed up in two words: *nobody came.* Not a word or a flower from Daisy. A drizzle added to the sad mood around the grave, as though nature itself were taking part in this inutterably bereft moment, when not just a man was being buried but also, most important, the American dream; the central myth of America was being placed in its grave.

There was one exception to the little group at the grave; oddly enough one of the men who had been drunk at Gatsby's parties turned up at the funeral. Aghast, he cries, "Why, my God! they used to go there [to the parties] by the hundreds!" He adds the phrase the equivalent of which is present in every reader's mind, "The poor son-of-a-bitch." The funeral is like Willy Loman's in *Death of a Salesman,* except there is not even the handful of people to discuss what really went wrong.

Fitzgerald himself felt this deep loneliness. Only as a self-defeating effort to break through his loneliness can we understand his panicky cavorting and compulsive drunkenness. Indeed the rootlessness was present throughout the whole Jazz Age; it was not till the crash in the 1930s that we were forced to look directly at our problem and ask whether there was something wrong in our alienation from each other, our isolation from the fountain of life.

THE AMERICAN-STYLE GOD

Can this loneliness and carelessness be due to the fact that human beings have become estranged from God? This may

*Ibid., p. 165.

seem a queer question here, but it is implicit in *The Great Gatsby*. True, when people lose the capacity to experience myths, they also lose their gods. This question comes up in *The Great Gatsby* in a remarkable symbol, again a demonstration of Fitzgerald's genius, that of the eyes of Doctor T. J. Eckleburg.

Halfway between New York and West Egg a wasteland confronts the commuter, a desolate landscape as barren as the moon. Fitzgerald calls this wasteland the "valley of ashes," where ashes take the fantastic forms of houses and chimneys and "ash-gray men who move dimly . . . through the powdery air, swarming up an impenetrable cloud of ash dust and dismally gray surroundings."*

But above the gray land and the spasms of bleak dust which drift endlessly over it, you perceive, after a moment, the eyes of Doctor T. J. Eckleburg, . . . which are blue and gigantic—their retinas are one yard high. They look out of no face, but, instead, from a pair of enormous yellow spectacles which pass over a non-existent nose. Evidently some wild wag of an occulist set them there to fatten his practice in the borough of Queens, and then . . . forgot them and moved away.†

The whole scene takes on a strange—and hell-like—religious aspect. George Wilson, half-crazed after his wife is killed by Gatsby's car on the road in front of his garage, stands with his visitor Michaelis across the road from the valley of ashes. This young Greek neighbor has stayed beside George all night in his bereavement. But Wilson keeps staring at these gigantic eyes. Michaelis tries to console him, "In a time like this, George, a man needs a church." But George mumbles,

"I spoke to her, I told her she might fool me but she couldn't fool God." And he repeats, "I said, You may fool me, but you can't fool God!"
Standing beside him, Michaelis saw with a shock that he was look-

*This "wasteland" makes an obvious connection with T. S. Eliot's poem by that name, also written in this Jazz Age.
†Fitzgerald, *The Great Gatsby*, p. 23.

ing at the eyes of Doctor T. J. Eckleburg, which had just emerged, pale and enormous from the dissolving night.

"That's an advertisement," Michaelis assured him. Something made him turn away from the window and look back into the room. But Wilson stood there a long time, his face close to the window pane, nodding into the twilight.*

During his adult life Fitzgerald had continuously wrestled with his Catholic upbringing. The struggle is obvious in this novel, and the undercurrent of sin and hell are present in his other works as well.

In his biography of Fitzgerald, Le Vot argues that it was a lesser god, like Lucifer, who created the world and then abandoned it. In any case, he believes Fitzgerald's meaning is clear, "that it is not men who have abandoned God, but God who has deserted men in an uninhabitable, absurd material universe."†

It was the nostalgic, self-pitying aspect of the Jazz Age which led it to react with resentful rebellion against all restraints, which felt itself abandoned, a mood which comes out in Fitzgerald's own self-pity. (Hemingway tried to get this across to him; in a letter to Fitzgerald he wrote, "We were all bitched at the start—we are not tragic characters.") This was partially Fitzgerald's inheritance from the overprotection and overconcern of his mother in his childhood days, when he lacked an image of a strong and successful father with which to identify. But more extensively, the "pampered child" psychology was a central part of the 1920s, when people believed in their rights for everything, when legal and other standards of justice were sneered at by persons high and low, and the eat-drink-and-be-merry philosophy seemed to hold everyone in its grip.

The most significant thing about Dr. T. J. Eckleburg's billboard was the fact that it was a huge, blown-up *photograph*. Susan Sontag has pointed out that our modern age confuses

*Ibid., p. 160.
†Le Vot, *F. Scott Fitzgerald*, p. 156.

photographs with reality. Many people when traveling assume that if they can only take a photograph of a treasure in a distant land then they *have* it; they do not need genuinely to *look* at the statue until it becomes part of their imagination, until they have absorbed it into their being. With the "shot" taken in a jiffy, they have "captured" the scene. We note that both words—to shoot and to capture—are from the hunter's or soldier's vocabulary. The traveler has the "treasure" in its minute form in the camera roll which he can take home. It is filed away, only a name and a number to call it forth to show other people. This is the meaning of God-has-abandoned-man; the substitute God, filed away in these photographs, makes it impossible for the genuine God to return.

These gigantic eyes, which George Wilson worships as the eyes of God, are, as Michaelis has pointed out, an *advertisement*. Its purpose is to sell eyeglasses; it was put there with the hope of sprucing up an occulist's business. Commercialism, the buying and selling, the rattling of silver dollars in one's pocket, has usurped the role of God. The advertising man, the person who is skilled at making photographs of things in order to sell them, the triumph of profit making—these capacities were part and parcel of the 1920s, of the culture of Gatsby and Fitzgerald and the tragedy that is presented in this book. This triumph of advertising and commercialism ironically appears "in a place where ruin is the sole residue of industrial prosperity."*

A prophecy made by Edmund Concourt, concerning the new deity in industrial societies, appeared in a Paris journal:

Sometimes I think that a day will come when modern peoples will be blessed with an American-style god . . . his image no longer elastic and adaptable to painters' imaginations, no longer floating on Veronica's veil, but caught in a photographic portrait. . . . Yes, I picture a god who will appear in photographs and who will wear glasses.†

*Ibid., p. 158.
†Ibid.

This god will not have the face of a Carnegie or a Rockefeller or a Whitney. Indeed, it will have no discernible face at all, only the man in the gray suit, anonymous, a mirror representation of the Advertising Man, who is not concerned about what he believes—indeed, beliefs are irrelevant—but only about how much he can sell. He knows that in the Jazz Age he must first of all sell himself. The man who worships this god of commercialism is a strangely robot-like type of person who fittingly is spawned by this wasteland, has no "up" or "down," no "north" or "south," and probably doesn't even want any. This myth does not involve the pioneers of production or invention, but only of marketing. The new goal, what Le Vot calls the "new hero of daily life," the myth that still is convincing, is the seller, the hustler, the "ad man." The only real tragedy written by an American playwright, says Le Vot, "the one deeply rooted in the people's mythology, is *Death of a Salesman*."* Willy Loman is a salesman in the full meaning of the word. If you are selling yourself—a smile on your face and a shine on your shoes—you make yourself into an object, you then have no identity, and so it makes entire sense that they should say at his grave, "He never knew who he was." We only know he "was the best liked." This fits the way much of the technology has been moving in the West, and especially in America, to the extent that our chief goal, our sought-after myth, is to "keep our country one in which anyone can become rich."

CONSCIOUSNESS IN AMERICA

After Gatsby's burial, Fitzgerald, through the person of Nick, muses about his own consciousness of America. In his musing the tragedy of Gatsby becomes explicitly identified with the loss of American myths and the demise of our American

---

*Le Vot forgets Eugene O'Neill, but his point is clear.

dream. He recalls the long trips home from prep school at Christmastime, meeting with old friends in the Chicago station, the railroad trip across Wisconsin when he and the other young people were "unutterably aware of our identity with this country for one strange hour, before we melted indistinguishably into it again."

That's my Middle West—not the wheat or the prairies or the lost Swede towns, but the thrilling returning trains of my youth, and the street lamps and sleigh bells in the frosty dark and the shadows of holly wreaths thrown by lighted windows on the snow. I am part of that.*

He recognizes that this story has been about the west— Gatsby and Tom and Daisy and he himself are all from the middle west. Not the far west, whence came our myth of the lonely cowboy; nor the Horatio Alger myth, the collapse of which he is describing. But the middle west, which, however one may want to get away from it, is the birthplace of modern American morality and literature. Perhaps, Nick ponders, we people from the middle west "possessed some deficiency in common which made us subtly unadaptable to Eastern life." For the east was Babylon, where one can only sit by the waters and weep. The real soul of the nation was beyond New York, "back where the dark fields of the Republic roll on under the night."

"Gatsby's whole story," writes Andre Le Vot, "and, behind it, that of a grand dream gone awry center on this symbol of Contemporary America and its companion vision. . . . *The collapse of Gatsby's dream is implicitly paralleled . . . with the failure of the American dream.*"†

With the genius of a great novelist, Fitzgerald is struggling to make clear the crisis in which America was and is existing. The novel bears a curious resemblance to another myth, beginning, in Genesis before the flood, with the crowd surrounding

*Fitzgerald, *The Great Gatsby*, p. 177.
†Le Vot, *F. Scott Fitzgerald*, pp. 147–148.

the ark and jeering at Noah's efforts to prepare to meet the holocaust toward which his world was sliding headlong.

Nick decides to leave the east and go back to his home. But before he leaves, he feels he is haunted by Gatsby's house in those last days:

I could still hear the music and the laughter, faint and incessant. . . .

One night I did hear a material car there, and saw its lights stop at his front steps. But I didn't investigate. Probably it was some final guest who had been away at the ends of the earth and didn't know that the party was over."*

On his last evening, he went down to the beach and, sprawling out on the sand, gave himself over to his reminiscing. The big shore places were closed and there were "hardly any lights except the shadowy moving glow of a ferry boat across the Sound." America had its flowering in the prosperity of this lush countryside with its great mountains and fertile plains.

And as the moon rose higher the inessential houses began to melt away until gradually I became aware of the old island here that flowered once for Dutch sailors' eyes—a fresh, green breast of the new world. Its vanished trees, the trees that had made way for Gatsby's house, had once pandered in whispers to the last and greatest of all human dreams; for a transitory enchanted moment man must have held his breath in the presence of this continent, compelled into an aesthetic contemplation he neither understood nor desired, face to face for the last time in history with something commensurate to his capacity for wonder.

Nick then remembers Gatsby and his capacity to wonder.

He had come a long way to this blue lawn, and his dream must have seemed so close that he could hardly fail to grasp it. He did not know that it was already behind him, somewhere back in that vast obscurity beyond the city, where the dark fields of the Republic roll on under the night.†

*Fitzgerald, *The Great Gatsby*, p. 181.
†Ibid., p. 182.

"Gatsby believed in the green light," like millions of other good Americans. But Nick knows this "orgiastic future that year by year recedes before us. . . . It eluded us then, but that's no matter—tomorrow we will run faster, stretch out our arms farther. . . . And one fine morning—"

This last sentence hangs in the air with only a dash and no period to conclude it. In the silence Nick gropes in momentary despair. He pauses as he gropes. Is there any sense to it all? Is there any principle, any wisdom, any thought that will shed some light on this apparent hopelessness in American consciousness? Or are we doomed to live in a world nobody can make sense of? Nick gropes for a *myth* that will cast light, as a man seeks a light switch, to turn on whole heavens. He seeks a myth to absorb this ceaseless failure, a myth which will make of the eternal return something that we human beings can endure, a myth that can lend meaning to our absurd existence. Nick then adds the last line in the book, a paragraph in itself, almost like a postscript:

"So we beat on, boats against the current, borne back ceaselessly into the past."*

THE MYTH OF SISYPHUS

Out of that moment of despair is born this myth which is new but eternally old, the only myth that fits this seemingly hopeless situation. This is the myth of Sisyphus. The one myth which directly counters the American dream, this myth denies progress, goes no place at all, seems to be a repetition, every day and every act being forever the same in perpetual monotonous toil and sweat.

But that is to omit its crucial meaning. One thing Sisyphus can do: he can be aware of each moment in this drama between himself and Zeus, between himself and his fate. This—because

*Ibid., p. 182.

it is most human—makes his reaction completely different from that of the dark night of the mountain up which he rolls his rock.

Punished by Zeus for deceiving the gods, Sisyphus is described by Homer:

> With many a weary step, and many a groan,
> Up the high hill he heaves a huge round stone:
> The huge round stone, resulting with a bound,
> Thunders impetus down.*

Indeed, Homer tells us then that "Poor Sisyphus" could hear "the charming sounds that ravished his ear," which came from Orpheus' flute in Pluto's realm.† The myth of Sisyphus is sometimes interpreted as the sun climbing to its apex every day and then curving down again. Nothing could be more important for human life than these circular journeys of the sun.

Out of the melancholy brooding about Gatsby comes the monotony which all human creatures must endure—a brooding which the Jazz Age with its boozing and dancing and parties and endless agitation went crazy trying to deny. For we face monotony in all we do; we draw in and exhale breath after breath in ceaseless succession through every moment of our lives, which is monotony par excellence. But out of this repetitiveness of breathing the Buddhists and Yoga have formed their religious meditation and a way of achieving the heights of ecstasy.

For Sisyphus is a creative person who even tried to erase death. He never gives up but always is devoted to creating a better kind of life; he is a model of a hero who presses on in spite of his or her despair. Without such capacity to confront despair we would not have had Beethoven or Rembrandt or Michaelangelo or Dante or Goethe or any others of the great figures in the development of culture.

---

*Homer (Pope's translation), in H. A. Guerber, *Myths of Greece and Rome* (London: George Harrap, 1907), p. 144.
†Ibid., p. 60.

Sisyphus' consciousness is the hallmark of being human. Sisyphus is the thinking reed with a mind which can construct purposes, know ecstasy and pain, distinguish monotony from despair, and place the monotony—the rolling of the stone—in the scheme of his rebellion, the act for which he is condemned. We do not know Sisyphus' reveries, his ruminations, as he performed his act, but we do know that each act may have been again a rebellion against the gods of conformity, or each act could have been an act of penance. Such is the imagination, the purposes and human faiths which we construct. Sisyphus takes his place in that line of heroes who declare their rebellion against the inadequate gods for the sake of greater gods—an illustration and inspiring line consisting of Prometheus, Adam, and hopefully even down to our own myths and gods. Out of this eternal capacity to see our tasks, as Sisyphus did his, comes the courage to move beyond the rock, beyond the monotony of day-to-day experience.

Sisyphus, furthermore, must have noticed in his trips some wisp of pink cloud that heralds the dawn, or felt some pleasure in the wind against his breast as he strode down the hill after his rock, or remembered some line of poetry to muse upon. Indeed, he must have thought of some myth to make sense of an otherwise senseless world. All these things are possible for Sisyphus—even, if he had been Gatsby, to be aware that the past cannot be relived but in every step he can leave the past behind. These capacities of human imagination are the hallmark of our paradoxical condemnation and our epiphany as human beings.

The myth of Sisyphus needs to be held in juxtaposition with the Green Light to lend some balance, some dialectic to us as individuals as well as to America. It is a safeguard against unallowed arrogance of the chosen people, and it makes clear that Horatio Alger only leads us astray. Sisyphus balances the myth of the Promised Land: it requires us to pause in our exploitation of this promised America-the-beautiful to meditate on our purposes and to clarify our aims.

It is the one myth which Gatsby so clearly lacked. At the very least the myth of Sisyphus can help us understand why the dream collapsed; and at the most it can show us the way to an ecstasy which balances our hopelessness and inspires us to a new age in which we can directly confront our despair and use it constructively.

We know then that the meaning of human existence is infinitely deeper than Gatsby's dream and the American dream. No matter how far we are borne back into the past of fatigue and ultimate death, we have harbored some ecstatic thoughts, we have wondered and experienced some poignancy as well as sadness in our wondering. And for a while the sadnesses are freed from guilt and the joys are relieved of anxiety. When eternity breaks into time, as it does in myths, we suddenly become aware of the meaning of human consciousness.

The myth of Sisyphus thus makes sense of our otherwise senseless efforts; it throws light on the darkness of our routine labors and lends some zest to our monotony. This is true whether we row our boats against a current that blocks progress, or work like a robot in a factory, or struggle day after day to express some recalcitrant thoughts in words that always seem to elude us.

The myth of Sisyphus is the ultimate challenge to the American dream. We are required—"destined," if you will—to recognize our human state of consciousness in progress or without it, with the Green Light or without it, with Daisy or without her, with the disintegration of our world or without it. It is this which saves us from destruction when our little rules prove unavailing.

This is what led Albert Camus to conclude his essay on Sisyphus, "We must consider Sisyphus happy."*

*Albert Camus, *Myth of Sisyphus and Other Essays* (New York: Random House, 1959).

PART III

MYTHS OF THE WESTERN WORLD

NINE

The Therapist and the
Journey Into Hell

No one who, like me, conjures up the most evil of those
half-tamed demons that inhabit the human breast, and
seeks to wrestle with them, can expect to come through the
struggle unscathed.

Sigmund Freud

THERAPISTS BELONG to a strange profession. It is partly religion. Since the time of Paracelsus in the Renaissance the physician—and afterward the psychiatrist and psychological therapist—has taken on the mantle of the priest. We cannot deny that we who are therapists deal with people's moral and spiritual questions and that we fill the role of father-confessor as part of our armamentarium, as shown in Freud's position *behind* and unseen by the person confessing.

Therapy is also partly science. Freud's contribution was to make therapy to some extent objective, and thus to make it teachable. Third, therapy is partly—an inseparable part— friendship. This friendship, of course, is likely to be more contentious than the familiar camaraderie of social relationships.

Therapists best aid their patients by "evoking their resistances." Even those in the general public who have not entered therapy know this beneficial struggle from published case studies and from popular films like *An Unmarried Woman* and *Ordinary People.*

These three ingredients make a strong brew. Four centuries ago Shakespeare has Macbeth take his physician to hide behind the curtain to watch and hear Lady Macbeth, as she moans in her hysterical guilt feelings. Macbeth then begs the physican,

> Canst thou not minister to a mind diseased,
> Pluck from the memory a rooted sorrow,
> Raze out the written troubles of the brain
> And with some sweet oblivious antidote
> Clean the stuffed bosom of that perilous stuff
> Which weighs upon the heart?*

Macbeth was indicating that human beings need some new mixture of professions. When the physician answers, in what seems to our age a platitude, "Therein the patient / Must minister to himself," Macbeth rightly retorts, "Throw physic to the dogs, I'll none of it." For physic—no matter how many forms of Valium or Librium we invent—will not basically confront the rooted sorrow or raze out the written troubles of the brain.

Science and technology have, of course, proposed new myths as they displaced or exploded old ones, but the history of technology, so exhilarating at first, has increasingly repelled believers. Now, in the post-industrial age, humanity feels itself bereft of faith, like Matthew Arnold when he wrote more than a century ago the classic epitaph for his dying culture:

> Ah love, let us be true to one another. . . .
> . . . the world, which seems
> To lie before us like a land of dreams
> So various, so beautiful, so new,

*Shakespeare, *Macbeth*, act. 5, scene 3.

Hath really neither joy, nor love, nor light,
Nor certitude, nor peace, nor help for pain;
And we are here as on a darkling plain
Swept with confused alarms of struggle and flight,
Where ignorant armies clash by night.*

We have shown earlier in this book how a loss of this magnitude leaves people en masse without any reliable structure; each one of us feels like a passenger in a rowboat, loose upon the ocean, having no compass or sense of direction, with a storm coming up. Is it any wonder, then, that psychology, the discipline which tells us about ourselves, and psychotherapy, which is able to cast some light on how we should live, burgeoned in our century?

DANTE'S *DIVINE COMEDY*

We propose another such myth, Dante's great poem, *The Divine Comedy*. We shall ask what light it throws on the therapeutic process. This dramatic myth is that of Virgil's relation to Dante as therapist-patient in their journey through hell in *The Divine Comedy*.

Many therapists have no knowledge of Dante's great drama. Even such a humanist as Freud, when asked in 1907 to name his favorite books, cited Homer, Sophocles, Shakespeare, Milton, Goethe, and many others, but ignored Dante. It is a radical deficiency that, in the education of post-Freudian psychotherapists, most students are left illiterate about the humanities. Our literature is the richest source of the presentation of human beings' self-interpretation down through history. For therapists the peril is greater than for naturalists because the imagination is specifically their tool and object of study, and any abridgement in understanding its workings will significantly limit professional progress.

*Matthew Arnold, "Dover Beach," in *A Treasury of Great Poems* (New York: Norton, 1955), p. 922.

This *Inferno* starts on Good Friday, when Dante was thirty-five,

> Midway in my life, I found myself in a dark
> wood, where I had lost the way.*

This opening line of *The Divine Comedy* has left an indelible impression on many figures in history. James Joyce once said, "I love Dante almost as much as the Bible; he is my spiritual food, the rest is ballast."†

Dante is so lovable because he admits his human problems at every step and never pretends to artificial virtues. He became aware that he had reached an impasse, a psychological place akin to Arnold's in "Dover Beach." As Dante writes in the Prologue of his poem,

> . . . I went astray
> from the straight road and woke to find myself
> alone in a dark wood.**

The *"selva oscura"* is not only the dark world of sin but of ignorance. Dante does not understand himself or the purpose of his life and requires some high ground, some elevation of perspective, by which to perceive the structure of his experience in its totality. He sights high above him the Mount of Joy, but is unable to make his journey there by himself. In this sense he is like our patients. On the mountainside his way is blocked by three beasts: the Lion of violence, the Leopard of malice, and the She-wolf of incontinence. About the last Dante writes:

> And down [the Lion's] track,
> a She-wolf drove upon me, a starved horror
> ravening and wasted beyond all belief.

---

*Quotations from Dante are from *The Divine Comedy: Dante Alighieri*, trans. John Ciardi (New York: Norton, 1970).

†Mary T. Reynolds, *Joyce and Dante: The Shaping of the Imagination* (Princeton: Princeton University Press, 1987).

**Ibid., I, 1–3.

> She seemed a rack for avarice, gaunt and craving
> Oh many the souls she has brought to endless grief!*

Freud's insight that sexual disturbances were the invariable causes of neurotic afflictions receives support from Dante's confession that it is the *concupiscent appetite* that drives him away from the prospect of joy. But we need not read the allegory narrowly. What for Dante were dispositions to sin we would call mechanisms for rationalizing the private hell of the neurotic: repression, pride, distortion, pretense, and so on. These block our way as effectively, if less interestingly, than the Lion, Leopard, and She-wolf.

A person's hell may consist of confronting the fact that his mother never loved him; or it may consist of fantasies of destroying those a person loves most, like Medea destroying her children; or undergoing the hideous cruelty released in wartime when it becomes patriotic to hate and kill. The private hell of each one of us is there crying to be confronted, and we find ourselves powerless to make progress unaided against these obstacles.

Dante's condition on that Good Friday, then, will remind us of numerous testimonies, not excluding our own. His situation recalls Hamlet at Elsinore, or Arnold at Dover Beach, or, to move backward toward Dante's own sources, St. Augustine's, who compared his licentious life in Rome, and its resultant despair, to a journey through hell, and St. Paul's, whose unhappy confession in Romans (7:18–19) resounds through the literature of psychoanalysis no less than through Dante's poem: "To will is present with me, but how to perform that which is good I find not. For the good that I would, I do not; but the evil which I would not, that I do."

---

*Ibid., I, 47–51.

VIRGIL
AND TRANSFERENCE

At this psychological moment in the poem, Dante sees a figure near him and cries out: "Have pity on me, whatever thing you are, / whether shade or living man." The figure is Virgil, who has been sent to guide him through the Inferno. After some explanations about himself, Virgil concludes:

> Therefore, for your own good, I think it well
>
> you follow me,
> and I will be your guide
> and lead you forth through an eternal place.
> There you shall see the ancient spirits tried
> in endless pain, and hear their lamentation.

To whom Dante answers:

> Poet, by that God to you unknown,
>
> lead me this way. Beyond the present ill
> and worse to dread, lead me to Peter's gate
> and be my guide through the sad halls of Hell.*

So Virgil, as guide and counselor, accompanies Dante to interpret the various levels of evil in hell (or, as Freudians would say, the depth of the unconscious). Virgil had shown in his own practice, especially in the *Aeneid,* a thorough familiarity with the dangerous moral landscape they will now traverse. Most of all, Virgil is to be a friend, an accompanying presence for the bewildered pilgrim.

This "presence" (see Chapter 8) in the relation of therapist to patient is the heuristic method most important but the one we understand least. Virgil will not only interpret these levels in hell but will be a *being,* alive and present in Dante's world.

*Dante, *Divine Comedy,* I, 105–109, 123–126.

Dante may be taken here as both patient *and* therapist. Some therapists, as John Rosen shows us in his active therapy with schizophrenics, need to have some friend present in order to let themselves go into the depths of the patient's disorder. The friend, who walks slightly behind Rosen, may say nothing at all, but his presence changes the magnetic field; and Rosen can then throw himself into the treatment without himself getting lost in the schizophrenia. Sometimes called empathy or simply relationship, this presence is central to the world of all therapists, I believe, and has a powerful effect upon the patient quite in addition to what the therapist says or the school in which he or she was trained.

In Dante's drama the first hurdle occurs immediately after the "contract" with Virgil and has an amazing similarity to what happens in present-day therapy. Dante is overcome with the conviction that he is not worthy of such special treatment. He cries to Virgil:

> Poet, you who must guide,
>> before you trust me to that arduous passage,
>> look to me and look through me—can I be worthy?*

How often, in doing therapy, do we hear that question, at least with the inner ear, if the patient does not verbalize it directly: why is *he* singled out, among all other people in the world, for this special guidance? Dante, like our patients, cannot "accept acceptance," in Paul Tillich's phrase. Dante recalls to Virgil the images of St. Paul and Aeneas, the hero of Virgil's epic poem, and avers that he can see why *they* were chosen:

> But I—how should I dare? By whose permission?
>> I am not Aeneas. I am not Paul.
>> Who could believe me worthy of the vision?
>
> How, then, may I presume to this high quest
>> and not fear my own brashness?

*Ibid., II, 10–12.

In his pleas to Virgil, he then adds what we might call a statement of positive transference: "You are wise / and will grasp what my poor words can but suggest."

Does Virgil respond in a way that many inexperienced therapists would, namely, to reassure the other person, "Of course you are worthy"? Not at all. He attacks Dante:

> I understand from your words and the look in your eyes . . .
>   your soul is sunken in that cowardice
>
> that bears down many men, turning their course
>   and resolution by imagined perils,
>   as his own shadow turns the frightened horse.*

This can be interpreted as a kind of challenge, which we use in therapy with patients addicted to any kind of neurosis (or habit-forming drug). Reassurance should be rarely used. Psychologists must *not* take the crucial initiative out of the patient's hands, especially at the beginning of therapy.

That sentence of Dante's, "You are wise/and will grasp what my poor words can but suggest," would be, in familiar terms, a buttering up of the therapist. Such a compliment is not going to be met by verbal denial (indeed, we may secretly believe we *can* read his mind!) but rather by a gesture or a wide grin—anyone who grins cannot be all-wise.

There is in Virgil's response to Dante an important sentence: "I was a soul/among the souls of Limbo."† We are all in limbo; we are all struggling along in the human condition, whether we be prince or pauper, patient or therapist, at that particular time. But therapists will not get across to the patient the humanness of it all by telling him their own problems. Frieda Fromm-Reichmann sagely remarks, "The patient is burdened enough with his own problems without having to hear the therapist's also." Again, it can best be communicated to the patient by gesture and attitude, rather than moral lec-

*Ibid., II, 31–35.
†Ibid., II, 51–52.

tures, that everyone who lives is in limbo, that the sin (if I may put this in Dante's language) is not to have problems but to fail to be aware of them and fail to confront them.

In any case, Virgil does give some explanation of why he is there. Beatrice in heaven has sent him to help Dante. But Virgil is firm throughout, never sentimental. He concludes:

> And now what ails you? Why do you lag? Why
> this heartsick hesitation and pale fright?

This rebuke has a strong effect upon Dante, who responds,

> As flowerlets drooped and puckered in the night
>   turn up to the returning sun and spread
>   their petals wide on his new warmth and light—
>
> just so my wilted spirits rose again
>   and such a heat of zeal surged through my veins
>   that I was born anew. . . .
>   My Guide! My Lord! My Master! Now lead on:
>   one will shall serve the two of us in this.*

And so they set out on what Dante calls "that hard and perilous track into hell."

We need not be too concerned about the "directive" language here. We must search continually for the inner meaning, which is that Dante cannot find his way alone through human misery. He requires not only the stability of a myth, which Virgil provides, but a myth that he can assimilate to his own purposes. The guide and pilgrim cannot be at cross-purposes or share radically dissimilar cultural myths. Likewise, to be a metaphorical Lord and Master, the therapist must paradoxically remain a humble friend, a figure of trust.

Virgil does, however, reassure his friend at certain crucial points in the narrative. In one experience later, when Dante is seized by genuine and profound anxiety, and cries to Virgil:

> O my beloved Master, my Guide in peril, . . .
> stand by me now . . . in my heart's fright.

*Ibid., II, 4–35.

Virgil does respond:

> Take heart . . .
>
> I will not leave you
> to wander in this underworld alone.*

This is a reassurance which leaves the task of the journey still with the patient, and so does not take over his responsibility. In my own work, I have reached stages parallel to this when the patient is afraid to go farther for fear he will not be able to come out again, or afraid that I will drop him. I may say, "I am glad to work with you so long as it is helpful to you." This puts the emphasis on active help rather than passivity (always a temptation) or stagnation. In the *Inferno,* one is impressed by Virgil's attitude, as Dante describes it: his "gentle and encouraging smile."

THE JOURNEY
THROUGH HELL

As they begin their journey, they pause in the vestibule of hell, where they hear the cries of anguish from the Opportunists. These are the souls who in life were neither good nor evil but acted only for themselves. They are the outcasts who took no sides in the rebellion of the angels. In modern psychology these opportunists would be called well adjusted; they know how to keep out of trouble! But Dante sees them as guilty of the sin of fence-sitting. Hence they are neither in hell nor out of it. John Ciardi describes them thus: "Eternally unclassified, they race round and round pursuing a wavering banner that runs forever before them through the dirty air; and as they run they are pursued by swarms of wasps and hornets, who sting them and produce a constant flow of blood." Dante's hell enacts the law of symbolic retribution: since these opportunists took no sides

*Ibid., VIII, 94–105.

they are given no place. Ciardi remarks, "As their sin was a darkness, so they move in darkness. As their own guilty conscience pursued them, so they are pursued by swarms of wasps and hornets."*

It is highly interesting that classical literature, whether the author is Dante or Sophocles or Shakespeare, has no sympathy with the sentimental or *superficial idea of human perfection.* These authors and myth makers saw the reality of man's inhumanity to man, and they viewed the human condition as essentially tragic. Any character who is neither good nor evil—like Peer Gynt in the first part of Ibsen's drama—is simply not living an authentic life. The great dramatists take care to punish the evil they depict, but they understand profoundly the passion that drives human beings away from the moral life. With Ibsen they believe that "it takes courage to be a real sinner."† The lovers Paolo and Francesca, who gave way to the concupiscence Dante had been warned against in the poem's opening, provide the most complex case of flawed humanity, sympathetic *because* flawed. Dante, the literary character, must learn by his traversal through hell how to evaluate the variety of sinful examples he witnesses. Again the analogy is apt, for the patient in therapy learns to cope with his problems (not to "cure" them) in part by means of the therapist's superior familiarity with disordered human types, what St. Augustine called "the land of unlikeness."

I will not describe the various levels Dante experiences as he journeys deeper into hell, such as the gluttonous, the hoarders and wasters, the wrathful and the sullen. The *content* of these evils, for which the perpetrators are in hell, varies from era to era; the content of modern sins differs from that of the Middle Ages. The important thing is not the specific evils with which one struggles but the journey itself. In any quest-romance the recognition of negative states leads to a purification of the self,

---

*Dante, *The Divine Comedy,* Ciardi's introduction to canto III.
†Ibsen, *Peer Gynt* (New York: Doubleday Anchor Book, 1963), p. 139.

a casting off of the dead/diseased self in favor of a new life. Likewise the function of psychoanalysis, from one point of view, is a movement toward health by traversing the morbid landscape of one's own past. Freud's remark that "hysterical patients suffer mainly from reminiscences" might be extended to include all those who are inwardly compelled to autobiographical narrative. The significant difference is that modern patients, like modern authors, tend to prefer personal reminiscences to the historical people and events of Dante's poem.

The "Inferno"—or hell—consists of suffering and endless torment that produces no change in the soul that endures it and is imposed from without. But in the "Purgatorio" suffering is temporary, a means of purification, and is eagerly embraced by the soul's own will. Both must be traversed before arriving at the celestial "Paradiso." I think of these three stages as simultaneous—three coexisting aspects of all human experience. Indeed, modern literature in the epic tradition of Dante's spiritual poem, such as Joyce's *Ulysses*, Pound's *Cantos*, or Eliot's *Four Quartets*, makes no radical separation of moral landscapes.

I wish to turn now to the problem of the limits of therapy. Does *The Divine Comedy* cast light upon the limits of our work as therapists? I propose that it does.

Virgil, whose relation to Dante I have been taking as parallel to that of therapist to patient, symbolizes human reason. This is made clear by Dante time and again. But "reason" in Dante does not at all mean our contemporary intellectualism, or technical reason, or rationalism. It stands for the broad spectrum of life in which a person reflects on or pauses to question the meaning of experience, especially of suffering. In our age reason is taken as logic, as it is mainly channeled through the left hemisphere of the brain. This does not describe Virgil: he is a great imaginative poet, not a logician. Reason can, if we take it in Dante's broad sense, guide us in our private hells.

But reason even in his amplified sense cannot lead us into the celestial paradise. Dante has need of other guides in his journey. These guides are *revelation* and *intuition*. I shall not present any brief for these two functions of human experience. But I do wish to state out of my experience with supervising inexperienced therapists that therapists cut themselves off from a great deal of reality if they do not leave themselves open to other ways of communication than human reason. (I recall Freud's statement that his patients so often saw through any "white lie" he might tell them that he had decided never to lie: this he proposes as his "moral" belief in mental telepathy.) It is interesting to me that Dante identifies intuition as the supreme form of guidance. Therapists who have succumbed to the sin of dogmatic rationalism, if I may be permitted to add it to Dante's hell, might consider the legitimacy of this mental power.

The limits of therapy are illuminated by Virgil's leaving Dante when they have passed through hell and almost through purgatory. When the poets come in sight of the earthly paradise, as Ciardi points out, Virgil "speaks his last words, for the poets have now come to the limit of Reason, and Dante is free to follow every impulse, since all notion of sin has been purged away."* Thus they bid goodbye to each other, with mixed emotions of sadness at leave-taking, comradeship, and loneliness but zest for the future. Once (three cantos later) Dante cries out for Virgil:

> I turned left with the same assured belief
> > That makes a child run to its mother's arms
> > when it is frightened or has come to grief. . . .

> [But] he had taken his light from us. He had gone.
> > Virgil had gone, Virgil, the gentle Father
> > to whom I gave my soul for its salvation!†

In place of Virgil, Beatrice appears as a redemptive and beatific presence. The parallel is that *our therapy is the prologue to*

---

*Dante, *The Divine Comedy*, Ciardi's introduction to canto xxvii.
†Ibid., XXX, 43–51.

life rather than life itself. We, like Virgil, seek to help the other person to the point where he can "gather the fruit of liberty," not without understandable lapses of need for the therapist's presence, and he moves forward to a place in time where "his will is free, unwarped and sound."

THE FREEDOM TO LOVE

Note that this self-directed life to which Dante, and our patients, go forth, is *life as community,* or more specifically, a freedom to love. This seems to be why the guides at the end of "Purgatorio" and in "Paradiso" are women and why Beatrice is portrayed as saving Dante by sending Virgil to him in the first place. It is in the summoning of Beatrice that Dante most reminds us of a modern analysand.

Beatrice is an entirely personal myth, a Florentine girl of Dante's acquaintance whose death inspired his first great poetic work, *La Vita Nuova.* Her reappearance in the "Purgatorio" shows us Dante successfully overcoming a morbid sense of loss—perhaps the trauma that steered him to the dark wood?—by means of a mystical reunion with this beloved figure from his childhood (they first met when he was nine years old). She is a reality in Dante's own mind and heart. One wonders what she stands for in Dante's mind—we propose the kernel (heart) of Dante's own inspiration, his spiritual longings, his sense of being guided by ethereal means. This imaginative encounter might be compared to the secular resurrection scene in Wilhelm Jensen's novel of Pompeii, *Gradiva,* about which Freud wrote a book-length study. In both works, a female figure from the protagonist's youth reappears in a radically different landscape in order to restore love and joy to the craving soul of her admirer. We recall other classics which put women in this crucial position: Goethe's *Faust,* where so much importance is given to the inspirational force of Helen and "the Mothers," or *Peer Gynt,* when Ibsen has Peer Gynt come back for his salvation to Solveig. In his essays on the *anima* concept, Jung singled out three novels of H. Rider Haggard—*She, The Return of She,* and *Wisdom's Daughter*—as supreme descriptions of the replenishing libido-object. This myth is of special importance, he claimed, to patients who have reached middle age.

I suggest that women here are symbolic of community. We all experienced life first in the womb and then in the journey from the womb out into the daylight. We were not born alone but in partnership with our mothers. Whether girls or boys, we nursed at our mother's breast, actually or metaphorically. It is in the reunion with a loved one in the sexual function that we participate in the ongoingness of the race. In this sense we experience the world as we experience love. Thus after our journey through hell and purgatory, life itself is the therapist. *Our patients leave us to join the human community of life itself.* This is why Alfred Adler made social interest—the commitment to life in community—the test of mental health.

This view of the limits of therapy implies again that our task is not to "cure" people. I wince to think of how much time has been wasted by intelligent men and women arguing about whether psychotherapy cures and trying to fit psychotherapy into the mode of Western nineteenth-century medicine. *Our task is to be guide, friend, and interpreter to persons on their journeys through their private hells and purgatories.* Specifically, our task is to help patients get to the point where they can decide whether they wish to remain victims—for to be a victim has real benefits in terms of power over one's family and friends and other secondary gains—or whether they choose to leave this victim-state and venture through purgatory with the hope of achieving some sense of paradise. Our patients often, toward the end, are understandably frightened by the possibility of freely deciding for themselves whether to take their chances by completing the quest they have bravely begun.

All through history it is true that only by going through hell does one have any chance of reaching heaven. The journey through hell is a part of the journey that cannot be omitted—indeed, what one learns in hell is prerequisite to arriving at any good value thereafter. Homer has Odysseus visit the underworld, and there—and only there—can he get the knowledge that will enable him to get safely back to Ithaca. Virgil has Aeneas go into the netherworld and there talk to his father, in which discussion he gets directions as to what to do and what not to do in the founding of the great city of Rome. How fitting it is that *each of these gets a vital wisdom which is learned in the descent into hell!* Without this knowledge there is no success in finding directions by which to go, or achieving the things of paradise—purity of experience, purity of heart. Dante makes the journey in person; he himself goes through hell and then is enabled to discover paradise at the end of his journey. Dante writes his great poem to enable the rest of us also to go ultimately to paradise.

Human beings can reach heaven only through hell. Without suffering—say, as an author struggles to find the right word with which to communicate his meaning—or without a probing of one's fundamental aims, one cannot get to heaven. Even a purely secular heaven has the same requirements. Poincaré, for example, struggles for weeks and months, faces depression and hopelessness, but then struggles again, and finally through hell arrives at a new discovery in mathematics, the "heaven" of his solution to the problem that he had posed.

At the beginning of this chapter I stated that Dante started his journey on Good Friday. The significance of this is that the mordant despair of this day is a necessary prelude to the triumphant experience of Easter, the resurrection. The agony, the horror, the sadness, are a necessary prelude to self-realization and self-fulfillment. In Europe multitudes go to church on Good Friday to hear testimony that Jesus is crucified, for they know that the ascent to heaven must be preceded by death on earth. In America we seem, by our practice, to act on the wish that we could pass over the despair of mortification and know only the exaltation of ascent. We seem to believe that we can be reborn without ever dying. Such is the spiritual version of the American Dream!

The Divine Comedy, like so many other great literary classics, gives the lie to such simplistic illusions. Dante's harrowing and exemplary journey remains one of the greatest case studies the profession of psychotherapy possesses, and is a presentation of a radiant myth of the methods and aims of the best of modern therapy.

TEN

Peer Gynt:
A Man's Problem in Loving

The visions of Malapaga, those of Peer Gynt, seem, all of
them, now to apply to me.*

Yevgeny Yevtushenko

PEER GYNT COULD be called the myth of males in the twentieth century, for it is a fascinating picture of the psychological patterns and conflicts of contemporary man. The drama
reveals a pattern that many psychotherapists find in their practice in the twentieth century. Presented to us as a work of art in
Ibsen's drama, it is a product of the particular stresses of our
time.†

Peer Gynt is the myth, that is, the life pattern, of a man
characterized by two desires, and in the contradiction between

---

*From "I Don't Understand," in *The Poetry of Yevgeny Yevtushenko, 1953–
1965*, trans. George Reavey (New York: October House, 1965).

†This is another illustration of how the images and vision of life presented in art
tend not only to give the quintessence of the psychological problems but to *predict*
them. Ibsen's drama was written in 1867, thirty-three years before Freud's book on
dreams, and a half century before *The Great Gatsby*, but this pattern of the breakdown
of self has come into our overt consciousness only in our twentieth century.

them his self is lost. One desire is to be *admired* by women, and the other desire is to be *taken care of* by the same women. The first desire leads to machismo behavior: a braggart, he swaggers and is grandiose. But all of this apparent power is in the service of pleasing the woman, the figurative Queen, in order that the second desire be satisfied. The power thus leads to passivity, to dependence upon the woman, and this ends up undermining his power. Thus these two desires are contradictory. The woman is the one who holds the final judgment and, correspondingly, the power over him. No matter how much he appears to be the swaggering master with his various women, he is in reality a slave serving the Queen. His self-esteem and his self-image depend upon her smile, her approval. He owes his being to her just as a courtier depends on his Queen to knight him.

THE LOSS OF ONE'S SELF

Peer Gynt is a myth developed from an old Scandinavian tale. But beyond the fact that Ibsen is Norwegian, the myth and the drama have a universal quality for our time. Ibsen has Peer himself say in this play, "Everyone feels akin to Peer Gynt."* When he wrote this drama Ibsen thought that it wouldn't be understood outside Scandinavia. He found rather quickly that it wasn't entirely understood *in* Scandinavia, but was very much understood in other parts of the world. Peer was acclaimed everywhere as national prototype. George Bernard Shaw wrote, "The universality of Ibsen, and his grip upon humanity, makes his plays come home to all nations, and Peer Gynt is as good a Frenchman as a Norwegian." Even in Japan it is claimed that Peer Gynt is "typically Japanese." The contemporary Russian poet, Yevgeny Yevtushenko, in an intro-

---

*Peer Gynt, trans. Michael Meyer (New York: Doubleday Anchor Book, 1963), p. 29.

spective poem, "I Don't Understand," writes that he feels *he* is
Peer Gynt.

Actually the reason Peer Gynt is a man for all nations is that
the character and the myth are the product of Ibsen's own
profound self-knowledge. The deeper the level to which any
writer penetrates his own individual experience, the more these
experiences will be archetypal, will have something significant
in common with other nationalities—the Japanese, the
Frenchman, the young Soviet Russian. Ibsen writes in his introduction, "The poem contains much that has its roots in my
own childhood."* Ibsen's own mother is particularly the model
for Aase, Peer Gynt's mother in the drama.

Another reason the drama speaks profoundly to us is that it
comes out of the period of our immediate forefathers. It was
written in 1867, the period following hard upon the time of
Kierkegaard, the period that gave birth to Nietzsche and to
Freud. As these other prophets spoke *out of* the nineteenth but
to our twentieth century, this drama is about the essential
problems that contemporary man in the twentieth century has
to face.

Running through *Peer Gynt* in the myth and in Ibsen's
drama is the theme of the lost self and the arduous process of
recovering it. Ibsen put it well—and he meant it as simply and
profoundly as he said it—"The issue is how to be yourself." It
sounds very much like Ibsen's fellow Scandinavian, Kierkegaard, and we immediately wonder how much Ibsen was influenced by Kierkegaard. One of his translators, Michael
Meyer, says that Ibsen read little of Kierkegaard and understood less. But, remarks Meyer astutely, many authors have
been influenced unconsciously by writers whom they only partially understood. I shall go further and propose that many
authors are influenced *more* by writers they only partly understand than by those they fully comprehend, for the former

*Ibid., p. xxiii.

leaves unfinished business going on in one's mind. The most powerful influence is that which grasps us as a totality, on levels Jung would call the collective unconscious. Kierkegaard is so close to everybody in our twentieth century that it is often hard to see him. Living and writing in Denmark just twenty years before this play was born, Kierkegaard has an influence on people in echoes that are intimate, personal, and subjective. The lost self is the central theme in Kierkegaard: his greatest condemnation is directed to the "conforming citizen."

The drama opens with the young Peer Gynt, now the braggart, telling his mother that he rode a buck into Gjendin Edge, down the glacier, over the cliff, and down the precipice. At first his mother believes him and is seized with anxiety, but then she catches on that Peer is bragging again as he always does.

Then Peer Gynt starts off to the wedding of his old girl friend, a celebration to which he has not been invited. Ibsen presents immediately in the play the broken self-esteem that is characteristic of this type of man and how vulnerable he is to humiliation. On the way down the country road toward the village where the wedding is to take place, Peer says to himself:

> People always snigger behind your back,
> And whisper so that it burns right through you. . . .
>
> If only I had a dram of something strong.
> Or could go unnoticed. If only they didn't know me.
> A drink would be best. Then the laughter doesn't bite.

He hears people coming and hides among the bushes beside the road. Some guests carrying gifts go by on the way to the wedding talking about him. The man remarks, "His Dad was a boozer and his ma's a ninny," and the lady rejoins, "It's no wonder the lad's a good-for-nothing."

His face red with shame, Peer gives a forced toss of his head, "Well, let them talk. That won't kill me." He then lies down on the grass nursing his wounded self-esteem and looks up at the clouds and fantasizes:

What a strange cloud! It's like a horse. . . .

It's mother.
She's scolding and screaming: "You brute! Stop. Peer!"
    (Gradually closes his eyes.)
Yes, now she's afraid. Peer Gynt rides at the head
Of a mighty army. His horse has a crest
Of shining silver and four shoes of gold.
He has gloves on his hands and a sword and a scabbard,
And a trailing cloak lined with scarlet silk
It's a fine bold body of men he has with him,
But none sits his horse as proudly as he.*

It is important not to confuse Peer Gynt with the Walter
Mitty pattern. There is nothing Walter Mittyish about this
kind of man; the Peer Gynt types are genuinely talented. They
are swashbuckling, true; but they use their strength—real as it
is—in the hit-and-miss way that Peer Gynt exemplifies. He is a
strong man speaking out of a broken self-esteem and trying to
find himself, as Peer Gynt will presently tell us in many ways,
despite the fault (I use that word meaning a deep crevice in the
ground) in his self-image. These men never amount to anything not because they don't have talent but because they *are
always a reflection.* Their myth is constructed as a consolation.
Somebody else has the power for their validation and not they
themselves. They are like an automobile in which the motor
spins but is always unengaged with the rest of the car.

Arriving at the wedding, Peer Gynt meets Solveig, who,
though still a girl, is destined to come back into the play as the
heroine. Peer experiences a strange ecstasy, a subterranean
charge in this first meeting:

How fair she is!
I never saw such a girl! She dropped
Her eyes to her shoes and her
    white apron,
And clutched tight to her

*Ibid., pp. 16–17.

> mother's skirt,
> And carried a psalmbook
> wrapped in linen,
> I must look at that
> girl.*

He begs Solveig to dance with him in phrases that sound sincere for almost the only time in the first half of the drama. She refuses, but she is obviously touched deeply with sympathy for Peer. Though he goes back to his bragging to the other young men ("I'll ride over the lot of you like a storm/The whole parish shall fall at my feet!"), he can never forget Solveig throughout the drama. One learns in psychotherapy that there is in everyone, no matter how distorted in neurosis or psychosis the person may be, this spot that is genuine, honest, humanly responsive—this center of the capacity to love. At this point Peer's soul was touched.

At the wedding there are arguments; the young men try to get Peer Gynt and the blacksmith to fight, but Peer backs off, having just been beaten by the blacksmith a few days before.

Then Peer Gynt runs off with Ingrid, the bride, an example of the dramatic seductions of which this type of man, with his particular way of using sex purely as a tool, is so capable. He carries her up the mountain, where he seduces her and then, despite her pathetic begging, he pushes her away with, "Oh, shut up" and "Go back where you came from!"

Now he must leave the country under pain of execution, and he begins his wandering. He meets three troll girls, who taunt him with the challenge to make love to all three of them at once. Peer answers, "Try me and see!" and proceeds to accomplish this act.

We see in our patients in therapy how this kind of man perpetually goes through this pattern of behavior, *seduce and leave.* He has a powerful need to keep mother at home waiting for him, and then he can stretch the umbilical cord as he wan-

*Ibid., p. 26.

ders about the earth, always tied to his mother. The Peer Gynt men are the sexual athletes. But all this potency is performed in the service of the figurative Queen: if the troll girls command, he must perform. There is then no relationship; it is a triumph and a leaving. Yevtushenko sees this lack of relatedness as basic for,

> . . . people insist, and I can't cope with it,
>   that I'm no good,
>   have so few ties with life.*

These men don't want relationship; on an apparent level they want triumph. But in a more profound sense, what they want, and struggle so hard to achieve, is the power to be still a concern in the Queen's eye, to force her to acknowledge their significance. The flexing of the muscles is purposed to prove to the Queen that they are strong. The upshot is that they remain dependent on mother no matter how far from home they go.

At this point in the drama Peer Gynt glimpses for a moment what he is doing, sensing his phoniness and the contradiction in his self-esteem.

> The flight along Gjendin Edge—
> It was all a fake and a lie! . . .
>
> Sporting with crazy wenches—
> A bloody lie and a fake.

But he cannot confront this directly. He pushes it out of his mind and again gives himself over to grandiose fantasies.

> Peer Gynt thou wast born to greatness
> And to greatness thou shalt come!†

As he wanders on, he meets the daughter of the Troll King, whom he bewitches with his sweet tongue. They ride on a huge pig, which they pretend is a "bridal steed," to the Troll King-

---

*"I Don't Understand."
†Ibsen, *Peer Gynt,* pp. 36, 37.

dom. He is told by the king that if he stays and marries the princess, who will be the queen, he will become the Troll King and inherit the kingdom as her dowry. This is a literal presentation of the point we made above: the man is enthroned not by his own power but by virtue of his relation to the Queen.

THE MEANING OF TROLLDOM

The myth of *Peer Gynt* consists of the counterposing of human beings and trolls, subhuman beings who live in the dark under the earth and represent exclusively the animal side of human nature. As mythic creatures, trolls are often conceived as dwarfs and fabled to live in caves. The Troll King asks Peer, "What is the difference between Troll and man?"

PEER: No difference, as far as I can see.
Big trolls want to roast you, small trolls want to claw you.
It's the same with us, if we dared.

TROLL KING: True. We're alike in that, and more.
But morning is morning and night is night,
And there is a difference nevertheless.
I'll tell you what it is.
Out there, under the shining vault of heaven,
Men tell each other: "Man, be thyself!"
But in here, among us trolls, we say:
"Troll, be thyself—*and thyself alone.*"*

All the difference hangs on that little word "alone." It means, according to the Troll King,

> never to care
> For the world beyond our frontier.
> Renounce day and the things of light.

According to the translator of this drama, it means, "To hell with the rest of the world."

*Ibid., pp. 40–41.

The trolls have eyes that are squinted; Peer must give up seeing things straight, for the vision of the trolls is distorted. Trolls live in the dark, and they see the pig on which Peer rode into the troll camp as a steed, and see his wench as "queen." Peer accepts the tail which they pin on him, as the Troll King continues his instructions, stating that the trolls live by pure senses and the "old Adam is safely kicked out of doors." To all this Peer agrees. But when he is told that he can never leave the encampment, Peer demures.

> I've taken a tail, that I'll admit;
> I'll gladly swear that a cow is a woman:
>
> But: The fact that you can't go home
>
> The way the book says . . .
>   I'll never put my consent.*

The King then demands that Peer marry his daughter since Peer, having had sexual desires toward her, has already impregnated her.

> You human beings are all alike
> You think that desires don't matter.

When he refuses, they set upon Peer, flaying him with the aim of killing him. As he succumbs to their blows, he falls to the ground crying, "Help, Mother, I'll die!" Church bells then ring far off, and the trolls flee in a turmoil of howls and shrieks. Again Peer is rescued by mother.

Let us consider that crucial word, the central term in the original precept, "alone." The troll precept is the ultimate statement of individualism; it is Ibsen's view of the central myth of modernity. Quite apart from what individualism meant in the earlier centuries of the West, and especially in the seventeenth to nineteenth centuries in this country, it is now a statement of the failure of human life. It is the genius of the

*Ibid., p. 37.

creative dramatist, Ibsen, that he predicts the future and sings the death knoll of hyper-individualism.

The individualism that was a noble value in early centuries of our period and elicited in people a courageous self-reliance and a "healthy" independence has, in our anxiety that our modern civilization is crumbling beneath us, deteriorated in the second half of the twentieth century into the motto of Fritz Perls, "I do my thing, you do your thing . . . and if we don't meet it can't be helped."* Ibsen is saying, with the insight of the poet, that the "self alone" is the person who seduces Ingrid and then scorns her after the rape when she, weeping, clings to him. The "self alone" is the essence of the narcissistic personality, which we have described in Chapter 7. The troll insistence on "not caring . . . about what goes on beyond our own borders" in our nuclear age spells the ruin of our world and our civilization. Whatever one thinks of the Christian tradition, the Troll King here logically throws it overboard, for it has stood, despite its failures, for brotherhood and for concern about the others who *are* beyond our frontiers.

The precept, "Be thyself *alone,*" describes the egocentric self, a self without world, a self without love. The ideal is to be unrelated to everyone else, offensively independent. It is a self without *inter*dependence, narcissistic to the core. It is to try to be a self only on the level of wish without will or decision or responsibility.

The trolls are subhuman mythological creatures who psychologically are the archaic elements in the myth. Ibsen himself remarks in the introduction to his play that the "trolls are within the man himself."

---

*The whole poem of Perls follows:

> I do my thing and you do your thing.
> I am not in this world to live up to your expectations,
> And you are not in this world to live up to mine.
> You are you and I am I;
> If by chance we find each other, it's beautiful.
> If not, it can't be helped.

Everything that I have written is most minutely connected with *what I have lived through, if not personally experienced; every new work has had for me the object* of serving as a process of spiritual liberation and catharsis; for every man shares the responsibility and the guilt of the society to which he belongs. That was why I once inscribed in a copy of one of my books the following dedicatory lines: *To live is to war with trolls in heart and soul, To write is to sit in judgment on oneself.* *

The troll always "goes round," never goes straight through anything. This comes out in Peer Gynt: he keeps repeating throughout the first half of the play, "I am the master of the situation," which sounds like personal power, an echo of the Victorian, "I am the master of my fate." But it is in reality the statement of the Victorian man who manipulates himself in the same way one does coal cars and factories.

Ibsen then raises the corollary question in *Peer Gynt:* How can one become human? Our problem here, as in understanding any myth, is to go through this regressive side, represented by the trolls and the archaic creatures, to the *integrative* side. As will be indicated in a later part of the play, this can be done only by *responding.* What Peer Gynt cannot do in all his seducing, in all his running around the world, in all his bragging, is *to respond to another human being.* To make a relationship, to exercise empathy, to build. All of this is part of genuine relating to another person, which Peer cannot do.

Before we go further into the play itself, let us look more specifically at Peer Gynt's relationship with women. Peer Gynt cannot stay with Solveig, even though he knows she loves him and he knows, at least later on, that he loves her. Love is not what he wants. He wants rather to feel "free," like a man wandering at the end of the infinitely elastic and extensible umbilical cord, with the woman always waiting back home. The musician Grieg in his *Peer Gynt* suite shows Solveig spinning and singing as she awaits Peer Gynt in her little cottage. If she were not waiting at home, if she did not "stay put," the

*Ibsen, *Peer Gynt,* p. xxviii.

umbilical cord of course would break, and the alleged "freedom" would then vanish.

Thus the Peer Gynts in life never solve the paradox of *freedom by giving oneself.* Their freedom is not even a freedom *from* something: it is a simulated freedom, with mother always in the wings. Hence their compulsive activity: they must always be trying to prove something to the woman, whether she is present or fantasied, and at the same time they are always running away from her. In Kierkegaard's terms, the Peer Gynts try to *be* themselves without ever *choosing* themselves.

Several interesting exchanges illustrate this dilemma. Rather early in the play, Peer Gynt says as in fantasy to Solveig, "My princess! Now at last I've found and won her! Hey! Now I'll build my palace on firm, true ground!" and he seizes an axe to build. Into the clearing comes an old woman, who says, "Good evening, Peer *Lightfoot.*" Lightfoot refers to Peer's predilection for running from ship to ship, pier to pier, if I may be permitted the pun, never getting, staying, or even arriving, any place.

PEER: What? Who are you?
WOMAN: Old friends, Peer Gynt.
My cottage lies nearby. We're neighbours.
PEER: Oh? That's news to me.
WOMAN: As you built your house, mine rose beside it.
PEER (turns): I'm in a hurry—
WOMAN: You always were, lad.*

This perpetual hurrying is an expression of his dilemma of needing to appear free of the woman while he is always tied to her. The Boyg says about Peer, "He was too strong. *There were women behind him.*" And Peer asks Helga to tell Solveig, "I only meant—ask her not to forget me." What the Peer Gynt type wants is not women or love, but to have women behind him, always at home, the base of the umbilical cord.

*Ibid., p. 57.

We notice that the person with this myth *appears* to have a great deal of feeling; he emotes continuously and copiously. But it is not hard to see that he does not have real feelings at all. The women Peer Gynt purports to love—Ingrid, and later Anitra—these he gives up with the snap of a finger. There is no real relationship at any point in his life. His feelings go off like firecrackers: we see a big show, and it as quickly fizzles out. His action is empty: none of his many motions becomes *emotions*. Peer Gynt runs *all over the world but always stays in the same place*.

Peer Gynt *seems* sexually to have whomever he wishes, from Ingrid the bride through the troll girls, et al. But when a person is characterized by such compulsive activity, he never can stop or even slow down. There are two reasons for this: first the compulsive activity itself allays and narcotizes his anxiety. Second, the person, if he were to slow down, would have to confront himself, and this would make him most anxious of all. The important point is that the compulsive activity is never action *for its own sake* in the Peer Gynts, never *action for pleasure, power, or joy.* It is action in the service of flight; he is running hard to avoid confrontation with himself.

We find in the beginning of therapy that patients of this Peer Gynt pattern are often sexually very potent. But the potency turns out to be on an unsound basis which cannot last: pleasing the Queen as a gigolo. Later on such a patient, when he becomes more integrated, may go through a period of impotence. He cannot understand why the therapist may regard this impotence as a positive sign. The impotence is typically an uncovering of the damaged structure underneath, and as we stated earlier about myths as structure, it gives one a chance to change the faulty myth.

The genetic origin of this pattern lies in infancy in a particular and powerful relationship with the mother. Peer Gynt's father had been a drunkard, as the gossiping people on the country road indicated, and now was dead. The mother elevated Peer Gynt to the throne of the father, overtly when the father died, but covertly while the father was living. It is an Oedipus pattern not in the sense that the little boy wants his mother or chooses her, but he is shoved onto the throne in the role of prince consort. The mother is the one who puts the crown on his head. But this makes him actually a slave monarch. It is something like the pattern that Adler used to understand better than he described—the pattern which he called the "spoiled child syndrome." By this he meant a spoiled child and a broken child at the same time. This syndrome particularly emerges from the Victorian period, as we will indicate later.

We next find Peer in Morocco, where he becomes rich and influential. He practices the slave trade, having worked out a nice system of sending idols to primitive nations and then missionaries to correct the idols. He sends Bibles and rum to the heathen, keeping these well balanced so there is nothing to get in the way of his acquiring riches. He then proclaims, "I must be myself entirely," and proceeds to discourse on what this is.

> My self—it is the army of wishes, appetites, desires,
> The sea of whims, pretensions and demands. . . .
> All that swells here within my breast
> And by which I, myself, exist.*

The self for him, thus, exists on the *archaic,* infantile level of selfhood. The world of relationship, the complex, fascinating, difficult, endlessly new, this world is rich in demands but copious in rewards. In short, this world of people is wholly omitted from Peer's life. The secret, he says, lies in always avoiding commitment:

PEER: . . . The key to life
Is simply this. Close your ear against
The infiltration of a dangerous serpent.

*Ibid., p. 74.

COTTON: What serpent, my good friend?

PEER: A little one that is most seductive.
The one that tempts you to commit yourself.
The art of success is to stand free
And uncommitted amid the snares of life.
To know that a bridge always remains open
Behind you.*

In the next scene Peer, standing on the coast, looks out and observes that his friends are stealing his yacht. For a moment he is tremendously shocked. He cries for God to help him—he forgets God's name and only after some thought remembers it—instructing God, "Now listen carefully." And of course nothing happens: the friends make off with the yacht and Peer is left stranded on the seashore.

Pondering his grandiose plans as he wanders anew through the desert, he comes upon an emperor's camp, with horses, jewels, and clothes waiting at hand. Appropriating these, Peer now proclaims himself a prophet. Here Anitra comes on the scene and dances, both in the drama and in Grieg's music. He tells her, as an aid to seducing her, that he is a prophet sent by Allah, but this time the seduction doesn't succeed. Riding off on his horse, Anitra abandons him as his friends have done.

Like a typical Victorian, Peer than proclaims the clichés all over again,

> In short, I am master of the situation. . . .
>
> How fine to set oneself a goal
> And drive one's way remorselessly towards it!
> To sever the bonds that bind one to one's home
> And friends.†

Now Peer is beginning to lie to himself, a common plateau which precedes the breakdown in a typical neurosis. *Ibsen is indeed one of the group of persons in the last of the nineteenth*

*Ibid., pp. 72–73.
†Ibid., p. 99.

century, including Nietzsche and Freud, who produced the great psychoanalytic revolution.

We then find Peer in Egypt before a statue of Mennon, the god of the morning. The statue is trying to say something to him:

> O Owl of Wisdom, where do my birds sleep?
> You must solve the riddle of my song or die.*

The riddle means that Peer has sealed off his soul and he must unseal it or die. He pays no attention.

Next Peer arrives at an insane asylum. He is introduced in the hospital as "the prophet of self"—a man who is himself in everything. The director takes him through the hospital and announces that Peer Gynt is going to be the new director. Peer Gynt avers, "Here, as far as I can make out, the thing is to be beside one's self." The director assures him that he is mistaken, and goes on to describe the inmates of the hospital as follows,

> Here we are ourselves with a vengeance;
> Ourselves and nothing but ourselves.
> We go full steam through life under the pressure of self.
> Each one shuts himself up in the cask of self,
> Sinks to the bottom by self-fermentation,
> Seals himself in with the bung of self,
> And seasons in the well of self,
> *No one here weeps for the woes of others.*
> *No one here listens to anyone else's ideas.* †

Peer Gynt and the patients in the mental hospital have this in common: they cannot weep for the woes of others, they cannot respond or experience sympathy, they have no ear for anyone else's ideas. The fundamental human bond is lost. Yevtushenko correctly sees that the Peer Gynt type is the person who has "so few ties with life." He states, in contrast, the other side on the basis of his own struggle and experience,

*Ibid., p. 101.
†Ibid., pp. 106–107.

But if I connect with so many things,
I must stand for something, apparently,
         have some value?
And if I stand for nothing,
Why then
         do I suffer and weep?*

Now in the hospital there is a fellah with a mummy strapped on his back. It stands for the past not in the sense of mommy but the mummy of the grandiose dead self—"King Avis"—which still clings to this man. The fellah asks Peer how he can make people see that *he* is King Avis (i.e., he himself is the dead, archaic element strapped on his back). Peer Gynt answers, "Hang yourself," with the idea that, dead, he'll look like the mummy. The fellah goes and does it. Peer says to another man, "Cut your throat," and the man does so. This is a vivid presentation of the truth coming home to Peer that to *be only yourself you become the victim of everybody else's whim.* A powerful paradox indeed!

Peer Gynt becomes frantic. He sees that these people "are themselves and nothing but themselves" and realizes that this is what he has all his life tried to be. It is the first time in the play that Peer gets any genuine insight. He is at last aware that he is now the ultimate of the empty self—he is aware of the bankruptcy of the central and basic myth in his life.

He cries, "I am a blank sheet of paper that no one will write on" and "I'm whatever you wish."† The dilemma of being yourself by way of the drive to be admired and to be taken care of consists of getting your identity as a self from what others want and direct. This now makes the circle full: Peer ends up "I'm whatever you wish."

---

*"I don't understand."
†Ibid., pp. 111–112.

THE VALUE OF DESPAIR

At this point we generally meet this kind of person in psychotherapy. It is not by accident that Ibsen has Peer Gynt in a mental hospital here. We can almost literally hear the cracking of the timbers as Peer Gynt's structure of myth collapses to the ground. In his own words his whole life up till now has been a "fake and a lie." The state of despair that is characterized by the realization that he simply has no self, has no center, is similar to the disintegration of self-world relationship in schizophrenia. It is a terrifying experience, and the fact that everyone has it to some extent does not make the despair any less terrifying.

At long last, Peer Gynt wakes up to the fact that he is not the master of himself at all. He knows now that somebody could say to him, "Jump into the Nile and drown yourself," and he might well do it. This is the state of despair and emptiness which Tillich terms literally the fear of non-being.

It is a sad spectacle as we remember Peer's exuberance at the opening of the drama; we see the hulk of a man who was "destined for greatness, a man who rides a horse with a crest of shining silver and four shoes of gold, trailing a cloak of scarlet silk." Now we see the pathetic corpse of a myth which never worked!

After this realization of despair, we find Peer on a ship bound back to Norway. Becoming aware of the sailors who are with him on the ship, Peer suddenly wants to give money to the poor sailors—his first appearance of a genuinely generous impulse in response to the needs of others. But then he learns that these sailors have wives and children waiting for them back home, while "there is no one waiting for old Peer Gynt." Spite and envy now surge up in Peer, weeping for a lost time.

Candles on the table! I'll put out those candles!
[because] there's no one who ever thinks of me.*

The problem of *spite* is exceedingly interesting in that it re-
leases bitter hatred, aggression, and a desire in him to erase the
sailors' human bonds; he wants "all their love destroyed!" This
surge of hatred and aggression against persons who have done
him no harm whatever may seem surprising. But at least it is
genuine, the first strong, genuine emotion that Peer Gynt has
had in the whole play. The anger at least tells us Peer Gynt
feels something directly.

This is what also often happens with our patients when they
come to psychotherapy in this state of despair and emptiness.
First there surges up in them a surprising amount of spite and
envy (often put in the sophisticated form of cynicism) toward
others' loves and happiness. Obviously it does no good to mor-
alize to the patient about this. They *are* full of envy and spite;
they *have* been cheated, regardless of whose fault it was. Our
moralism is not only ineffectual and unconstructive but wrong
in a more important sense. For the patient's envy and spite is
the beginning of something positive, something that can be
constructively used. It is an emotion that is *sincere,* for one
thing; it is an emotion also that is *strong* for another. It comes
out in *Peer Gynt* as the play goes on, as it does with our patients, that spite and envy can be a prelude to other more
constructive emotions, and the spite and envy make available
to the Peer Gynts a power that they did not have before. In due
time with the patient we get to the most important question of
all, "What do you yourself have to do with the fact that no one
is waiting at home?"

Peer Gynt, of course, has everything in the world to do with
his inner despairing conviction that no one is waiting with a
candle at his table. The despair is a function of the contradiction in his subjective attitudes and is then projected on the
outside world. For it is objectively inaccurate: someone *is* wait-

*Ibid., p. 116.

ing for Peer Gynt, namely, Solveig, and on an intuitive level he knows it.* But Peer Gynt can't allow this fact into his own consciousness, cannot "accept acceptance," in Tillich's pithy phrase.

Now they pass a ship that has been wrecked on a rock in the storm, and Peer Gynt has the urge to rescue the men on the stricken ship. When the captain refuses to turn the ship around to save the drowning men, Peer Gynt tries to bribe the sailors to rescue the men on the sinking ship. Here comes out not only some genuine statement of concern, but active commitment in its behalf. Peer hears the screams on the ship that is going down near them;

> They're screaming again. Look, there's a lull!
> You, cook! Will you try? I'll give you money!†

Peer at last can hear the pain of others, can "weep for other's woes." As the other ship sinks, Peer Gynt speaks in soliloquy, "There is no faith left among men any more." The story wrenches from him a profoundly gripping cry, "On a night like this our Lord is dangerous."

Here emerges the daimonic in the service not of aggression and destructiveness but of awe and wonder. It is an entirely different mood from the time in Morocco when he commanded God to pay attention. It is a human being who stands in awe of the significance of life and death and the portentousness of their powers. With the closeness to death there comes an honesty—one can no longer take refuge in platitudes. The fact that Peer can experience this awe and wonder, this respect for Being, makes it also possible for him to affirm, as he does a few lines further, his human ties:

---

*The translator suggests that this last part of the play, starting with the wrecked ship, can be seen as occurring after death, Peer Gynt as it were seeing his whole life in a series of quick flashes. But regardless of whether that is the dramatic meaning, we can see the myth as Ibsen's description of the development and the meaning of this pattern of life.

†Ibsen, *Peer Gynt*, p. 117.

. . . A man can never be
Himself at sea. He must sink or swim with the rest.*

THE STRANGE PASSENGER

Now a character who is called by the curious name "Strange
Passenger" comes up to Peer Gynt at the ship's rail and puts a
question to him, "Suppose we, for example, should strike on a
rock and sink in the darkness." Frightened, Peer responds, "Do
you think there is a danger?" The Strange Passenger answers,
"I don't really know what I ought to say," but he continues to
remind Peer of the imminence of death. When Peer remonstrates, the Strange Passenger cautions,

> But, my dear sir, consider. It's to
>   your advantage.
> I'll open you up and let in the light.
> I want to discover the source of your dreams.
> I want to find out how you're put together—†

This Strange Passenger is indeed a curious character. Peer,
in angry "resistance," disposes of him by calling him a horrible
"scientist . . . you damned free thinker!" Does the Strange
Passenger not have the role of the psychoanalyst? Even his
language, though perhaps partially spoken in Ibsen's jest,
sounds like a prediction of psychoanalysis.

But most of all the Strange Passenger is Peer speaking to
himself. In a profound sense this scene is an endeavor to show
Peer Gynt's awareness of what is going on in his consciousness
in the hope that this may be the beginning of some reintegra-
tion.

Now we see several symbolic portrayals of the vicissitudes of

---

*Ibid.
†Ibid., p. 119. Recall that this drama was written in 1867, three decades before
Freud's book on dreams.

the longed-for integration. In one scene we see Peer Gynt
crawling up to a cabin in the woods, a cabin which he left. He
soliloquizes, "The old boy's had to crawl back to his mother."
Then comes the graphic scene in which he peels an onion,
which is himself:

>   . . . You old fake!
> You're no Emperor. You're just an onion.
> Now then, little Peer, I'm going to peel you, . . .
> That's the shipwrecked man on the upturned keel . . .
> And inside that is the digger of gold; . . .
> And here is the Prophet, fresh and juicy:
>   . . . he stinks of lies. . . .
>   . . . Living for ease and pleasure. . . .
> Surely I'll soon get down to the heart?
> No—there isn't one! Just a series of shells.*

It turns out that in the hut toward which he is crawling he
finds Solveig. She is singing, "I will wait for you, my love." But
Peer Gynt is not yet ready to accept a genuine relationship; he
gets up saying to himself, "One who remembered and one who
forgot."

> And the game can never be played again!
> Oh, here was my Empire and my crown!†

He goes away with the realization that he must become more
integrated before he can come back.

Scene after scene now piles up as symbols of the lost self. A
Button Moulder wants to melt down Peer Gynt in his casting
ladle. Peer Gynt has never been anything, charges the Button
Moulder, so why shouldn't he be melted down? Peer Gynt
protests, crying, "I have never been a real sinner," and the
Button Moulder rejoins, "That's just the trouble,"

> You aren't what one could call a whole-hearted
> Sinner. You're scarcely even a minor one— . . .

*Ibid., p. 133.
†Ibid., p. 134.

> . . . You are not virtuous either— . . .
>
> *A man needs strength and purpose to be a sinner.* *

This last powerful sentence, this demonstration of the dai-monic, Nietzsche would have loved. Peer Gynt would have amounted to more if he had been a real sinner. He now has to admit the truth of these judgments: "I just splashed about on the surface. . . . I have never been—? I could almost laugh!"And the Button Moulder later sums it up in this one proclamation: "To be oneself is: to kill oneself."†

In this nadir of despair, Peer Gynt is told in effect that he is nothing. The gospel of "being one's self alone" ends up in becoming nothing. The ultimate meaning of this myth, even more true today than it was in Ibsen's day, is that all such narcissistic egocentricity leads to self-destruction.

But from the profound nadir of despair life shows us, as in Alcoholics Anonymous, the way toward a resurrection of the self.

> . . . There are two ways in which a man can be himself.
> A right way and a wrong way.
> You may know that a man in Paris
> Has discovered a way of taking portraits
> With the help of the sun. Either one can produce
> A direct picture, or else what they call a negative.
> In the latter, light and dark are reversed;
> And the result, to the ordinary eye, is ugly.
> But the image of the original is there.
> All that's required is to develop it. **

The negative in the long run is essential to the positive—the original is there and what is necessary is to develop it, arduous as this undertaking may be.

Stumbling into the Troll King, to settle a long-ago score, Peer is assured that he has done well indeed in living up to the

*Ibid., p. 139.
†Ibid., pp. 139, 141, 148.
**Ibid., p. 153.

motto, "Troll, be thyself—and thyself alone!" Whenever they are writing a newspaper article extolling Trolldom, the troll adds, they cite him as their best example of one who really believed, "To hell with the rest of the world!" Peer gives Trolldom short shrift this time and hurries down the road toward Solveig.

In his experiencing of the abyss of heaven he sees a shooting star and is overcome with awe,

> We flash for a moment, then
>   Our light is quenched,
>
> And we disappear into the
>   . . . void forever.
>
> Is there no one in the Abyss—
>   —no one in Heaven—!

He gradually calms himself and then speaks one of the most beautiful passages of the play:

> How unspeakably poor a soul can be
> When it enters the mist and returns to nothing!
> O beautiful earth, don't be angry with me
> That I trod your sweet grass to no avail.
> O beautiful sun, you have squandered
> Your golden light upon an empty hut.
>
> There was no one within to warm and comfort.
> The owner, I know now, was never at home. . . .
> Then let the snow pile over me,
> And let them write above: "Here lies no one."
> And afterwards—let the world take its course.*

---

*Ibid., pp. 154, 155.

LOVE AND RESTORATION

This renunciation of the narcissistic self is the beginning of authentic selfhood. Now the Boyg who comes in for a final scene again repeats to Peer Gynt, "Always go around." But Peer finally can now commit himself. "Ah! No! This time straight through."*

He finally arrives back to Solveig. The poignant words they speak at the end are significant for us here:

PEER: Tell me, then!
Where was my self, my whole self, my true self?
The self that bore God's stamp upon its brow?
SOLVEIG: In my faith, in my hope, and in my love.

. . . .

PEER: My mother! My wife! O, thou pure woman!
O hide me in your love! Hide me! Hide me!
SOLVEIG: Sleep, O sleep, my dearest boy.
I will cradle you. I will guard you.
Sleep, O sleep, my love, my joy.
Sleep now, and rest.†

For some readers this ending will present a problem. Are we to assume that Ibsen is simply saying Peer Gynt goes back to mother? This is one conclusion that could be drawn, but it would be much too superficial. There is a great difference between the way Solveig relates to him here, and he to Solveig, and the way he related previously to his mother. Solveig waits for him out of her *own choice and integrity, whereas the mother clung to him out of her deprivation.* Solveig lets him come when he is ready to come, when he has gone through the experiences that he must go through. These experiences make him finally able to love her.

*Ibid., p. 156.
†Ibid., pp. 157–158.

Solveig is a symbol of the presence of some significant person in relation to whom it is possible for Peer Gynt to experience human ties and to love. Thus he too can at last become a self. Like the Strange Passenger, Solveig fulfills the role of the true human healer. A world of interpersonal relationship is made available in which Peer can at last experience and find himself. This world is characterized by consistency and has within it some person or persons who will accept Peer's rejection without withdrawing, accept his anger without retaliation, and steadily value him for his own worth.

It is the combination of these characteristics which we call *presence*. The Strange Passenger on the ship symbolized presence at the nadir stage in Peer's development; he was willing to face with Peer the ultimate state of loss of being, namely, death. The function of the therapist, applying this myth to psychotherapy, is to provide a presence which constitutes a human world within which the patient not only *can* find the polarity of the I–thou relationship but within which he must find it.

This presence, and the making of such a world possible, is the function of Solveig in the drama. As Dante can survive the long vigil in purgatory and continue his journey into paradise when he meets Beatrice, so Peer Gynt can now continue his journey into human integrity and joy in his love for Solveig.

ELEVEN

Briar Rose Revisited

> In a way this story tells that to be able to love, a person first
> has to become able to feel; even if the feelings are negative,
> that is better than not feeling. In the beginning the
> princess is entirely self-centered; all her interest is in her
> ball. She has no feelings when she plans to go back on her
> promise to the frog, gives no thought as to what this may
> mean for it. The closer the frog comes to her physically and
> personally, the stronger her feelings become, but with this
> she becomes more a person. For a long stretch of
> development she obeys her father, but feels ever more
> strongly; then at the end she asserts her independence in
> going against his orders. As she thus becomes herself, so
> does the frog; it turns into a prince.
>
> Bruno Bettelheim,
> *The Uses of Enchantment*

THE QUESTION THAT LEAPS OUT immediately is, how did this
tale's name get changed to "Sleeping Beauty" in our society? If you look into a collection of Grimms' fairy tales, you will
find no entry by that name. The tale is called *Briar Rose* by the
Grimm brothers, and rightly so. There is a vast difference between the connotations of these two names. Whereas "Sleep-

ing Beauty" connotes Hollywood and our American tendency from decades ago to romanticize the developing girl, "Briar Rose" implies that the girl is by no means so open to exploitation as the fairy tale implies.

For the "briar" is a form of feminine protection and assertion. It is a statement that even the girl child's "briars" are present as a warning against anybody who seeks to break in when she is not yet ready. We may take "rose" as a symbol of the vagina—a rose is lovely with its exquisite folds, its secret promises, and its unknown depths and joys for the chosen suitor. This symbol of the rose leads to the many vaginal-like creations, such as rose windows in cathedrals, which are regularly accepted as symbols leading into such great adventure. The tale is not at all a picture of passivity but an assertive statement which requires what I call later in this chapter "creative waiting."

In America and Western Europe we are living in the age of women's assertion after centuries in which women were passive responders to male desires and biologically prisoners of their own bodies. Now with contraceptives women can achieve pleasure of the body without the age-old penalty of pregnancy. And with abortion, apart from the difficult moral questions involved, women have some choice about whose child they will carry. Women nowadays can choose to have families on their own—single-parent families, with the woman impregnated by a man of her choice or by semen from a sperm bank, or by adoption of an orphan. *Briar Rose* had her natural protections by virtue of thorns; these briars were the protection the girl child possessed as she moved into adulthood.

The same is true concerning women's reactions to their men's affairs. Time was when men had a multitude of affairs, like the bee in the song in *The King and I* which goes into as many flowers as it can, whereas the flower must stay put in the ground. Nowadays women as well have choice about their sexual partners. In this sense "Briar Rose" was always the fitting title for this myth and was changed, we venture to suggest, in late centuries to fit the well-known clichés of women's passivity.

We turn to this tale "Briar Rose," which has not yet been infused with consciousness. As we read it literally in Grimms' fairy tales, it has a happy ending, and nobody has to work anything through—which is one distinction between a fairy tale and a myth. *Fairy tales are our myths before we become conscious of ourselves.* Only fairy tales were present in the Garden of Eden before the mythic "fall" of Adam and Eve. The myth, then, adds the existential dimensions to the fairy tale. Myths challenge us to confront our destiny, our death, our love, our joy. The myth adds the universal dimension because every adult has to confront his or her fate in love and death. Fairy tales can become myths, as does this one about passivity and freedom in a love which applies to all of us, male as well as female. But though "Briar Rose" is still a fairy tale, we see pushing through some aspects of human struggle and consciousness.

Students in my classes always take care to point out (and I agree) that there are many men in our culture who exemplify Briar Rose, and conversely not a few women who are Peer Gynts. We all confront the problems of our own freedom and our responsibility for our own selves, whether by active escape like Peer Gynt or by fortifying ourselves against the opposite sex like Briar Rose.

As a tale of awakening, Briar Rose begins as a description of the vicissitudes of emerging femininity. It is the presentation of the problem and dynamics which inevitably accompany this development. The contradiction and the conflict in the story are that this growing girl, Briar Rose, wishes to develop, but the motive power for her development is given over to another, namely, the prince who shall come and kiss her into womanhood.

If we see this in psychological terms, it is not unlike Peer Gynt. Briar Rose moves toward the emerging of her own powers, particularly her sexual capacities, but the movement is dependent upon some creature, some force outside herself, namely, the imagined prince. I believe this phenomenon—now taking the story as a myth rather than a fairy tale—reflects a profound contradiction in modern women and in the development of their femininity. In decades past, they have been expected by the culture to seek their development by exactly the process which no longer produces it—namely, making one's self dependent on the prince, who will suddenly come, riding on a white horse to hack with his sword a swath through the thorns.

Before we go into the fairy tale of Briar Rose itself, I will present some vignettes from a case of a patient in psychoanalysis who represents this dilemma. This woman of thirty, whom I shall call Sylvia, was married and had a daughter of three and a son just born at the time of her consultations. Her chief difficulties, which had hounded her for her whole life, were a lack of spontaneity, a lack of feeling in social relationships, and a general difficulty in experiencing herself as a woman. Along with these went a specific sexual problem—she had no sexual passion—and understandably a general feeling of profound emotional inadequacy. Her husband had affairs outside the marriage and was considering divorce because of her coldness and disinterest in sex. Indeed, she came for psychoanalytic treatment originally at the insistence of her husband and his family.

Like Briar Rose in the tale she had developed late, menstruation not coming till seventeen, her breasts and other feminine aspects of her body developing proportionately late. She had three older brothers, and in her position in the family she had had plenty of reason to experience herself as a little princess. As is often the case in this kind of configuration, her mother was a seemingly ineffectual person who controlled the father by masochistic behavior.

The pattern of Sylvia showed itself by a very great passivity, an inertia, and a tendency to go literally to sleep. Particularly on trains she would assume a fetal position as nearly as possible whenever she was faced with a problem. This tendency came out dramatically in her literal grogginess during psychoanalytical hours. One enlightening session she brought a dream which was a dream within a dream: she was explaining to me the following words, "I haven't come to terms with Orville Johnson." Orville Johnson was a boyfriend when she was seven or eight.

During that hour she described falling asleep as a "curling up and being like a fetus." "Going to sleep is a way of going back to the beginning, to be reborn—reborn not warped." At a later time she had dreams of herself and her daughter both in the kitchen, and she was afraid "I will grow old before I grow up," which is exactly what happens with women in this pattern. The night following that dream came one in which I was present: "You and I were sleeping in the same room. We were snowbound. You were on the couch and I was on the cot. You complimented me when we woke up that I slept with such serenity." This dream, she stated, refers to her therapy, as a womb in which she was waiting to be born, and she is complimented by the therapist for being so "child-like."

We see already in these simple terms a scene with the dramatic personae of the Briar Rose tale: she sleeps sweetly, the man (myself) is present, though she ostensibly has me sleeping too rather than awakening her. My complimenting her has the effect of constituting her biologically. What is especially important is that being passive also can have a positive function; it may be a method of transformation.

Sylvia had an extensive feeling of being "transported" by men, being lifted up and experiencing sexual feeling at the same time. She used "transport" as meaning to carry, and to carry her away; one is "transported" by love and sex and ecstasy. We are also transported by trains, and Sylvia had the same feeling of pleasure and sexual excitement when riding on a train as she had had when she, as a little girl, had been lifted up and carried by her father. When I asked about her feelings when such experiences occurred, she retorted, "I don't want to talk about it or dissect it, I'm afraid I'll lose it." Through this portion of the therapy, she was often prickly; I could often feel the "briar" without the rose.

Let us pause at this point to go directly to the Briar Rose tale and later return to Sylvia to discover the dynamics that underlie this tale.

The fairy tale goes as follows:

A long time ago there were a king and queen who said every day: "Ah, if only we had a child!" but they never had one. But it happened that once when the queen was bathing, a frog crept out of the water on to the land, and said to her: "Your wish shall be fulfilled; before a year has gone by, you shall have a daughter."*

What the frog had said came true, and the queen had a little girl who was so pretty that the king could not contain himself for joy, and ordered a great feast. He invited not only his kindred, friends and acquaintances, but also the Wise Women, in order that they might be kind and well-disposed towards the child. There were thirteen of them in his kingdom, but, as he had only twelve golden plates for them to eat out of, one of them had to be left at home.

The Wise Women bestowed their magic gifts upon the baby: one gave virtue, another beauty, a third riches, and so on with everything in the world that one can wish for.

When eleven of them had made their promises, suddenly the thirteenth came in. She wished to avenge herself for not having been invited, and without greeting, or even looking at anyone, she cried with a loud voice: "The king's daughter shall in her fifteenth year prick herself with a spindle, and fall down dead." And, without saying a word more, she turned round and left the room.

---

*A feminist group with whom I discussed this fairy tale proposed that the queen, in her trip to the bath-house, had been impregnated by another man. This is certainly a possible interpretation; It reflects what we said earlier, that modern women take steps on their own, cuckolding the men if necessary as a way of getting back at them.

They were all shocked; but the twelfth, whose good wish still remained unspoken, came forward, and as she could not undo the evil sentence, but only soften it, she said: "It shall not be death, but a deep sleep of a hundred years, into which the princess shall fall."

So far we recognize a tale that we already have long known. Many readers will be familiar with the usual biological and psychoanalytic interpretation of this tale, namely, that it has to do with the onset of menstruation symbolized in the princess pricking her finger, after which there comes a latency period and then she is awakened into sexual awareness and sexual excitement by the kiss of the man. There is validity, albeit oversimplification, in this biological interpretation; it can be accepted from a biological point of view.

But our concern here is to see this tale as a myth, putting it into a broader perspective, and to ask not only how this child develops as a biological organism but how she becomes a *human* being. It is the story of a *being*, Briar Rose, in the process of *becoming*. It is a tale of the girl caught in passivity but needing to act responsibly for her own life. Our search is to clarify the problem of the affirmation of her freedom and responsibility.

The story begins with a wish. In one sense every tale, every myth, every emergence of a new element in one's development starts with a wish, a yearning for some new element of being, a longing for some fulfillment. Here it is, also appropriately, a *conceiving*. We conceive many different things: an idea, a plan, a work of art, a baby.

The birth is predicted by an archaic element, namely, the frog. Appearing in many of Grimms' fairy tales and in mythology of all sorts since, the frog is that creature with one foot in our previous evolutionary development, the water, and another foot on land. It represents the archaic element in its cold and slimy qualities, and also in its big eyes, primitive as they are, which can at least peer powerfully. The frog here stands for the point in evolution when our human forebears crawled out of the swamps and slime but kept the possibility of living in water as well.* Some persons regard the frog as symbolic for intercourse and thus conclude that the queen met a man at her bathing spot and cuckolded the king. This is entirely possible since frogs in Grimms' tales often have this sexual role.

Then come the wise women, highly significant figures. We may see them as the women with whom this growing baby girl will have to identify. The developing child will be helped to get virtues and abilities from identifying with her mother, aunts, schoolteachers, and, as it turns out in this myth later, grandmother. These and other women—hopefully women of wisdom in real life—will be there living out certain virtues and abilities which have an educational (*e-ducere*—to draw out) effect upon the girl-child. The identification that goes on is a normal and healthy part of all development.

But there are two cautions to be made about it. One is that identification should be as much in awareness as possible. That is, one should know what and whom one is identifying with. Identification will always go on; but our autonomy and future growth are protected by the fact that it is not blind and compulsive but occurs in the subject's awareness as well as in unconsciousness.

Another point which becomes critical later in this tale is that the little girl-child must not only identify with these women but also get free from them. The identifying *with* and getting free *from* is the ever recurring paradox of the umbilical cord as it comes out in tales and myths of every kind. It is the fundamental problem of all human individual development: each person must negotiate the biological tie in order *to gain his or her being, and then to go beyond it* to more highly differentiated dimensions of consciousness.

There enters the evil element at exactly the dramatic time, for while we are taking the new steps, we are most vulnerable to

*The relation of this level of water and slime to levels of the unconscious, by way of both Freud's and Jung's theories, is obvious.

evil. It was easier to describe this in the older religious myths of Satan's tempting us most strongly at exactly the time when we are achieving some spiritual good. The thirteenth old woman embodies a particular kind of evil, *spite* and *envy*, which often go together, as we will presently see. In her curse that Briar Rose will die at the age of fifteen, it is important that she will die before she has come into her full femininity.

Now enters the twelfth good woman—those numbers, twelve and thirteen, are obviously symbolically significant— who can commute this ultimate fate from death into the sleep of one hundred years. One hundred years is a century: we take it as meaning the girl will sleep from one age to another in the sense of one age of hers to another. In other words, Sylvia must "come to terms with Orville Johnson."

The king, who would fain keep his dear child from the misfortune, gave orders that every spindle in the whole kingdom should be burnt. Meanwhile the gifts of the Wise Women were plenteously fulfilled on the young girl, for she was so beautiful, modest, good-natured, and wise, that everyone who saw her was bound to love her.

The king here is doing what every father is tempted to do, namely, to overprotect his daughter. To prevent her death he tries to hedge her in: he seeks to avoid the non-being by preventing being, to use Tillich's definition of neurosis. We are afraid of non-being and so we shrivel up our being. The king thinks that he can protect her by blocking her growth: by burning all the spindles, stopping all activity, and keeping her simply shut up within the castle. But of course this shrinking never works; and we shall find Briar Rose very humanly, if not entirely judiciously, going out to explore the world, to look into the different rooms in the castle.

A rusty key was in the lock, and when she turned it the door sprang open and there in the little room sat an old woman with a spindle, busily spinning her flax. "Good day, old mother," said the king's daughter, "what are you doing there?" "I am spinning," said the old woman and nodded her head. "What sort of thing is that, that rattles round so merrily?" asked Briar Rose, and she took the spindle and wanted to spin too. But scarcely had she touched the spindle when the magic decree was fulfilled and she pricked her finger with it.

Here we see the growing girl moving out into the world. She does this when she's alone, as she's always bound to be at some time no matter how much her father overprotects her. The word "alone" here is especially significant, because this kind of development, this leap of freedom, must always contain some element of being done alone, taking responsibility for one's own steps oneself. Going out into the world, she wants to learn the feminine tasks, the capabilities that go with what women do, such as spinning. Then comes the bleeding, biologically the point of menstruation and the harbinger since the beginning of time that she will be able to conceive a new being. "Becoming" now is becoming able to be impregnated.

Time then stops in this tale. Menstruation, indeed, is named time, *menses* being the Latin word "months."* In our vernacular we refer to menstruation also in terms of time, one's "period."

And, at the very moment when she felt the prick, she fell down upon the bed and lay there in a deep sleep. And this sleep extended over the whole palace. The king and queen, who had just come home and had entered the great hall, began to sleep, and the whole court with them.

But round about the castle there began to grow a hedge of thorns, which every year became higher, and at last grew close up round the castle and all over it, so that there was nothing of it to be seen, not even the flag upon the roof.

In this stopping of time, even nature is quiet and comes to a halt. This is indeed what happens when human development is blocked: growth is frozen, the developmental level is fixated. But it is never possible for growth to stop fully: neurotic de-

---

*Time is of great importance to the existential writers. Heidegger wrote *Being and Time*. Eugene Minkowski wrote *Le temps vécu*. I have a section on "Of Time and History" in my book *The Discovery of Being*.

fenses are required to effect the halt, and a vicious circle sets in. Figuratively speaking, nature takes part in the defenses of the girl, the hedge of thorns grows round the castle and every year grows higher, i.e., the neurotic pattern becomes more evident.

The shrinking into oneself characteristic of neurosis is symbolized in the fairy tale by this hedge growing around the castle. The hedge hides not only Briar Rose but the other people as well and covers the castle so that not even the flag on the roof can be seen. The identity of the palace is lost. The place becomes only a memory.

But the story of the beautiful sleeping "Briar Rose," for so the princess was named, went about the country, so that from time to time kings' sons came and tried to get through the thorny hedge into the castle. But they found it impossible, for the thorns held fast together as if they had hands and the youths were caught in them and could not get loose again, and died a miserable death.

The youths try to storm the thorns, to force their way in to Briar Rose before the time is fulfilled and she is ready to be awakened. We can assume, now from a psychoanalytic viewpoint, there will be rage in Briar Rose that she is so completely blocked off from life. I propose that her rage shows itself in the fact that the briars around the castle *kill the suitors.* In every neurotic pattern others are dragged down and made to suffer by virtue of the anger—in this case, Briar Rose's anger. It may seem strange to talk of rage on the part of such a "sweet" creature as Briar Rose, but that is the unexpected effect neurotic patterns have on one's world.

The princes represent *wishing without mutuality.* Wishing becomes willful defiance when it does not take into account the needs and readiness of the other, when it is not genuinely *inter*-personal. This storming of the hedge happens when the princes are driven by their own needs and desires without relation to the girl's. Their behavior has the character of forcing Briar Rose, the attitude of rape rather than mutual love. Their behavior presupposes Briar Rose as a love object to be attained rather than a woman to be loved. They represent what we call the *daimonic:* they are under the sway of the daimonic gone awry. True, the princes get caught in Briar Rose's defenses; but otherwise she would become the mere victim of their desires. If the body is forced open before it is ready, there is the likelihood of considerable trauma, including the possibility that the body will never then open of its own accord.

There then occurs a new development in the story.

The many young princes had tried to get in but they had tried to get through the thorny hedge, but they had remained sticking fast in it, and had died a pitiful death. Then the youth said: "I am not afraid, I will go and see the beautiful Briar Rose." The good old man might dissuade him as he would, but the prince did not listen to his words.

Here we have the beginning of the *courage of relationship.* It is one aspect of the "courage to be," as Tillich would put it. The old man who tries to dissuade the prince reminds us of Jocasta in the famous drama of Oedipus. As Jocasta adjures Oedipus to rest, take it easy, not to bother himself, not to insist on being "present to himself," the old man tries to dissuade the prince with the counsel of common sense and adjustment. But the prince refuses such advice: "I am not afraid. I will go and see the beautiful Briar Rose."

But by this time the hundred years had just passed, and the day had come when Briar Rose was to awake again. When the king's son came near to the thorn-hedge, it was nothing but large and beautiful flowers, which parted from each other of their own accord, and let him pass unhurt.

This is a beautiful dénouement: the thorns become roses and the hedge becomes flowers by virtue of "creative waiting." The fairy tale would have it that this occurs simply by waiting. I believe differently: it is inner growth, the external manifestation of *kairos.*

This mythic approach to time is opposite to the routine—

and often boring—concept of time as automatic passage of "tomorrow and tomorrow and tomorrow" creeping on "in petty pace from day to day." This demonstrates that this great change did not occur because of the special qualities of this prince (others were as courageous and died in the thorns). This prince, we assume, sensed the *kairos,* the moment when "all creation trembled and groaned."

Briar Rose and everything in her world is asleep until the man in the form of the Prince comes to awaken her, and then the thorns become large and beautiful flowers which part from each other of their own accord. This is a very meaningful and graphic symbol of the hymen and other protections of the girl from sexuality, protections which now change into their opposite of their own accord. When the time is ripe, the thorn becomes a flower, a rose—a vaginal symbol as beautiful and exquisitely fitting as could be imagined. We are reminded that in mythology and cultural history the word "deflowered" is used for the intercourse in which a woman gives up her virginity in her first sexual relationship. A recurrence of the same symbol is present in such folk songs as "My Wild Irish Rose,"

> Some day for my sake
> She may let me take
> The bloom from my wild Irish rose.

This tale binds up in symbolic form not only the biological meaning but the psychological meaning of this significant experience. The prince is *present* when her time arrives in fullness. The tale says, "He could not turn his eyes away," which indicates an interpersonal relation very different from the previous youths' desire to storm the castle. He kisses her and she then awakes—specifically awakes sexually, but we may assume the meaning is an awakening in all aspects as well.

There now is an interpersonal relationship. There is love, we are told; there is capacity for creating new being in procreation, and there is, as in all fairy tales, the happy ending. They marry in splendor and live contentedly to the end of their days.

But we cannot help thinking at this point of the *Three Penny Opera* and its charming satirical song, "Happy Ending," as well as another of its songs, "Sad To Say It Never Has Been So." Now sad to say it never has been so that any woman's development in real life is as simple as being asleep in the pre-adolescent age and then, on being awakened by the kiss of the prince, she then lives happily ever after. The vicissitudes of development and individuation are difficult in the best of ages, and particularly in our age of psychological alienation, when we are all to some extent emotionally displaced persons.

There are within this tale, nevertheless, deeper dimensions which make the myth more than a fairy tale. We see first of all the phenomenon of *presence*.

The loss of the presence means we are not fully alive to ourselves and so not fully alive to others. Thus the central issue in the myth is the presence of Briar Rose to herself. The spokesmen in contemporary Western civilization for this loss of presence to ourselves are Kierkegaard and Nietzsche; they are the prophets who saw the consequences of our alienation from our culture, from our friends, and especially from meaning in life. Nietzsche was passionately concerned with the fact that we have become vapid, empty, powerless in ourselves. He represents the phase in the myth of these young men who try to storm the thorns and citadel, who try to take it by force but, since the time is not yet ripe, fail.

The next phase is that in which the sleeping girl's presence can be restored only by waiting. Heidegger is the representative of this phase, for he was aware of the death of God—if we put it in a theological context—and he lived in the awareness that this presence is lost. Heidegger knew how to "wait for Godot," to borrow the title of Beckett's play.

Whether or not one likes this specific language and these illustrations, one must grant that the concept of *presence* is a fruitful one for understanding this tale and myth. "Man is only man," writes Heidegger, "when he is spoken to by Being," which is the enlarged, universalized form of what is going on concretely in this tale. Woman is only woman when she is spoken to by her true being. She gains presence to herself when her feelings, passions, and capabilities are not only hers but are called forth by other people and by her community. The same thing is in W. H. Auden's poem, "The Age of Anxiety":

> .... for the ego is a dream
> Till a neighbor's need by
> name create it.*

These are all endeavors to highlight a fundamental aspect of human relationship, namely, that the birth and development of the self take place in an interpersonal field. We call to each other, we awaken each other; hopefully we are present to each other, either through books, or art, or relationship.

CREATIVE PRESENCE

We return now to a topic broached earlier, the capacity for *creative presence.* We saw that the premature youths who stormed the hedges and "died a miserable death" were those who lacked the capacity to wait until the time of *kairos,* the time when Briar Rose's sleep was fulfilled. I refer to waiting until something is ready to be born—whether it be a baby, an idea, an invention, or an artistic vision. This waiting is not passive and empty; the one who waits is an active participant in the gestation. Too much emphasis on conscious *intention*— like the active pushing of the premature suitors in the tale of Briar Rose—blocks the capacity to wait. *Intentionality,* the condition that everything has meaning which is given by our consciousness, is possible only when we have this capacity for creative waiting.

It is fascinating to compare the waiting of Briar Rose in the fairy tale with the lady Eliot evokes in "The Waste Land," a

*Rollo May, *Man's Search for Himself* (New York: Norton, 1953), p. 88.

lady who is rich and beautiful but jaded, bored with everything, including sex, although she is with her lover. Both are waiting. The jaded lady says, "What shall we do tomorrow. What shall we ever do?"* Both are expressions of wishing for something. Both imply some hope that there may be a "knock upon the door."† But Briar Rose is the waiting of innocence, the waiting of dreaming; she sleeps, her eyelids are closed. Whereas Eliot significantly tells us that his lady presses "lidless eyes"; her eyes are fixed open, she cannot close them. Now it is well known clinically that in anxiety a person's eyelids tend to be distended, to be fixed rigidly open in the face of danger. Artists observe this; Michelangelo's sculptures and his paintings of persons who are anxious have the eyelids distended, frozen open.

Briar Rose was in pre-awareness; Eliot's lady is post-awareness, her tragedy being not that she has not gained awareness but that she has *lost* it. For Briar Rose the chance for awareness had not yet arrived and does so only with the coming of the prince; for the lady, the possibilities for awareness are present, but she is blocked off from seeing them, even though her eyes are pried open. She is in the state not of innocence but of despair; she is in the Waste Land. Briar Rose is asleep without consciousness. The lady is sexually emancipated, "free," with all the riches of technology and culture at her fingertips; however, what she experiences is not gratification but the satiety of sex and appetite. Eliot is saying that one must wait through the age of despair for the gestation to occur which will lead us to a birth of consciousness on a higher level, that is, to *kairos*.

The myth, we have said, presents *creative waiting*. The distinction between this and passive waiting, which in psychotherapy can be quite unconstructive, lies in the question, What is one waiting *for*? Waiting is self-destructive, emptying, when the person, whether a patient in therapy or Eliot's lady, takes no responsibility for what he or she is waiting *for*.

---

*T. S. Eliot, "The Waste Land," in *Collected Poems, 1909–1962* (New York: Harcourt, Brace, Jovanovich, 1970).

†Beckett, *Waiting for Godot*, p. 43.

Clinically speaking, I believe this pattern of the patient's refusing to take cognizance of what he is waiting for is when he or she is actually waiting for some infantile wish, possibly omnipotent, to be gratified: "Mother will finally knock upon the door." Also it involves relatively severe anxiety, which has to be confronted before one can dare to ask and see what she or he is waiting for. The lady's waiting in Eliot's poem strikes one like the problem in much modern art and drama: waiting through nihilism and satiety until some new meaning can be born.

At the beginning of this chapter, we cited some dreams of Sylvia, whom we proposed as a modern example of the Briar Rose motif. As Sylvia's analysis proceeded, patterns emerged which were not at all the sweet young princess waiting to be awakened. She uttered in various forms the stubborn cry from Peter Pan, "I won't grow up!" This is a defiant statement when seen outside its fairy-tale setting. But even this defiance can be a harbinger of some valuable insights to be born.

Sylvia brought in the following dreams:

You [the therapist] and I were in a session. It was at some sanatorium. You complimented me by saying I was very bright and cute. Part of my being cute and bright in the dream came naturally, part of it was learned. I kissed you spontaneously on the cheek. I was in my nightdress. Then you left. I looked in the mirror and I saw I had mumps and my face was swollen. Then I thought that you must have been sorry for me.

Her associations with this dream came immediately: the Nutcracker legend. In this story a princess is deformed with swollen jaws the way Sylvia was in the dream, and only a man who has never shaved and always worn boots can save her. Soon the young man comes and is kissed by the princess, who thereupon gets over her deformities and becomes beautiful. But the man gets all her deformities, including the swollen jaws, and she thereafter will have nothing to do with him.

This is obviously a sexual and angry dream. She is in her nightdress and she kisses me. But in her associations, she transfers her deformities to me. No person can experience being robbed of talents, as Sylvia had been robbed of freedom and other capacities—all involved in her being put to sleep—without experiencing anger. And against whom should her anger be directed? Surely a large part of it toward those who are fated to kiss her to overcome the spell ("Why is my Prince so long in coming?"). In therapy this is expressed toward the therapist, and understandably so. Regardless of the motives, such a client would feel shortchanged. No one would choose this pattern if other patterns were open to her; but when it is forced upon her—as it was in Sylvia's experience—she is, rightly, angry.

Now this poses a serious contradiction. The very ones who are supposed to rescue Briar Rose in her powerlessness at the hands of a cruel fate, the ones who are supposed to validate her as a woman and as an awakened self, get their power by her forcing them. The fact that her deformities are placed on them adds vengeful, sadistic fuel to the fire and it keeps the vicious circle going.

This is a contradiction parallel to what we saw in Peer Gynt—he got his self-validation out of the same pattern which destroyed it. Such a pattern, then, becomes more and more self-destructive, until it cracks up in neurosis.

The anger toward men consists, when we track it down, of anger that the man did not save her from the spiteful woman. As I suggested this interpretation to Sylvia in the hour in which she brought the princess/Nutcracker dream, she responded, "It just occurred to me that my mother was envious of me. She had so much rejected the woman's role, but there I was, bright and cute."

In *Peer Gynt,* we recall Peer's spite and envy toward the sailors who had candles waiting for them at home. We emphasized then, as we do now, that envy and spite are the first, imperfect but honest, emotions which show the emergence of the person's self-affirmation. These are not idle feelings but the harbingers of more acceptable emotions to come later on.

As a neurotic feeling this is the expression of the state where the person has potentialities that he or she does not live out. Envy is the characteristic of the person who has not developed. Thus it is fitting that envy should be a problem in the whole tale of development of femininity. Envy is found in those who try to develop by the very means—giving the power for one's development to another—which block development. If Briar Rose cannot experience her feelings as her own, cannot experience her sexuality as hers, her capacity for procreation, her spontaneous awareness as hers, but always in hock to an envious mother, she will indeed always feel powerless no matter how many princes kiss her.

But I propose that the envy, in the last analysis, is within the girl, Sylvia, herself. We have seen that the fairy tale objectivizes the problem, puts it outside the person, and presents it in naive innocence. But the myth puts it in the person; it adds the highly significant subjective dimension, and if you can imagine this myth written as a drama you would need to assume that the struggle, the conflict surrounding envy, is spite within the person, Sylvia, herself. She is the person who was undeveloped, and the envy arose with her, as with all of us, to the extent that the neurotic form blocks her, or our, development. Sylvia herself is characterized by envy, which is a neurotic perversion of the undeveloped potentialities within herself. As an expression of this conflict her potentialities are expressed in a negative, destructive form that is sheer power, validating herself by her power to command others. This first comes out toward men (toward me as in the Nutcracker dream) and later on toward women. A central part of the therapeutic problem with the Briar Rose type is helping them find and experience the positive strength that is present in the whip cracking. Sylvia, indeed, got a good deal of gratification and sense of significance out of experiencing how she had been able to control her brothers, and to some extent her father, those years of childhood. The negative, resentful, revengeful power that goes with envy needs to be shifted into the wishing and willing that will serve constructively to help her get what she wants and needs for her own freedom and responsibility.

About this time in the therapy Sylvia met a man at a concert committee meeting who interested her greatly. He was of high position and seemed to have real charm; his skin was of a different color from hers. They met a number of times when she could arrange it and he was free from his duties. One significant thing about this relationship was that Sylvia turned out to have powerful sexual energy. They spent passionate nights in which they made love all night long, not bothering to sleep. This seemed to have no particular effect on her marriage; she did not tell her husband, keeping the experience as her own. But she was more relaxed at home. The experiences gave Sylvia proof that she was capable of intense response to a man, and demonstrated to her that she could abandon herself in a sensual relationship. It confirmed her femininity in many different ways.

Toward the conclusion of her therapy Sylvia brought the following dream:

There was a woman who was an author. She and her husband ran a short-order lunch counter. The husband stood at the counter, the wife back by the stove. When the order was taken by the husband, the wife immediately heard it and started to make it. This was to prove how unnecessary and affected were the usual ways of domestic servants when you have to spell everything out. The woman was more intelligent and efficient than anyone gave her credit for being as a domestic servant.

Sylvia explained that the woman "heard" the order by a kind of telepathy, and then she would move automatically to fill it. From the angle of the Briar Rose motif, the dream is exceedingly enlightening. The woman now earns her admiration, her identity by being so efficient, picking out of the air the order someone gives at the other end of the room.

The dream seems to be saying that at last the woman finds her unique contribution, her special ability, her uniquely feminine aspect of the relationship with a man. Perhaps due to their biological role in bearing and understanding children, women are often better at telepathic ways of communicating than men. This dream salutes the fact that Sylvia is now finding her own abilities, her own unique capacities as a woman. She also points out that the woman is an author. The dream is a mark of genuine human progress, and I silently cheered.

In the Sleeping Beauty fairy tale, the adolescent is one who never adolesces, the person who wants to be awakened without ever awakening herself or himself. This has a parallel in the togetherness of premature "going steady" that characterizes the social life of many young people. Too soon they become sources of presence for each other, and it thus becomes a presence without content. A premature awakening sexually means that sex can be used in the service of avoiding an awakening on all other levels of the self. We—adolescent or adult—often hurry into sex to avoid confronting the *meaning* of the relationship. Togetherness then consists of truncated development that is pegged at a partial level; part of the girl and young man remaining unawakened. If one's awakening consists of knowing only a single person—and now we are speaking particularly of adolescents—one will likely have an undeveloped and truncated perspective on the rest of the human world.

REVISITING BRIAR ROSE

We must ask what happens with this Sleeping Beauty tale now that we've turned it into a myth? If Ibsen were to write it, or Arthur Miller, what would it be? There is a story, for which we are indebted to Theodore Reik, about the finding of a little piece of manuscript after the bombing of a German city during the last war. The manuscript was badly damaged, and the one page of it that remained was only barely legible. But it pur-

ported to be the final page of the fairy tale of Briar Rose. It
went like this:

... and they lived happily ever after. Some months passed by and the
king's son began to feel restless and bored. He wanted to leave the
castle in search of new adventures. There must be, he thought, other
sleeping beauties he could awaken with a kiss. And he imagined how
they would open their eyes—which he imagined as being sometimes
blue, sometimes hazel, or dark brown—and look at him sweetly. One
day when he was walking about the castle ground he noticed that
what used to be a wall of flowers was now again a hedge of thorns so
high and so thick that he couldn't work his way through it. Every day
after that he slipped out of the castle by a side entrance and tried to
find some opening in the hedge. Every day the hedge grew thicker
and higher. He took a sword and tried to hack his way through, but
the thorns held fast together as if they had hands.

At last the young prince gave up and returned to his wife Briar
Rose. She told him all about her troubles with the cook and the
kitchen maid, and what the butler had said to the laundress and what
the laundress answered, and what she herself had wanted to say to the
chambermaid, but didn't.

While she was talking, the eyelids of the young prince grew heavier
and heavier, and, in spite of all that his wife and the courtiers could
do to prevent it, he fell into a sleep that lasted a hundred years.

That was Theodore Reik's answer to the conclusion of this
myth-tale. There is no reason why one cannot write one's own:

... and they lived happily for a couple of years. But increasingly the
queen began to feel bored by the enclosed life of the castle. No one
went out of the castle yard and almost the only people who came in
were delivery men.

As she was walking around the castle one morning, she began to
think of these other men who had stormed the castle in the old tales
about her being asleep, and she wondered how and who they were. It
was only a falsehood that they had been killed; she knew many were
still alive, one or two in the village below, others throughout the land.
So she pulled on her slacks and sweater and strolled down to the
village, where she met one of them in the bar. He had become a

writer of fairy tales and had traveled all over the country, and he interested her greatly. So she went back to the castle and summoned the gardener. "Cut down all this hedge," she said, "And let's have a lawn that stretches all the way down to the village. I'm tired of being cooped up here!"

In the village she found a painter who, strange to say, turned out to be one of her erstwhile suitors. So she took several lessons from him and found to her delight that she had a great deal of talent. She had exhibits in the village town hall, and there were two others of the old suitors, whom she met. One of them turned out to be a master piano player, so she instituted afternoon soirées and invited all her friends from the village to the palace to hear the music.

One day at her musical soirée the king came in and sat down in the back row. But just as the pianist was doing a Chopin nocturne, the king began to nod and soon he was fast asleep and snoring!

The queen saw him and laughed to herself, "Thank God I got out of this cage!"

TWELVE

Faust:
The Myth of Patriarchal Power

> Today we simply no longer know what a myth is; for it
> is no mere aesthetically pleasing mode of representing
> something to one's self, but a piece of the most lively
> actuality that mines every corner of the waking
> consciousness and shakes the innermost structure of being.
> . . . [Myths] were about one all the time. They were
> glimpsed without being seen. They were believed in with a
> faith that felt the very thought of proof as a desecration.
> . . . In the old days men did not "enjoy myth." Behind it
> stood Death.
>
> Oswald Spengler, *The Decline of the West*, vol. 2

THE POWERFUL MYTH of Faust fit the deep psychological
and spiritual needs of Europeans in the radical transition
from the Middle Ages to the Renaissance and Reformation.
Faust became the mythic narration for the Northern peoples.
A number of versions of the myth were written: Marlowe's *The
Tragical History of the Life and Death of Doctor Faustus*, pub-
lished in 1591; Goethe's *Faust*, the first half published when
Goethe was forty and the second when he was eighty, in 1832.

During World War II, Thomas Mann wrote his version, *Dr. Faustus,* published in 1947. In addition the myth has been spread far and wide through opera, philosophy, and creative writings of all sorts. Mozart's *Don Giovanni* is a musical rendition of the Faust legend. *The Great Gatsby* is itself a Faust-like novel. Benet's *The Devil and Daniel Webster* is another example, as is *The Year the Yankees Lost the Pennant,* which became the musical *Damn Yankees.*

"It is depressing," writes René Dubos, in his contemporary book *The God Within,* "that the only myth the modern age has contributed to civilization is that of Faust."* But the most powerful contemporary demonstration of the significance of the Faust dramas is given by Oswald Spengler in his classical work *The Decline of the West,* published in 1918, the year World War I ended. With his encyclopedic mind, Spengler compares other cultures, such as the Persian and Arabic, with our modern Western culture, using the contrast of *Apollonian* and *Faustian* as his categories. Coming from the Greek myth of Apollo, the Apollonian stands for cultures characterized by reason, harmony, balance, and justice. The symbol for Apollonianism is the *circle.*

The symbol for Faustianism, on the contrary, is the *straight line,* always moving ahead in progress, which is our contemporary belief. But our dilemma is that progress applies only to technical things—we invent better automobiles, electric dishwashers, and nuclear bombs. The concept of progress does not hold in spiritual and aesthetic realms, such as religion, philosophy, art, and literature, all of which thrive in the classical Apollonian ages. Spengler argued that the West (meaning chiefly Europe and America) is Faustian in our great love of competition and our overweening materialism.

Spengler's book was greeted with immediate horror and rebuttals on all sides. But if he had lived through World War II, the dropping of the atom bomb, and the use of the nuclear

*Rene Dubos, *The God Within* (New York: Scribners, 1973), p. 264.

bomb to obliterate Nagasaki, he would have made his Faustian emphasis in the West even more emphatic!

Our existence in the nuclear age, with our arsenals filled with nuclear warheads, makes ours a Faustian age in the extreme. Where previous ages have only knocked on the door of the mystery, we have broken into the building itself. Will our ending be self-chosen destruction like Marlowe's *Faust?* Or will we experience some *deus ex machina,* like Goethe's *Faust,* and be given the chance to repent before the fatal bell tolls at midnight?

Nuclear physicists are well aware of the dangers that they have helped to discover. Dr. Hans Bethe at Cornell has talked of the catastrophic Faustian danger we face. When the director of the nuclear laboratory in Los Alamos, Dr. Alvin Weinberg, needed to find a term to describe the dangers of our predicament with respect to nuclear arms, he seized upon the myth of Faust. Pondering our warheads and the dismal fact that we are able to blow up most of the globe in one hour, or cause a perpetual nuclear winter, plus the great difficulty in the disposal of nuclear waste, which threatens to contaminate much of our land for future generations, Dr. Weinberg pondered Faust's experience. His article, "Our Faustian Bargain," comes to the conclusion that our only possible answer is "eternal vigilance."* We can indeed understand what Spengler means when he says that "behind the myth stands death."

THE FAUST STORY

Some changes of great psychological and spiritual significance occurred in the fifteenth century, which marked the end of the Middle Ages and the beginning of the Renaissance. We can see this most vividly by comparing Dante's *Divine Comedy*

*Weinberg, "Our Faustian Bargain: Social Institution and Nuclear Energy," *Science* (Dec. 27, 1971), p. 27.

with the myth which was to come in the Renaissance, namely, Faust. Dante wrote his *Divine Comedy* as an expression of the struggle through hell, purgatory, and finally to paradise to achieve ultimate blessedness in the peak of Divine Love. There is in Dante's writing a serenity, a sense of faith, divine blessing, and pure love. All these are mediated by Beatrice, a figure who reconciled these great capacities with what had been taught by the Church at its best.

In medieval times the Church held women in high esteem. Mary, the Mother of God, made up the triangle with God and the Christ and was adored in the Middle Ages in countless assignments of "Hail Mary's." Cathedrals like Notre Dame were named after women.

But in the Reformation in Germany and in England the trinity was changed to "God, Christ, and the Holy Spirit." And the luscious, colorful, even if sometimes gaudy Catholic churches were exchanged for the masculine severity—though still often beautiful—Protestant churches of the Reformation. It was a new world and the peasantry and burghers were filled with fright at this world and cried out for a new dominant myth.

Renaissance people were told by Mirandella that they as individuals had the power to make themselves into whatever they chose. And they had been instructed by Nicolaus Cusanos early in the fifteenth century that each person had the center of the universe in himself. Many other spokesmen lauded the individual power of Renaissance individuals. Calvin and Luther were to tell them that they were free in religion, and Kepler, Copernicus, and Galileo were showing them the movement of the stars. No wonder they felt spiritually uprooted and needed a new myth!

The myth which fit these excited people of the Renaissance was the narration of Faust. This was a man who was born in that spiritual and psychological maelstrom and who partook of that lust for knowledge to be gained by magic, since the new discoveries on every side seemed to the ordinary person to be magical. This mythic Faust would live out his lust for knowledge and his twenty-four years of voluptuous power on this earth, but he would do this by selling his immortal soul to Lucifer, after which he would suffer the tortures of hell for eternity. The myth must show this figure representing the hopes and fears of these citizens as Faust succeeds in his great aim to partake of divine power. The myth then must furnish a catharsis to assuage the citizen's fears and guilt in Faust's punishment at the conclusion of the twenty-four years of magical power.

The Faust myth began as the story of the exploits of a certain John Faustus, who actually lived in northern Germany in the mid-sixteenth century and spent his life in continual magical pranks on his fellow men. Some of his life was spent in jail, and he was reputed to have gone to hell when he died and there suffered eternal fire and brimstone. A pamphlet published in Germany in 1587, called the "Chapbook," detailed the sins of this Faustus, including his alleged sexual intercourse with Helen of Troy, which was believed to doom a man forever to hell. Entitled "The Damnable Life and Deserved Death of Dr. John Faustus," this booklet caught on like wildfire at the end of the Middle Ages and was made into a traveling morality play. It united the yearning for new knowledge (which often seemed magical in reality) with guilt, punishment, and the dreaded fires of hell and eternal torture.

Regardless of their not understanding the language of the pamphlet, the people of Holland and Belgium could see the burning fires of hell and smell the flesh burning. They could experience the sense of doom and the catharsis they so desperately needed. They had seen copies of Bosch's paintings of hell and damnation and those of Grunewald of the punishments of the dying. To watch this myth enacted and to hear the groans of the damned in eternal punishment was to experience their own conscious and subconscious fears. These fears were allayed by the catharsis of observing Faustus writhing and agonizing in his punishment. The vivid myth gave them a sense of vicarious penance. Faustus suffered before them and they were thus freed to accept what they perceived as the magic of their new age.

MARLOWE'S FAUST — GRANDEUR AND TRAGEDY

Christopher Marlowe, a Renaissance man in his own right, had a checkered career. He was born the same year as Shakespeare, 1564, studied for some time at Oxford, and was killed in a brawl when he was twenty-eight. But he wrote several dramas of great power, any one of which would have assured him of immortality. His *The Tragical History of the Life and Death of Doctor Faustus* is written, as one critic states, with "terrifying beauty."

As the drama opens we see Dr. Faustus, a respected professor, ruminating in his study on the great boredom of his life. Though he has degrees in medicine, philosophy, and theology, he is overpowered by his lust for vast, new, *magical* knowledge, a lust which was common in the Renaissance.

> Philosophy is odious and obscure,
> Both law and physics are for petty wits,
> Divinity is basest of the three,
> Unpleasant, harsh, contemptible, and vile;
> "Tis magic, magic, that hath ravished me!"*

Faustus especially castigates the subject that was most important in the Middle Ages, divinity, which is called "harsh, contemptible, and vile." Like Icarus, writes Marlowe, is Faustus;

> Till swollen with cunning, of a self-conceit,
> His waxen wings did mount above his reach,
> And melting, heavens conspired his overthrow!†

---

*Marlowe, *The Tragical History of the Life and Death of Doctor Faustus,* in *The Norton Anthology of English Literature,* vol. 1 (New York: Norton, 1974), p. 769.
†Ibid., p. 770.

It is a myth of conscience, springing from the pride, greed, lust, and despair of a man which commit him to Eternal Darkness. He strives against the faith, against repentance or belief in God's mercy and love, all of the things which give a person grace.

Faustus cries out as he plans to give himself up to Lucifer:

> O what a world of profit and delight,
> Of power, of honor, and omnipotence
> Is promised to the studious artisan!
> All things that move between the quiet poles
> Shall be at my command. . . .

Faustus cannot accept being a mere man. He demands that he be like God, indeed that he *be* God.

> Yet art thou still but Faustus, and a man.
> Couldst thou make men to live eternally
> Of being dead, raise them to life again.*

So Faustus gives up his human status and tries to be God. He summons Mephistopheles and tells him of his decision to join the forces of Lucifer. In answer to Faustus' question about his life before he was thrown into hell, Mephistopheles—the representative of the devil—answers with one of the most haunting passages of the drama:

> . . . Think'st thou that I who saw the face of God
> And tasted the eternal joys of heaven
> Am not tormented with ten thousand hells
> In being deprived of everlasting bliss?†

In this strange reversal of roles, the *devil pleads with Faustus to forgo his plans to join Lucifer,* the chief of the underworld. But Faustus is adamant and tells Mephistopheles to go back and "bear these tidings to great Lucifer," so that Faustus, for "four and twenty years, will

*Ibid., p. 771.
†Ibid., p. 778.

> live in all voluptuousness,
> Having thee always to attend on me:

How great he will be!

> ... I'll be great emperor of the world,
> And make a bridge through the moving air
> To pass the ocean with a band of men:
> I'll join the hills that bind the Afric shore
> And make the country continent to Spain,
> And both contributory to my crown.*

Thus Faustus will dominate both nature and man.

The hundreds of people who flocked to see this morality play, into which Marlowe's myth was made, quivered at these words, aware on some level of consciousness that this was their secret desire as well. This new sense of power, control, omnipotence, the very rival of divinity, this vast power to change the boundaries of the world, gave them a fright along with a great sense of their power. For they were living in the new world of Copernicus and Galileo, and this lust for knowledge gave them new freedoms on every side. Living "in all voluptuousness" was profoundly tempting, and the height of evil at the same time.

The drama gives a continuous picture of Faustus struggling with the decision, shall he or shall he not? He then stabs his arm for blood to sign away his soul to Lucifer, but his body does not follow his aims—the blood is blocked: "My blood congeals and I can write no more." And he rightly sees this as a psychosomatic sign,

> Is it unwilling I should write this bill?
> Why streams it not, that I may write afresh?
> "Faustus gives to thee his soul"—
> Ah, there it stayed.†

The myth hinges on this phenomenon, which we see in therapy and in ourselves, that the conscious mind and the un-

---

*Ibid. It is interesting that Marlowe predicts what has actually happened; we do now make bridges to pass through the air in our airplanes.

†Ibid., p. 781.

consciousness have a *complementary* relation to each other. Carl Jung saw this clearly: when a person is overcome with joy, there comes a warning and an opposite tendency in one's unconsciousness. A patient who was a theological student and a homosexual in the days when homosexuality was strictly taboo was ordained at a big service in his church, which service he greatly appreciated. But the same night after the service he went directly to Central Park to pick up a stranger for a homosexual fling. The next day in therapy he was full of guilt and horrified about the risk he had taken of being found out. It is not unusual for a much appreciated event like this man's ordination to be followed by some act which is considered to be just the opposite.*

Marlowe has the remarkable insight of a great poet when he asks whether his body is "unwilling" that he sign away his soul. And Mephistopheles shows this complementary character: he, the agent of evil, argues *against* Faustus' signing the document! We are also amazed at Marlowe's astuteness later in having the good angels battle the bad angels. An old man (whom we may take to be the therapist) also tries to bring Faustus back to his original human destiny as only a man. But Faustus brushes aside these cautions, even this congealing of his own blood, and acts out the longing of everyone in that period: "I want to be wanton and lascivious."

Faustus then asks Mephistopheles, "Tell me, where is the place that men call hell?" The devil answers,

> Within the bowels of these elements,
> Hell hath no limits, . . .
> . . . for where we are is hell
> And where hell is, there must we ever be.

This reminds us of Sartre in the twentieth century, "Hell is other people."

---

*The contemporary admission of fundamentalist preachers that they are guilty of sexual misconduct—Jimmy Swaggart and Jim Bakker—are present-day examples.

But Faustus brushes these questions aside by sexuality. He demands,

> The fairest maid in Germany,
> For I am wanton and lascivious.

He then asks Mephistopheles for a book of magic,

> . . . Wherein I might behold all spells and
> incantations, that I might raise up spirits
> when I please.

When Mephistopheles gives that to him, he requests another,

> a book where I might see all characters and
> planets of the heavens, that I might know their
> motions and dispositions.*

Even the angels join in the psychological and spiritual struggle for this human soul. Faustus is not evil in our sense; he does not kill anyone as Goethe's Faust does, or participate in tragic cruelty (as Goethe's Faust does with Gretchen), or cause the burning to death of two aged persons because he wants to see the view of his accomplishments from their cottage site (again as Goethe's Faust did). Marlowe presents on the stage only those longings the persons in the audience have been struggling with in their own breasts. He pictures the psychological and spiritual doubt, dismay, conflict which all these human beings had felt in their own lives as citizens in the Renaissance with its great opportunities and great evils.

It is the fact of Faustus' denial of God, his setting himself up as opposed to God, that constitutes the tragedy. It is similar to Thomas Mann's later interpretation of the myth; Faustus is damned by his thoughts, by his very wish for godlike control, not simply by his actions. This is why the crowds were so responsive, for everyone has such desires, deep-down evil fantasies, wicked daydreams. Wishes, rather than actions, are the

---

*Marlowe, *Doctor Faustus*, p. 782.

cause of neurosis, as Freud would later assure us.

We have already seen how Mephistopheles himself has implored Faustus not to go through with the signing of the compact. And throughout there are not only bad angels but good angels who implore Faustus to repent while there is still time. This spiritual struggle is seen from a different angle when Faustus rationalizes his predicament and accuses Mephistopheles of having seduced him:

> When I behold the heavens then I repent
> And curse thee, wicked Mephistopheles,
> Because thou has deprived me of those joys.*

But Mephistopheles rightly answers, "Twas thine own seeking, Faustus, thank thyself." Then the devil goes on to question the idea that heaven is so wonderful; he takes his stand, curiously enough, *with human beings!*

> I tell thee Faustus, it [heaven] is not half so fair
> As thou or any man that breathes on earth.

This reveals the great humanism of the Renaissance. One felt good to be alive and to look about the world with joy, which Giotto had shown in his painting and Brueghel was even then showing when he covered his canvases with the joys of gathering wheat, skating, and just being alive. These Faustus myths have an obligation to try to find the best of human life at the same time as they envy the divine. Humanism lies in the terrible struggle in that period, between the free inquiring of science and the powerful remnant of absolute ecclesiastical authority.

The good angel begs Faustus again to repent, while the bad angel argues that Faustus must remain with his bargain; God cannot pity him. And Faustus answers,

> My heart is hardened;
> I cannot repent.*

*Ibid., p. 784.

THE HARDENED HEART

This "hardened heart" is a heart that cannot love. It expresses the patriarchal side of the energy sought by these men of the Renaissance who were concerned with power, ambition, self-assertion.

Again and again the good angel and the bad angel return; Faustus is never actually hardened. Shall he, *can* he, repent and throw himself upon God's mercy? That this issue remains vital all through the drama contributes to its great power over the audience.

Mephistopheles then takes Faustus on a trip in which to demonstrate his magical prowess. But the much-sought-after power has become trivialized. Faustus plays pranks on the Pope, whose nose he tweaks; he steals the wine from in front of the Pope at table while he, Faustus, is invisible.

All the while Faustus is aware that his time of death draws nearer. He ruminates:

> What art thou, Faustus, but a man condemned to die?
> Thy fatal time draws to a final end;
> Despair doth drive distrust into my thoughts.

An old man enters, pleading, "O gentle Faustus, leave this damned art, This magic that will charm thy soul to hell."

> I see an angel hovers over thy head
> And with a vial full of precious grace
> Offers to pour the same into thy soul;
> Then call for mercy and avoid despair.

This old man seems to be playing the role of the therapist.

Faustus makes his last demand; he pleads with Mephistopheles to let him make love to Helen of Troy.†

*Ibid.

†Helen in the Greek sense is "the form of forms," as Dr. Richard Wiseman has put it in personal conversation. Form is beauty in the profound and infinite sense.

> One thing, good servant, let me crave of thee
> To glut the longing of my heart's desire
> That I might have unto my paramour
> That heavenly Helen which I saw of late,
> Whose sweet embracings may extinguish clear
> Those thoughts that do dissuade me from my vow,
> And keep mine oath I made to Lucifer.*

"Heavenly Helen" is the customary phantasy of contemporary men as an escape from difficult decisions. Many a man has fantasized, "if I could only have a beautiful woman!" But the very patriarchal nature of Faustus' power precludes that solution. For how can one love authentically when the motive is actually not love but power? To love we need grace.

Helen also is the touchstone for great poetry. Marlowe is inspired to go even beyond his previous scenes to write in these oft-quoted and much loved lines:

> Was this the face that launched a thousand ships?
> And burnt the topless towers of Ilium?
> Sweet Helen, make me immortal with a kiss,
> Her lip sucks forth my soul—see where it flies!
> Come, Helen, give me my soul again.
> Here will I dwell, for heaven is in these lips
> And all is dross that is not Helena.
>
> Oh thou art fairer than the evening air
> Clad in the beauty of a thousand stars!†

The Old Man, whom we met a moment ago, stands nearby and watches. He then pronounces what all these watchers of the morality play knew, namely, that if one makes love to a demon, that person is automatically excluded from heaven. Helen now represents a spirit from the dead, which is a demon.

How different is the use of sex and love in the sixteenth century from what it was in the Middle Ages of Dante! Here it is a tool, an instrument to use Helen in order to give him his

*Marlowe, *Dr. Faustus*. p. 813.
†Ibid.

soul again. Sexual love is allied with power. In all of the Faust myths sexual love is a mechanism by which one avoids one's guilt and sorrow. But in Dante love was grace; Beatrice was always related to paradise. In Dante love is beatified.

As the end nears, the sad friends of Faustus gather on the last day to say good-by. Even his good angel must leave him, for, "The jaws of hell are open to receive thee."* The audience must indeed have gasped, for hell is now pictured and reproduced openly on the stage in this miracle play;

> But yet all these are nothing, thou shalt see
> Ten thousand tortures that more horrid be.

And all Faustus can say is, "O, I have seen enough to torture me!"

The clock strikes eleven, and Faustus is in great spiritual agony presented in poetry which is so magnificent it can only be quoted:

> The stars move still, time runs, the clock will strike,
> The devil will come, and Faustus must be damned.
> O I'll leap up to my God! Who pulls me down?
> See, see, where Christ's blood streams in the firmament!—
> Rend not my heart for naming of my Christ;
> Yet will I call on him—O spare me, Lucifer! . . .
> Where is it now? Tis gone, and see where God
> Stretcheth out his arm and bends his ireful brows.
> Mountains and hills, come, come, and fall on me
> And hide me from the heavy wrath of God,
> No, no—
> Then will I headlong run into the earth;
> Earth, gape! O no, it will not harbor me.

We can only imagine how powerful is the drama as the myth is played out to the end, and must indeed have deeply grasped every observer;

*Ibid., p. 816.

(The clock strikes twelve)
It strikes, it strikes! Now, body, turn to air . . .
(Thunder and lightning)
O soul, be changed to little water drops
And fall into the ocean, never to be found.
My God, my God, look not so fierce on me!

The devils come and bear Faustus away to the adders and serpents of ugly hell. Faustus cries out as his last words, "I'll burn my books—ah Mephistopheles!"

The issue is the secrets gotten from books! The struggle between the free inquiring of science and the remnants of the dictatorial power of the Church is still alive and active. This final begging promise of Faustus is indeed a reference to the lust for learning that, in those days, was a considerable part of evil. The Renaissance was inebriated with this lust to such an extent that the burning of the books was deemed the most important element in giving up Renaissance power.

The chorus, taking its cue from the Greek myths, cries:

Cut is the branch that might have grown full
straight,
And burned is Apollo's bough
That sometime grew within this learned man

The evil shown in this version of the myth of Faust is that man tries to be omnipotent, to usurp the position of God. It is a situation of hubris, the unseemly pride, the negation of humility and repentence. The crime is *the refusal to accept the human role* (which, we recall, Mephistopheles said he valued more than heaven!). It is instead the demand that one's self be God. The Greeks put this sin above all: Agamemnon, we recall, is met by the chorus when he returns from Troy with a warning not to commit hubris over his victory. Socrates repeats time and again the need for acceptance of one's limitations. But Renaissance man, having tasted the joys of knowledge, has not yet learned to transmit it into wisdom.

Faustus cries twice in this drama that he could not accept the fact that he was *"only* a man,"

> Yet art thou still but Faustus and a man.
> What art thou, Faustus, but a man condemned to die?*

It requires Mephistopheles, the devil's emissary, to appreciate the stage of humankind. It is a strange result of the development of consciousness that along with the fact that we can see ourselves, that we are self-conscious of our own status, there comes the presence in consciousness of the sin of pride. This is the problem particularly of great men and women; they most of all are in danger of hubris and most often commit this sin. Faustus was guilty of this from the beginning; hence there is little suspense in the story, for we know to start with how it will end. It carries us along by the great power of the myth and Marlowe's dramatic vision and beautiful poetry.

THE CATHARSIS OF MYTH

This myth gives us rich opportunity to imagine the effect Faustus' death in the drama would have upon the audience. The strong physical and emotional experience would give the people who watch it a sense that they too are personally going through the same experience vicariously. They will feel the same quality of emotion, if not in the same degree, as Faustus felt on the stage. Each will get an emotional and moral release; each will feel his own desires to sell his soul for magic and power, and his own punishment for such, as each of us sells our soul along with the bargain Faustus made.

In myths, which means in the psychic world that surrounds us all, we experience catharsis by identifying with the performers on the stage. Having made the vicarious descent into the underworld the people in the audience felt purified. This is the

*Ibid. p. 806.

openness of the myth: it spreads its arms, and all whom it takes in gain some of the power of the catharsis. There is also in the catharsis the social effect, the cleansing of the community. We have shared an "id" experience; there is now a bond among us.

The cathartic experience of the myth cleanses us from our own need to do the things Faustus did. He did it *for* us. The experience of Christ on the Cross is built upon this expression of the myth; Christ died for each of us, we are told, meaning his crucifixion has an inward power for each of us. Faustus in this drama has a similar mythic effect on the people who watched. Faustus has done it for them, and his doing it wipes away our own drive to do it. This implies a community, and a communicative power in the myth.

The people who watched Faustus dragged into the horrors of the serpents and adders, the burning and the other tortures of hell, would not only feel scared; they would go away *relieved*. All of this inner activity is on a deeper level than morality. This underlying experience is the cathartic power of the myth.

THIRTEEN

Goethe's Faust
and the Enlightenment

Faust: When you are labeled Lord of
                Flies, corrupters, liars.
                All right—who are you, then?
Mephistopheles: ... Part of that force which would
                Do ever evil, and does ever good.
                        Goethe, *Faust*

WHEN WE HEAR THE NAME "Faust" in our day, we immediately assume the speaker is referring to Goethe's great drama. This masterpiece occupied Goethe, who lived during the Enlightenment in Germany, his whole life long, and he finished it only when he was in his early eighties. It was his work of destiny, as Schiller, in the heated correspondence between these two giants of literature, kept insisting to Goethe. This telling of the myth is great because it is done in such wonderful poetry; everyone seems to quote from this aesthetic triumph.

The drama is great also because it deals with the profound and forever-new problems of how we should live. Faust is a philosophical poem in that it centers on what life could be—its temptations, its catastrophes, and its joys. Goethe asks the profound questions, What is life and what are damnation and salvation? As a great humanist, he seeks at every point to deal with the question, What does it mean to be a human being?

Goethe's *Faust* is a poignant and powerful expression of the myth of our modern age in which people yearn to believe that the God of progress—our great machines, our vast technology, our supernational corporations, now even our nuclear weapons—all these, we yearn to believe, will have a beneficent effect upon us and will bring vast gains to humanity. Goethe was caught up in this dilemma, as were his confrères in the Enlightenment and the Industrial Revolution. On his desk he kept a model of the new steam engine and its track which stretched from Liverpool to Bath as a constant symbol of this great hope.

This myth grips the minds of people today because it demonstrates that evil, which in the puppet shows expressed Marlowe's fierce damnation in a literal hell, is now changed in Goethe's poem to good. This amazing tour de force is revealed early in Goethe's drama when Faust demands to know who Mephistopheles is. The devil answers that he is the spirit which seeks to do evil but it always turns to good. Yes, Satan is the apostle of strife, intense activity, even cruelty, but he still ends up after the killings in goodness, according to Goethe's position here.

The intelligentsia of Europe respected Goethe as their titular head. Indeed, Matthew Arnold wrote of him at his death,

> When Goethe's death was told, we said:
> Sunk, then, is Europe's sagest head;
> Goethe has done his pilgrimage.
> Physician of the iron age.*
>
> He took the suffering human race,
>
> He read each wound, each weakness clear;
> And struck his finger on the place,
> And said, "Thou ailest here, and here!"

*We note that, according to Matthew Arnold, Europe is in its "iron age." This points again to the industrial age in the early nineteenth century.

He looked on Europe's dying hour
Of fitful dream and feverish power.*

The drama of Faust begins just before Easter. Goethe describes this as the time when people

. . . exult in raising of the Lord
For they are resurrected themselves,
Freed from the shackles of shops and crafts,
From stuffy dwellings like narrow shelves,
From smothering roofs and gable lofts,
From the city streets with their smothering press,
From out the churches reverend night,
They have all been raised to light.†

This great vision of Goethe's of what industrialism could
bring was shared by a multitude of his fellow writers in this
period. His life spanned the Enlightenment in Germany, an
enviable time to be alive. Mozart was still living, Beethoven
was in his prime, there were important philosophers like Kant,
Schelling, Schopenhauer. The Declaration of Independence
was written in America when Goethe was twenty-seven. It is
indeed thrilling to realize that out of the same milieu came our
own political proclamation: "that all men are created equal,
that they are endowed by their Creator with certain inalienable
rights, that among these are life, liberty and the pursuit of
happiness." To read the drama of Faust is to participate in the
period when vast numbers of people were dedicated to inter-
preting evil in such a way that it would eventuate in good.

Faust thus ponders the age-old question of the meaning of
evil in a world presided over by a beneficent God. Does creative
effort involve the kind of strife which inevitably brings destruction? It is the ancient problem of Job: is there a servant of God
so devoted that he will remain true to God even in the worst of
human suffering? This fundamental question of human exis-

The Norton Anthology of English Literature, vol. 2 (New York: Norton, 1976),
p. 1343.
†Goethe, *Faust,* trans. Walter Arndt (New York: Norton, 1976), 1.

tence has been pondered by almost every sensitive person, a modern one being C. G. Jung in his book, *Answer to Job.*

GOD AND MEPHISTOPHELES

The drama opens with a heavenly council in which God is questioning Mephistopheles, to whom He makes this friendly overture, "I never did abominate your kind."* What does Mephistopheles think of things on earth? The devil answers that he "feels for mankind in their wretchedness," and humans have become "more bestial than any beast" because they have "reason." The Lord agrees that human beings too easily become lax; they need vigilance, even though "man ever errs the while he strives." God proposes that human beings should be "ever active, ever live creation."

These opening lines introduce the theme that is crucial to Goethe's whole drama: action, striving, effort. Forever the *active deed* takes supremacy over other forms of human existence. Goethe pictures Faust pondering the Biblical sentence, "In the beginning was the Word,"† and Faust shakes his head at that; the "word" is too intellectualistic. Perhaps sensibility will do, so he proposes "in the beginning was the Sense." But that is to be refused as well. Finally he comes up with, "In the beginning was the Deed." That is it! The expression of action and perpetual striving Faust accepts as final.

As the myth—or drama—unfolds we find ourselves immediately in the consulting room of the therapist. This demonstrates again that, when the would-be patient gives his complaints, he is talking about myths that in his way of life have collapsed. Here Faust is groaning over his failure to gain position or splendor or fortune, and he tells how this makes him feel:

*Ibid., l. 337.
†Ibid., l. 1224.

> Each morning I awake in desperation
> Sick unto tears to see begun
>   Yet one more day. . . .

> I dread to bed me down, wild visions cumber
> My dreams and wake response unblessed.
> Existence seems a burden to detest
> Death to be wished for, life a hateful jest.*

He sums up these morbid imprecations which have led him to consider suicide,

> A curse on faith! a curse on hope!
> A curse on patience, above all.†

Mephistopheles then appears and tempts him with a very different way of life:

> Be done with nursing your despair,
> Which, like a vulture, feeds upon your mind.**

The pact is made. Faust agrees that he will be forever unsatisfied, forever moving, forever striving.

> Should I ever take ease upon a bed of leisure,
> May that same moment mark my end!
> When first by flattery you lull me
> Let that day be the last for me! . . .
> Then forget the shackles to my feet,
> Then I will gladly perish there!‡

Faust signs this pact with a drop of his blood, saying,

---

*Ibid., ll. 1554–15.

†Ibid., ll. 1570–1571. In this very psychoanalytic portion, Faust throws aside with contempt our modern ways in which many people deal with such depression, namely, giving oneself over to money, drugs, and sex.

> Accursed be Mammon, when his treasure
> to deeds of daring eggs us on, . . .
> Cursed be the balsam of the grape!
> Cursed, highest prize of lovers thrall!

**Ibid., l. 1635.

‡Ibid., ll. 1698, 1702

So may then pleasure and distress,
Failure and success,
Follow each other as they please
Man's active only when he's never at ease.*

Goethe here reflects the essence of the behavior of modern man: rarely serene, always striving, always heaping task on task and calling it progress. The myth shows us the way of life for which Faust sells his soul.

Faust's first adventure is to fall in love with Gretchen, an innocent "child in bloom," and in their lovemaking he impregnates her. This affair between Faust, man of the world, with the fairy-like girl is all directed from the wings by Mephistopheles. Goethe reveals his own ambivalence in that his sympathies and his heart are with the unfortunate Gretchen, who, in her pregnancy, becomes driven out of her mind by her sorrow and by the condemnation of her fellow villagers. Faust, piling cruelty upon cruelty, then fights Gretchen's brother, Valentine, a soldier who has come back from the war to protect Gretchen. In the fight Mephistopheles holds back the brother's rapier so Faust kills him in cold blood. As he dies, Valentine adds his imprecations against the poor Gretchen.

One could make a case for the damnation of Faust simply out of this relationship with Gretchen, even though he so far expresses his love for her. This is the first revelation of Goethe's radical problem with women, which will be visible all through this drama; it is indeed a myth of *patriarchal power*. Goethe pictures Faust as experiencing a foretaste of damnation from the suffering of this fairy-child whom he has made pregnant. Faust, however, grieves at the agony of this fairy-child and is enraged by Mephistopheles' cold remark, "She's not the first." Faust cries,

*Ibid., ll. 1756–1759.

>I am rent to the living core by this single
>one's suffering; you pass with a carefree
>grin over the fate of thousands.*

It is clear that Faust has some love, however inadequate, for Gretchen, and he is deeply shaken when she must have her baby in jail. But she cries only that Faust doesn't kiss her with the passion he used to have.

Having the keys to the jail, Faust begs her to come out. Gretchen can leave the jail "at will," but she has no will to leave; she takes responsibility for her pregnancy and lives out her punishment.

The final scene grows in intensity toward its climax. Gretchen cries out from the jail, "You're leaving now? Oh Heinrich,† if I could too!"

FAUST: You can, Just want to! See, the door is open.

GRETCHEN: It must not be; for me there is no hoping. What use in fleeing? Still they lie in wait for you. . . .

FAUST: Oh love,—you rave! One step and you can leave at will!**

But Gretchen, in her mental derangement, sees the day as both her wedding day and her day of execution. "This day is my undoing," she cries. Mephistopheles can only sneer "Womanish mutter! . . . Vain chatter and putter."‡ When Gretchen catches a glimpse of Mephistopheles, she knows he is a devil who has come to take her to hell, but Faust cries out a phrase which links him again with our contemporary therapy, "You shall be whole!"***

How is this dénouement to be solved? Goethe feels profound sympathy for this creature and her troubles which he has created, yet he must, for the sake of his own integrity as writer,

---

*Goethe, *Faust*, ll. 4398 ff.
†Faust's first name.
**Goethe, *Faust*, ll. 4543–4544.
‡Ibid., ll. 4564, 4598.
***Ibid., l. 4604.

lead her to condemnation. He has Mephistopheles call out, "She is condemned."*

But Goethe inserts the exclamation, "Redeemed!" The notes tell us that this word was not in the first version but was inserted only in a later edition. In other words, Goethe must finally yield to the dictates of his own heart. And he must have some voice cry out "Redemption," whether it makes any sense or not. Thus Gretchen is condemned and redeemed in the same moment.

The first book ends with a voice: "[from within, dying away] Heinrich!"

The myth of unlimited power leads Goethe into the greatest of human complications. We can imagine his remembering another verse in his *Faust,* and we wonder if it applies to himself and this drama;

> Spirits sing,
>
> > Woe! Woe!
> > You have destroyed it,
> > The beautiful world,
> > With mighty fist.†

Is this why Ortega wrote that Goethe had never really found himself, never lived out his own indigenous form, his true destiny in life?

MYTHIC AGONY

Part Two was put together during the forty years following the publication of part one. We marvel at the thoughts Goethe must have had during all the years when he was turning this myth over and over in his mind. How was he to conclude this myth?

*Ibid., l. 4611.
†Ibid., ll. 1607–1610.

In this second part he deals centrally with the problems of sexuality and power. Some of the verses are slapstick, as when Mephistopheles molds magic gold into a gigantic phallus, with which he threatens and shocks the ladies. But on a deeper level power and sexuality are essential aspects of the Faustian myth. Sex has largely become an expression of power. This is partially seen in our own day with our pornography, our sexy commercialism, our advertising built on luscious blondes and shapely brunettes. There is a curious relationship between our society's attitude toward power on one hand and sexuality on the other.

In the Industrial Revolution there began the radical separation between the product of the worker's hands and his relation with the persons who use his product. Indeed, the worker normally saw nothing at all of the product he helped produce except his own little act. The alienation of labor added to the alienation of persons from themselves and from other people. Their personhood is lost. With the growth of industry and the bourgeosie, sex becomes separated from persons; one's sexual responses are bought and sold, as is the product of one's hands.

Faust demands to see and have for his lover Helen of Troy, the symbol of beauty and ultimate fulfillment in love.* He thinks it will be easy for Mephistopheles to conjure up Helen.

FAUST: I know it can be done with but a mutter,
Two winks and you can have her on the spot."†

But Mephistopheles has a very different view. Faust must go through the Mothers, a strange group which has raised an infinite number of questions since Goethe wrote the play. The Mothers seem to be the only ones who have the power to threaten and to frighten Mephistopheles.

---

*This relationship presents one of the most profound problems of human life. The connection of form with sex is shown in feminine beauty. This serves the evolutionary survival of the race mythologically and is bound up with the arts and with the relation between the sexes, as we shall see below.

†Goethe, *Faust,* l. 6203.

MEPHISTOPHELES: I loathe to touch on more exalted riddle—
Goddesses sit enthroned in reverend loneliness,
Space is as naught about them, time is less;
The very mention of them is distress.
They are—the Mothers.

FAUST: (starting) Mothers!

MEPHISTOPHELES: Are you awed?

FAUST: The Mothers! Why it strikes a singular chord.

MEPHISTOPHELES: And so it ought. Goddesses undivined
By mortals, named with shrinking of our kind.
Go delve the downmost for their habitat;
Blame but yourself that it has come to that.

FAUST: Where is the road?

MEPHISTOPHELES: No road! Into the unacceded,
The inaccessible; toward the never-pleaded,
The never-pleadable. How is your mood?*

We pause, for the above lines are for all the world like a session in psychotherapy, especially with that aside, "How is your mood?" The mother, from whom one is born, who gives us form to start with, who carries the survival of the race in her womb—no topic could be more important. Every patient, in learning to love, must confront the psychological remains of his or her mother's imprinting. Mephistopheles presses the point home by making Faust take responsibility for his own anxiety and his own distress—"Blame but yourself that it has come to that."†

Is Goethe writing in this myth to relieve his own guilt? And what does this passage have to do with assuaging the guilt of his age? The Mothers certainly seem hostile in this description. I am informed that Goethe never went to see his own mother from the time he was twenty-five until her death, even though he went through Frankfurt, where she lived, often enough. We

*Ibid., ll. 6224–6225.
†Ibid., l. 6221.

also know that Goethe was enthralled by women and they by him. Going into a relationship like a storm, he would use the woman up and then leave her. He puzzled his whole life long as to why he could write significant poetry only when in the presence of some femininity. He married late in life and then to his mistress, the last person who would seem suitable; he called her his "bed rabbit." Sixteen years his junior, she was a small vivacious girl, not really pretty or particularly intelligent, but full of spontaneity.

And now to Helen.

May we emphasize again that Helen has a mythic quality in each of these three approaches (Marlowe, Goethe, and Mann). Goethe has Helen herself say when she is questioned about her relationship with Achilles,

> I as a myth allied myself to him as myth
> It was a dream, the words themselves
> proclaim it so.
> I fade away, becoming to myself a myth.*

This tells us that Helen was a myth all the way back in history, and the Greeks, in the Trojan War, were fighting for a great myth, the myth of ultimate form. Helen stands for the feminine form, not in the sexual sense (although she may be given that role often enough) but rather in the sense of the Hellenic *arête*, with all the ideal quality that her name stands for in Greek culture.† Hence the phrase "form of forms" does indeed fit. It refers to feminine beauty raised to an ethical level, a goal for one's development of the virtue, *arête*, so prized by the ancient

---

*Ibid., l. 8878.

†We mentioned in Chapter 12 on Marlowe's *Faust* our radical separation of the symbol of Helen from modern Westerners' view of beauty and sex. Chiron, a centaur who had a special knowledge of medicine in Greek mythology, supports this when he says, in Goethe's *Faust* (ll.7400, 7405),

> Bah! Beauty's often lifeless; not in feature
> True loveliness is found expressed. . . .
> But irresistible is grace
> Like Helen's.

Greeks. The path to Helen, as Mephistopheles has already told us, leads only through the Mothers, i.e., it can be followed only by those who have confronted their own mother problem.

When he mentions the Mothers, Mephistopheles asks, "Are you awed?" The awe that Faust feels indicates that some deep conflict has been touched.

Mephistopheles then gives Faust a key with the counsel, "Follow it down—it leads you to the Mothers." At this Faust, like any sensitive client in therapy, shudders,

FAUST: The Mothers! Still it strikes a shock of fear.
What is the word that I am loath to hear?

MEPHISTOPHELES: Are you in blinkers, rear at a new word?

FAUST: Yet not in torpor would I comfort find;
Awe is the finest portion of mankind:
However scarce the world may make this sense—
In awe one feels profoundly the immense.

MEPHISTOPHELES: Well then, sink down! Or I might call it,
soar! It's all one and the same.*

Indeed it is all the same whether one reaches the Mothers by sinking or soaring, so important are they. Now that Faust has the key, he can "make them keep their distance," and he is suddenly enraptured by the challenge: "Yes, clutching it I feel my strength redoubled, My stride braced for the goal, for heart untroubled."† Mephistopheles informs him,

> A glowing tripod will at last give sign that
> You have reached the deepest, nethermost shrine;
> And by its light you will behold the Mothers. . . .
> Some may be seated, upright, walking others,
> As it may chance. Formation, transformation.
> The eternal mind's eternal recreation.**

*Ibid., l. 6265.
†Ibid., l. 6282.
**Ibid., l. 6275.

Then he directs Faust, "Sink down by stamping, stamping you will rise."* And Faust stamps and sinks out of sight.

The next scene is in a ballroom filled with persons exhibiting jealousy and repartee. Mephistopheles suddenly cries out, "O, Mothers! Mothers! Won't you let Faust go?"† Did he sense some abnormal tie to mothers on the part of Faust? And as Faust continues to seek Helen through the Mothers, Mephistopheles cries, "Mother! Mothers! it is yours to give!" So something of importance is occurring beyond the achievement of Helen, something that makes the "Mothers" of ultimate importance. The form of forms participates in the universe of reproduction of the species. There is in the smile of the Giaconda on Leonardo's canvas, though his insight is projected from the artist onto the painting. The one in whose womb life is created, the one who carries the implantation of new life, also has these powers such as intuition that alternate between knowledge and magic.

Here we must fall back upon the fundamental truth that Goethe, great poet that he was, possessed a degree of prescience, a capacity to speak from the unconscious depths of his society. The poets as well as the other artists of any culture tell us of myths that go quite beyond anything they consciously know. In this sense they are the predicters of the future. Wizards of femininity, they (the Mothers) must be rescued to help form and reform the new culture. The Mothers have, by nature of reproducing the race, whether they are conscious of it and take responsibility for it or not. They have the key to transformation as they had for the forming of the fetus in the womb at pregnancy.

But this Industrial Age is one of patriarchal power. Such power is gained by overcoming its competitors; it works by thrust, by attack, by mechanical activity. The seamy side of the Industrial Age is sweatshops, life-killing assembly lines, child

*Ibid., l. 6302.
†Ibid., l. 6367.

and women labor, smoke-filled skies over Liverpool and Detroit, the whole arsenal of competitive, adversarial systems. The feminine characteristics ideally are receptivity rather than aggression, tenderness and creating rather than destroying.

Is Goethe doing penance for his worship of progress and for his epiphany of industry? Ostensibly he believed in this patriarchal gospel and he had a long drawn-out battle within his soul as to whether it was good or bad. Faust's later building of the great dike to "give life to millions," where he is on the creative side, is one aspect of the acting out of these beliefs.

Power, attack, the thrusting mode—all these are called, somewhat as a cliché to be sure, masculine and patriarchal. Goethe was in a paradox about this chief myth of modern times, which includes our time in the twentieth century as well as his. The paradox comes out of his poetic soul in dealing with the Mothers as the source of love, tenderness, caring, instead of toughness, cruelty, slaughter. Could the "magic" be the hope that the transformation could occur without great loss of life and without cruelty? The episode of the saving of Gretchen at the very end of the drama would seem to rectify Faust's original cruelty; and the ultimate saving of Faust by having his immortal remains carried to heaven by flocks of angels—all this gives a positive answer to the question. Goethe may have meant it as an affirmative cheer for "progress"; this is the overall impact of this great poem. *We take the drama here as a demonstration that sole patriarchal power is bound to come to grief.* *

CULTURAL CREATIVITY

Faust does meet Helen and has a child by her. He seems then to change his character, becoming more sensitive to human need. Does this mean that his change of character has some-

*See Chapter 16.

thing to do with his having loved the "form of forms"?
He rebukes Mephistopheles,

> What do you know of human need?
> What can your mind
> Know of the longings of mankind?*

Faust then becomes a man of wealth, inhabits a castle, rises
to the position of Generalissimo and Emperor. He grows in
power and in far-reaching plans for improving life for human
beings. Faust's lands stretch out before him; he can now say,
"from this palace the world is wholly in my reach."† He is
completely absorbed in this cultural creativity:

> Still this planet's sail
> For noble deeds grant scope abounding,
> I sense accomplishments astounding,
> Feel strength in me for daring toil.**

Here in the drama we are introduced to an old couple living
in a little cottage on this land. Goethe calls them Baucis and
Philemon, the very names of the old couple in ancient Greek
mythology who gave hospitality to the gods, unknowing of
their identity, and were rewarded handsomely for their kindness.

Baucis takes tender care of her elderly husband Philemon,
cautioning a wayfarer who visits them to lower his voice so that
Philemon may finish his nap. The old couple are told about the
plans of Faust to clear all the land, but they have also been
promised that they will be allowed to stay. But Faust is ambivalent.

> Yet as I say it, I'm ashamed.
> That aged couple must surrender,
> I want their linden for my throne.

*Goethe, *Faust*, ll. 10190–10195.
†Ibid., l. 11225.
**Ibid., ll. 10182–10184.

. . . .
A look-out frame will soon have risen
To sweep the world in boundless arc.
Thence I shall view the new plantation
Assigned to shelter the old pair,
Who, mindful of benign salvation,
Will spend life's happy evening there.*

He sends Mephistopheles to deliver his message that they will be moved to a new house. But Mephistopheles comes back to report that a fight had ensued with a stranger,

They wouldn't hear, so didn't stir. . . .
The couple did not suffer much
From fear fell lifeless at our touch.†

About their house:

—and now it blazes free,
A funeral pyre for those three.

Faust bursts out in anger at Mephistopheles,

So you have turned deaf ears to me!
I meant exchange not robbery.
This thoughtless violent affair,
My curse on it, for you to share!**

But now Faust finds himself wholly involved in his great cultural creativity,

From every source
Find me more hands, recruit with vigor
Spur them with blandishment and rigor,
Spare neither pay nor lure nor force!
I want a tally, daily to be rendered,
How much the trench in hand is gaining room.

*Ibid., ll 11238, 11342.
†Ibid., l. 11362.
**Ibid., l. 11373.

> To drain this stagnant pool of ills
> Would be the crowning, last achievement
> I'd open room to live for millions.*

This is surely the best aspect of the Industrial Revolution, an illustration of laudable progress! The building of dikes and making farms for human beings is the noble use of tools. It is interesting that Kenneth Clark, in his pictures of art through the ages, shows in the nineteenth-century photographs not of paintings but of trains, tunnels, bridges, and other constructions of engineering in the art of the nineteenth century, the work of men and not women. In contrast to Vasari's book, *Lives of the Painters* written in the Italian Renaissance, Samuel Smiles wrote *Lives of the Engineers* in nineteenth-century England, when the triumph of patriarchal power was almost complete.

But not quite. Faust still cannot accept Care, a curious character introduced to test Faust.† Leaving him sadly, Care remarks:

> Man commonly is blind throughout his life,
> My Faust, be blind then as you end it.**

Faust now arrives at the fateful words which bring him close to breaking his original pledge to Mephistopheles,

> Yes—this I hold with devout insistence,
> Wisdom's last verdict goes to say:
> He only earns both freedom and existence
> Who must reconquer them new each day.
>
> And so, ringed all about by perils here,
> Youth, manhood, age will spend their strenuous
> year.

---

*Ibid., l. 11552.

†We found "care" coming up in other myths, like *The Great Gatsby*, *Peer Gynt*, and so on. I have described the meaning of care in *Love and Will* under the caption "Myth of Care."

**Goethe, *Faust*, l. 11498.

> Such teeming would I see upon this land,
> On acres free among free people stand
> I might entreat the fleeting minute:
> O tarry yet, thou art so fair!*

Mephistopheles does not hear that word "might." But the statement is subjectively a *loss to the devil* in any case. As Freud would say, Faust *considers* this satisfaction, and that is in effect capitulating to Mephistopheles. Negations have no meaning in dreams or other phases of the unconscious; one calls the item or person to mind, and that is enough. Faust here at least considers the serenity and the happiness. So the great wager is lost!

THE SALVATION OF FAUST

Faust sinks backward and the devil gathers up his body with the speech,

> There lies the corpse, and when the soul would flit
> I'll show it straight the bond with blood cemented.†

The "ghastly jaws of hell open at left," says the stage direction.

But to our great surprise the devil's plans are thwarted by a chorus of young angels, messengers of grace, who arrive with roses, which they strew in front of Mephistopheles, while singing,

> Roses, you glowing ones,
> Balsam bestowing ones!
> Floating and flickering,
> Stealthily quickening,
> Spring, . . . burst out blooming,
> Emerald, red;

*Ibid., l. 11573.
†Ibid., l. 11613.

> Send grace perfuming
> The sleeper's bed.*

Mephistopheles is not only confused by the rose petals floating all about, but—of all things—he becomes sexually at-
tracted to the young angels. It is indeed a comic and
enchanting scene—the devil caught in his own trap of sexual
desire! Goethe must have had a good chuckle as he wrote this;
for the devil tries to hold the angels off to no avail because of
his own uncontrollable sexual yearnings; "They seem so very
lovely all at once." The angels continue to sing,

> Blossoms of blessing,
> Gay flames caressing,
> Love they are spreading,
> Ecstasy shedding.†

Mephistopheles must break down and admit,

> My liver burns, my heart, my head as well,
> Some super-devilish element
> More pointed far than flames of hell.—
> That's why you so prodigiously lament,
> Unhappy lovesick lads, who wander, spurned,
> Their craning necks to the beloved turned.
>
> I too!**

He forgets Faust as he, now the lovesick lad, loses his senses
over bare sex in these young angels. He cries,

> What ails me!—Job-like,
> boil on boil my skin,
> All sores I stand and shake with self-disgust.‡

In this strange confusion, erotic and beautiful at the same
time, Faust's immortal essence is born up to heaven in a scene

*Ibid., l. 11700.
†Ibid., l. 11724.
**Ibid., ll. 11748, 11759.
‡Ibid., ll. 11809–11810

made up not only of angels but the "Chorus of the Blessed Boys," amid Church Father galore. It is as though God himself now takes a hand in having Faust born off to heaven! But Goethe, caught in his own paradox, must again get in his lauding of the active man,

> Whoever strives in ceaseless toil,
> Him we may grant redemption.*

At the end, Goethe comes back to the central emotional and psychological theme, namely, the significance of Woman, now in the form of the Virgin. From the "highest, purest cell," there comes the song,

> Here is the prospect free,
> Spirit uplifting.
> Womenly shapes I see
> Heavenward drifting.†

This scene, the highest level of spiritual perfection attainable for human beings, is a radiant contrast to Dr. Faustus' dreary and dark study at the very beginning of the drama. Goethe is saved by Dante, in this ending: Gretchen imitates the intercession of Beatrice on behalf of Dante in *The Divine Comedy.* These two great poets unite in this wonderful ending finally published by Goethe when he was eighty years old. Gretchen, now from the celestial vantage point of the Saved, takes part in the singing that welcomes Faust into blessedness. Goethe now lists the four kinds of women that one should serve: Holy Virgin, Mother, Queen, and Goddess. The drama ends with a verse which lauds action again, but now the final words again sing out the saving quality of the eternal feminine,

> All that is changeable
> Is but refraction;
> The unattainable

*Ibid., l. 11936.
†Ibid., l. 11989–11993.

> Here becomes action.
> Human discernment
> Here is passed by;
> Woman Eternal
> Draws us on high.

At this ending we are immediately struck by the fact that Marlowe's Faust was thrown into hell, while in Goethe's myth Faust is carried away into heaven! How shall we explain this conflicting interpretation of the same myth? Indeed, in Goethe's version it is more than merely a "happy ending." It is a delightful scene with Gretchen symbolizing the forgiving love for Faust, gay humor in Mephistopheles' uncontrollable sexual desire for the "sweet, lovely things," and everyone surrounded by a charming ballet of the dancing angels.

Each myth in human history is interpreted according to the needs of the society which it reflects. Marlowe's Renaissance needed an opening of hell to represent the audience's own guilt; they would experience the abreaction they so much needed only by Marlowe's bringing literal hell into the picture. But Goethe's Enlightenment needed a quite different abreaction. The people then needed to leave the theater with the feeling that God was on their side in the form of Providence, that their culture was a great step in advance, that progress was a holy thing, that the highest calling is, in Goethe's words,

> To drain this stagnant pool of ills
> Would be the crowning, last achievement
> I'd open room for millions.*

This made sense because the Enlightenment was a greatly expanding economy and a time of the expression of noble ideas, as we recall in the American Declaration of Independence and the Rights of Man.

We have said that the divine element of the forgiveness of Faust is in the last two lines of the drama,

*Ibid., l. 11552.

Woman Eternal
Draws us on high.

One of Goethe's purposes in writing this great drama was to explore the myths of the life of humanism, to search out every way to help human beings discover and live by their greatest callings. He is said to have died with this last word on his lips, "Progress." Progress for him did not mean simply mechanical achievements or achieving wealth. It meant human beings learning to be conscious of their richest unique capacities, and thus have "life and have it more abundantly." Hence he begins his myth of Faust with a description of Easter, the time of the rising of Christ.

There is in Goethe's writing an element of eternity, a sense of the true use of myth. He stretches up toward the divine; he seems always related to transcendent being. This becomes explicit in his last sentence, "Woman eternal/Draws us on high." We have said the principle of forgiving love is present in the person of Gretchen. This is embodied in the "eternal feminine," a force which is an expression of the *deus ex machina*. This brings us back again to Mephistopheles' statement in his first encounter with Faust: his evil acts are changed to good. The devil is duped, betrayed by his own powers. The motif of the "betrayed Satan" or the "duped devil" has been present in Western theology and philosophy for many centuries, all the way back to Origen. Here it turns up specifically in the ending of Goethe's *Faust*. Thus Mephistopheles is at least partly right when he says that he "does evil out of which there comes good."

FOURTEEN

Faust in the Twentieth Century

Germany . . . was reeling then at the height of her dissolute triumphs. . . . Today, clung round by demons, a hand over one eye, with the other staring into horrors, down she flings from despair to despair. When will she reach the bottom of the abyss? When, out of uttermost hopelessness—a miracle beyond the power of belief—will the light of hope dawn? A lonely man folds his hands and speaks, "God be merciful to thy poor souls, my friends, my Fatherland!"

Thomas Mann, *Doctor Faustus*, 1948

IT REMAINED FOR THOMAS MANN, the great novelist of the first half of the twentieth century, to describe the destructive power and despair present in the myths of Faust. Nobel laureate, Mann had already chronicled the bourgeois culture of his Germany in *Buddenbrooks*, writing with special sensitivity of the challenges and dilemmas of modern Western society. He had pictured the sickness of Europe in *The Magic Mountain* in the 1920s. But with the advent of Hitler and World War II, Thomas Mann, humanist in the best sense of the term, was thrown into a deep convulsion as he experienced the destruction of his country and the West. He found the ultimate form of the myth of Faust in the context of World War II, the greatest destructiveness our Western world has yet known.

I was made especially aware of the depth of the ambivalence and grief that affected such Germans because of my close friendship with Paul Tillich, a man of similar honors and, like Mann, a refugee from Hitler's Germany. One night in the early 1940s when World War II was in full tilt, Hannah Tillich, Paul, and I had gone to the cinema to see some long-forgotten movie. Preceding the picture a newsreel was shown which turned out to be photographs of the bombing of Dresden, the city which had been the center of creativity in Germany. Now its great buildings and many art museums came crashing down in the fire and smoke of complete destruction. Paul and Hannah burst into tears in such complete agony of the heart that I thought their tears would never stop. I had never seen such deep-felt agony of spirit.

Thomas Mann endured a similar agony. Mann's wife was Jewish; he escaped with her into Switzerland and then ultimately to the United States and Princeton's Institute for Advanced Study. He could observe the conflagration from the quiet of Princeton, but this made the contrast even sharper. What was happening to his native land?

There never was the slightest question of the loyalty of these Germans to America. Tillich had been the first Christian exile under Hitler, and Mann had been Europe's foremost novelist in the first half of the twentieth century. Yet Germany was where their relatives were, and Germany had given them a profound education in the humanities, music, and art. Now Germany's great symbol of humanism was being ground into dust by that bombing of Dresden.

Humanistic to the core, Thomas Mann desperately grasped for a myth that might give some meaning, if not a release from sorrow, some sense of community in the long history of human self-destruction. Hitlerism was no longer simply an illness; it was a cancer of the German soul. Had not Germany sold its birthright to the devil in permitting and embracing the degradation of all culture in Hitlerism? Mann was thus irresistibly drawn toward the myth of Faust.

No one can open Mann's *Dr. Faustus* and read a few sentences without realizing that great convulsions were occurring in the author's soul. He rewrote the myth of Faust, emphasizing what did not concern Marlowe and Goethe, namely, the cultural destruction of the Western world. Indeed, Mann was so caught up in his portrayal of this cancer of the soul that he himself became ill in the process of writing and had to spend time in the hospital in Chicago.

The story, or what there is of narration in Mann's *Dr. Faustus,* is about Adrian Leverkuhn, a talented musical composer and the inventor of the twelve-tone scale.* The narrator of the myth, Serenus Zeitblom, is an old friend from childhood, perhaps the only friend Adrian had, who himself was a good German. Zeitblom was a classical scholar, professor at the university, happily married; he speaks of his wife as "my good Helen." He is greatly distressed when his sons support Hitler, and he resigns from his professor's chair when he is told that he is required to teach Nazi doctrine.

The narrator, Zeitblom, tells us that Adrian's hell begins when he loses the only human being he had ever truly loved, a sweet and innocent child of five, son of his sister. The little boy dies in the agonies of cerebral spinal meningitis. Thereafter Adrian can love no other human being. He lives as a recluse.

In his early twenties Adrian had been tricked into going to a brothel, and in his embarrassment he had walked over to the piano and struck a chord from Weber's *Freischutz.* This was the same chord that Nietzsche had played on the piano when he also was brought to a brothel. Here Adrian has his only sexual experience in his life, with a prostitute named Esmeralda. She warns him that she is infected, but he neverthe-

---

*This twelve-tone scale is important because it is one of the experiments in "new art" which the devil will castigate later on in the novel.

less has intercourse with her and contracts syphilis. This makes the story parallel in this regard with the life of Nietzsche, who also contracted syphilis in his early twenties in a brothel.

Some students of Thomas Mann, such as Professor Richard Wiseman, believe that Mann's book, *Dr. Faustus,* is about Nietzsche all the way through. This may be so, especially when we consider that Nietzsche was the ultimate nay-sayer, the philosopher, in his writings like the *Death of God,* who makes it clear that the modern epoch is at its end.

Mann seems to feel that, had European culture listened to Nietzsche, its collapse could have been avoided or at least mitigated. For Nietzsche was one writer who predicted what would later happen to Europe if it continued on its ambivalent course.

CONVERSATION WITH THE DEVIL

The mark of Cain—or the equivalent in our society—is on Adrian's forehead, placed there by the devil in the most fascinating chapter of the book, a dialogue between Adrian and the devil.* The bargain Adrian signs with his blood is stated by Satan at the end of this chapter and then the devil adds:

We are entering into times, my friend which will not be hood-winked by psychology.... Thy life shall be cold, [therefore] thou shalt love no one.... Love is forbidden you, insofar as it warms. Thy life shalt be cold, therefore thou shalt love no human being.†

Mann's novel is difficult reading, but it becomes captivating when the devil appears and holds a conversation with Adrian, who has been ill with a severe migraine attack, retching and spewing all day. We recall that migraine often is accompanied

*Thomas Mann, *Dr. Faustus* (New York: Knopf, 1948), chap. 12. For those who do not wish to read the whole novel, I recommend this one chapter as the heart of the book.
†Ibid., p. 249.

by out-of-body experiences and psychological breakthroughs. Icy drafts blow through the room, and Adrian remarks on how cold it is—all of which make a fitting atmosphere in which to hold a conversation with the devil. Adrian states in this conversation that the devil says only those things that already are in himself, Adrian—which is a description of what happens when our subconscious talks back to us. Thus the thrusts and the obsessions *are the breakthrough of Adrian's own preconscious and subconscious ideas.*

Satan is an amazing conversationalist, but the conversation is one-sided—Adrian tries in vain to shut up his adversary, as we all do when accosted by Satan. But the devil lords over the talk with his irony and sarcasm. When Adrian demands to know who he is, the devil wards off the question except to say that he is "in fact German, German to the core."

The devil scorns the profession of psychology; it is a "nice, neutral middle point and psychologists the most truth-loving people."* He talks of Luther's having thrown an inkwell at the devil, though he keeps calling Luther Dr. Martinus. He discusses Oswald Spengler at length and the latter's two-volume work, *The Decline of the West,* a book damned by the bourgeoisie when it was published because of its pessimistic prophecy.† In his own agony about what was occurring in Germany, Mann seems to find in Spengler as well as Nietzsche his prophetic statements.

The whole novel is about the illness of the twentieth century. It requires us to rethink the meaning of health in a declining civilization and to reconsider how we use our great progress

---

*Ibid., p. 229. The fact that Mann has Satan level these attacks on psychology tells us again that there is a curious connection between the spread of psychology and the decline of Western culture. Is it the prevalence of emotional sicknesses, the special need for help on adjustment, etc., that occurs in a declining or, as Mann would say, a sick culture? Whatever the reason for these attacks on psychology, we know that Mann was very sympathetic toward Freud and modern depth-psychology.

†Published the same year as *The Magic Mountain.* At that time Mann was opposed to Spengler's pessimism, but Hitler was yet to show how ruthless human beings can be.

in medicine. For the sickness which Mann (and Hesse in *Steppenwolf* before him) are talking about is a spiritual illness. About this the devil says some pithy things:

"What is sick, what well, my friend, about that we must not let the philistines have the last word. Have you forgotten what you learned in the schools, that God can bring good out of evil?" And he adds, in language which sounds surprisingly like the New Testament, "A man must have been always ill and mad in order that others no longer need be so. And where madness begins to be malady, there nobody knows at all."* The passion of modern human beings is to conquer the world of medicine and therefore of health—to arrive at a concept of health which Mann believed is our vanity rather than actually health—"more than the piddling condition of so-called healthiness."

The devil tells him, by way of persuading him to make the pact, that real creativity comes that way, i.e., from the devil. A genuine inspiration, immediate, absolute, unquestioned, ravishing, where there is no choice, no tinkering, no possible improvement; with shudders of awe from head to foot, with tears of joy blinding his eyes. It comes but from the devil, the true master and giver of such rapture.

But what is most crucial in this chapter, in which Adrian confirms his bargain with the devil, is the discussion of modern art and music. Mann believed, as Paul Tillich, Oswald Spengler, and other great students of our age have believed, that *the best measure of the spiritual health or illness of a culture is its art.* The chief symptom of the twentieth century, the age of the despair and dissolution Mann has described, is the *trivialization of art.* Arthur Miller, we recall, has warned us of the contemporary "trivialization of drama," which is another

---

*Ibid., p. 235. This reminds one of Rilke, who found his devil necessary for his creativity, and William Blake, who in his drawings of God always put hoofs on the feet of the Almighty, and all the other artists and musicians who secretly believe their creativity requires the presence of the devil. Mann is saying that if we cure all disease we will have wiped out our creativity.

similarity with our own day. This is the proof of the work of the devil; it is a gnawing away at the soul of modern culture.

"What is art today?" asks the devil rhetorically. "A pilgrimage on peas. There's more to dancing in these times than a pair of red shoes."* He dismisses the "stylists," for they persuade "themselves and others that the tedious has become interesting, because the interesting has begun to grow tedious."† All artists have become powerless, "but the sickness is general, and the straight-forward ones show the symptoms. . . . Composing itself has got too hard, devilishly hard." Here Mann must be saying that the twelve-tone scale is without harmony (he charges at one point that in it the harmony is irrelevant) and that the art of music is part of the new triviality, an avoidance of the great forms which were in the past so important. Beethoven's *Ode to Joy* is the foil; Adrian's new scale, and music, does away with Beethoven's "joy." "But music too by untiringly conforming her specific concerns to the ruling conventions has so far as she could played a role in the highbrow swindle."**

The devil continues regarding the relation between sickness and creativity:

And I mean too that creative, genius-giving disease, disease that rides on high horse over all hindrances, and springs with drunken daring from peak to peak, is a thousand times dearer to life than plodding healthiness. I have never heard anything stupider than that from disease only disease can come. [The creative person] takes the reckless product of disease and as soon as it takes it to itself it is health. . . . On your madness they will feed in health, and in them you will become healthy."‡

In other words, out of consciously admitted illness can come great creativity, which is why there has been such a close rela-

*Ibid., p. 238. We are in the decade when paintings that were done by poverty-stricken artists, e.g., Van Gogh, a hundred years ago, are now sold at auction for $53 million. This shows not the valuation of Van Gogh but rather what one does to avoid income tax.

  †Ibid.
  **Ibid., p. 241.
  ‡Ibid., p. 243.

tionship through history between disease and creativity.

Again Mann argues that creativity thrives on illness, and disease is the process by which the creative person shifts forms; he or she creates from formlessness to a new form. The trouble is that our culture is in the midst of this process and has not yet found its new Renaissance. We have not found our own method of creating health by healing works of art.

Satan then repeats the sentence that love is forbidden to Adrian and his life will be cold. "A work-filled eternity of human life shall you enjoy." When the hourglass runs out, the devil will have "good power to deal and dole with, to move and manage the fine-soul Creature after my way and my pleasure, be it in life, soul, flesh, blood or goods—to all eternity."*

THE LAMENTATION
OF DR. FAUSTUS

Toward the end of Mann's rendering of this myth, Adrian invites his acquaintances and admirers to his recluse home under the pretext of playing for them his crowning achievement, a symphonic cantata entitled *The Lamentation of Dr. Faustus.* But when the group has assembled, Adrian launches into a confession. "Since my twenty-second year, he confesses, I have been married to Satan." He continues about his life, all in the semi-gibberish that is the telltale mark that the syphilis has done its work. A strained and painful stillness now reigns in the room. The audience becomes restive as they begin to see that Adrian has lost his sanity. One of the doctors present says in a loud stage whisper that Adrian is mentally deteriorated. Some persons in the audience who are embarrassed get up to leave. Adrian continues in his gibberish until he collapses at the piano with a paralytic stroke.

The peasant woman who takes care of Adrian's house pushes

*Ibid., p. 249.

through the guests and takes Adrian in her arms, rebuking all
these renowned people for not having the human kindness to
take care of him. He is taken off to the hospital. His one faithful friend, Serenus, goes later to the hospital to see him and
finds that he is in complete senility.

There follows the epilogue about the deterioration of Germany, the most important paragraphs of the whole book. In
this epilogue Mann cries aloud what the reader feels about
those years, that Hitler and his mates are a "monstrous national
perversion . . . its prime movers have had themselves poisoned
by their physicians, drenched with petrol and set on fire . . . evil
men willed that Germany be destroyed down to the ground."*
Mann ends this tortured book with his beseeching God to be
merciful to his people, his friends, his Fatherland.† "It is finished. An old man, bent, well-nigh broken by the horrors of the
times in which he wrote and those which were the burden of
his writing."**

One is deeply gripped by this "lamentation." But the question immediately arises in the myth, What evil was Adrian
guilty of? What was the Faustian character who bore the guilt?
In Mann's interpretation, it is a nation of people, Germany.
Marlowe's Faustus and Goethe's Faust clearly sinned, the first
by usurping the role of God and the second by his passion to
have all power and all sensuality for his own power and sensa-
tion. But Adrian is not guilty of any clear sins, certainly not the
death of the little boy he loved; nor did he destroy or kill any
other person. And whether one likes the twelve-tone scale or
not, it is surely not a sin to invent it.

Above all, Mann is concerned with the guilt each of us bears
as a part of the sins of our society. The basic source of guilt and
evil, which this myth is about, namely, that *Germany itself had
become the Faust, and Germany itself bears the punishment.*
Thus the "guilty person" is not a person but a nation, and *this*

*Ibid., p. 504.
†Ibid., p. 501.
**Ibid., p. 504.

nation represents the Faustian evil in all the nations of the West. It is a collaborative guilt, a collective guilt of whole peoples.

It is significant that this was the Germany which had made such great contributions to art, philosophy, music, and science. This excellence made it possible for the philosopher Hegel to argue, half a century before Hitler and the Nazis, that the epitome of attainment in all evolution was Germany with all its supreme culture. This Germany was the Icarus which soared to its too great height—and fell to its grizzly death and destruction in Nazism.

The guilt must also be borne by all of us in the West—we who saddled Germany with impossible war debts in the Treaty of Versailles. But Germany itself was the modern Faustus and crashed in the ruins of the bunkers in Berlin, where these evil men, the Hitler leaders, "poisoned by their physicians . . . willed that Germany be destroyed down to the ground." The crashing down of the great art in Dresden, the slaughter of 20 million Russians, the torture and killing of 6 million Jews—all these things are so evil as to beggar our imagination. They present us with the most gripping and authentic picture of the myth of Faust since the "Damnable Life and Deserved Death of Doctor John Faustus."

Thus *Dr. Faustus* is the myth which shows us the meaning of vicarious evil and cathartic salvation. Mann is describing human life as he saw it in those terrible years. He is presenting the fact that we all are guilty even though we did not commit the specific evil. We are saved by a virtue beyond ourselves; and perhaps our virtue will aid someone else. Life is never a question of adding up particular sins. The child of a sharecropper, or the starving child in Africa, did not themselves do anything particularly evil; they suffer for someone else's—or perhaps fate's—mistake. *Our hyper-individualism in the West is already part of the evil.* God is no bookkeeper: the innocent and guilty are part and parcel of the same evil and same salvation. All three of these Fausts—Marlowe's, Goethe's, and Mann's—we have noted had degrees in theology, which means that goodness is never very far from evil.

Mann specifically cites the trivialization of art as the basic flaw in our civilization. But no particular person or group is responsible for that, whether they like to play twelve-tone music or not. The book is saying that all Germans, indeed all of the West, share in the common guilt. We have sold our souls to Satan, and we all hope for the grace of salvation. To be human is to exist in the paradox of Mephistopheles on one side and the good angels on the other.

PSYCHOTHERAPY
AS FAUSTIAN

We noticed above that Thomas Mann, in his *Dr. Faustus*, makes frequent criticisms of psychology. One, for example, is the remark of the devil, "Psychology—God warrant us, do you still hold with it? That is bad, bourgeois nineteenth century."* This is certainly not because Mann was opposed to psychology in real life; he was very appreciative of it and gave an excellent lecture to honor Freud in celebration of the latter's eightieth birthday. But there is plenty of evidence that our twentieth century in the West is a Faustian culture. How is this related to psychology? Our booming stock market, our increasing multitudes of millionaires, our nuclear arms race, and star wars—all these make our age a playground for the myth of Faustianism more profound than Marlowe's age and certainly Goethe's.

There is a curious relationship between the spread of psychology and this myth of the Faustian age of Western culture. Is it the prevalence of emotional sickness, the special need for help in adjustment, a society of *Waiting for Godot,* or as Mann would say, a culture in which there is a trivialization of God? The remark of the Viennese wit, "Psychoanalysis is the sick-

*Ibid., p. 249.

ness which its therapy purports to cure," expresses some deep relationship between this very sickness and the cure for it.

Indeed, the devil's own methods have the flavor of psychoanalysis. "What you don't feel, you won't hunt down by art," says the devil, "unless it wells from your own inward source." And again, the devil remarks, "We only release, set free. We let lameness and self-consciousness, scruples and doubts go to the devil."*

We noted above, especially in the Goethe and Marlowe versions, that Faust, in presenting his problems, sounds like modern persons who come for psychotherapy. When Goethe's Faust complains, "Each morning I wake in desperation," and "Existence seems a burden to detest," he is speaking exactly like our patients.† Indeed, the myth of Faust so permeates our culture that it is part of the corrective endeavors—in this case, psychotherapy—as well as the problems.

Persons who come for therapy do so because they lack power; they complain that they cannot achieve. Shall they sell their souls to the devil—in our day called heroin, cocaine, alcohol? Some of them have of course tried those ways, seeking at least some surcease of sorrow even if they can't expect cures.

People who come for therapy also want sensual gratification. The advertisements over television and in the slick magazines hammer home by sheer repetition the doctrine that if you are not rich and sexy and don't drink champagne every night you are missing out on life.** Patients want "magical knowledge,"

---

*Ibid., p. 233.
†Ibid., p. 236.
**What is anathema in these days of self-expressionism is what Goethe's Faust said when he was making up his mind to sell his soul to Mephistopheles,

> What does the world hold out by way of gain?
> Abstain! it calls. You shall abstain!
> Thus goes the sempiternal song
> That every mortal creature hears,
> Each hour comes rasping to our ears,
> Each morning I awake in desperation.

Instead of "abstain" we would use the word "repress." It is easy to see why Faust finds this process unsatisfying.

and no matter how correctly the therapist explains that insight is not magic, it still feels that way to the person when an insight "dawns."

In the early Freudian forms of therapy, when it was believed that repression was the great and universal evil and one should express oneself in all situations (even though this is a misreading of Freud), we detect a particular Faustian flavor. Many of these early forms of therapy operated on the assumption that one needed to clear away the blockages so that patients could achieve all the power and sensual gratification possible. Scream your head off, have as many sexual experiences as possible, let nothing stand in your way!

This use of psychoanalysis was itself based on Faustian principles. Erich Fromm entitled one of his books, *Ye Shall Be as Gods*. People should cultivate the free expression of moods and desires that Marlowe's Faust lived by (and that led to his doom). The unending crusade "to get more and more out of life," as was shown in the wide sale of such pop psychology books as *I'm O.K., You're O.K.*, is itself a form of Faustianism.

Psychotherapy surely tries to meet the problems of our day. When people feel guilty at making their million, they can go to a therapist and be reassured that they are only using their abilities and no one should feel guilty about that. When one is caught up in breakneck competition, one can go to a therapist and learn that success would be a proof of his value rather than the reverse. When one marries a dazzling blonde—just like the advertisements—and the marriage goes sour, we can go to a therapist and be strengthened to try again. In conversation one can often assume that the person to whom one is talking has participated in psychotherapy of some sort. One hears from time to time statements that one's friend is in a hurry; he had a "bad dream" and is rushing off to see his therapist to get his anxiety relieved. In New Hampshire where my family spends its summers, there appeared an ad in the local paper entitled, "Supportive, Transitional Counseling," and there followed a listing of the things this person and process can do for you:

"Treats stress and crisis management, goal selection, decision-making, life style orientation, imaging, pre-marital strategies, social net-working, personal evaluation."

This and similar advertisements are increasingly frequent in newspapers and the Yellow Pages as the therapists exhibit their wares. These surely are the problems we used to take to pastors in churches: guidance in making decisions, help in formulating goals, right life styles, and so on. The professions which give psychotherapy have been growing by leaps and bounds. This is especially in the five areas called the "helping professions"— psychiatry, psychology, social work, education, and pastoral counselors—all are now not dealing exclusively with the eternal symbols of religion but rather with counseling as psychotherapists.

There is no doubt the Faustian myth is all about us in the psychology of the late twentieth century. It is as alive—or more so—today as at any time in the four centuries past. It is present in our boredom, like Faust's, with knowledge of the past; in our allying ourselves with the devil in our nuclear warheads; in our demand for power (which is defined in terms of money); in our craze for fulfillment of all sensual desires; in our greed, our compulsive activity, our frantic pursuit of progress. Through all this is our refusal to pause and ask, What is the purpose of this mad race?

The myth is an unseen guide, a silent leader, a way of deciding what is acceptable and not acceptable; and it brooks no more questioning than did Satan in Marlowe's *Faust* when the clock struck twelve. As Marlowe's Faust says in a moment of insight, "The god thou servest is thine own appetite."

FIFTEEN

The Devil and Creativity

God allowed evil to exist, woven into the texture of the
world, in order to increase man's freedom and his will to
prove his moral strength in overcoming it.

                              The Philosophy of Gnosticism

THE RELATION OF MODERN PEOPLE to the myth of the devil
is startling indeed. In Chapter 1 we cited the study made
in the 1970s of beliefs in the devil and in God, in which it was
discovered that the belief in God was decreasing while the
belief in the devil was increasing.

The alarm this phenomenon calls forth is that it indicates
that great numbers of contemporary people are expressing their
disillusionment with life, their suspicion of their fellows, and
their frightening uncertainty about their future. The study implies that people have shifted from faith to fatalism.*

Most sophisticated and educated people in the West in our

---

*This shift is connected in the last half of the twentieth century with the growing
fundamentalism all over the world. *Life* magazine devoted a special edition during the
summer of 1989 to the increase in our present time of this belief in the devil. The
journal reported that over 70 percent of the people in this country now believe there is
some evil spirit in the universe they call the devil, while there are less than 40 percent
who believe in a God.

century had cast out the term "devil" as mere superstition. But strange things have been happening in the world during recent decades. By 1950 we had seen so much cruelty in the sheer destruction in Hitlerism and we had observed the use of concentration camps as an accepted technique of government. America had dropped the atom bomb on Hiroshima and the nuclear bomb on Nagasaki, reducing these two whole cities to groaning rubble in two hours. These things understandably led many thoughtful people seriously to wonder whether the term "devil" should not be brought back into our vocabulary, certainly not as a person but as a powerfully active myth.

We also recall the case referred to in Chapter 2, when Charles' critical point in his therapy was his identification with Satan. For Satan existed as a myth of Charles' identity. The devil empowered his soul. These were more than mere words for Charles; he emphasized that his belief was not a form of Manicheanism since Satan really believed in God. By means of the myth of the devil this man could accept his negativity—for it had suddenly changed into a positive term. "I am Satan," he kept repeating. "Satan was a rebel for God." At last he had found an outlet for his rebellion merged with his considerable talents. In Jungian terms he was freed to create something of real value by his acceptance of his shadow, Satan.

When we note the number of books written about Satan by recognized scholars in our day, the data become almost overwhelming. Some of these titles are *Lucifer, The Devil in the Middle Ages, Sanctions for Evil, Light at the Core of Darkness.*

An excellent study of the devil has been made by psychologist Henry Murray of Harvard in his essay, "The Personality and Career of Satan."* Murray first refers to Isaiah in the Bible for his description of Satan:

How art thou fallen from heaven, O day star, son of the morning! how art thou cut down to the ground, which didst lay low the nations!

---

*In *Endeavors in Psychology: Selections from the Personology of Henry A. Murray,* ed. Edwin S. Shneidman (New York: Harper & Row, 1981).

And thou saidst in thine heart, I will ascend into heaven, I will exalt
my throne above the stars of God; and I will sit upon the mount of
congregation, in the uttermost parts of the north: I will ascend above
the heights of the clouds; I will be like unto the Most High.

Murray then speaks of Origen. This Church Father

convinced his fellow theologians that these words could refer, not to
any earthly king, but to Satan only; and henceforth the Devil became
the prince of pride on whose brow was to be read: I will be like unto
the Most High. This puts Satan in a class which includes the giants
who tried to scale Olympus and replace Zeus, as well as a host of other
defeated defiant ascensionists, frustrated dictators, would-be deicides,
regicides, and parricides.*

Our task here is to look at the reality of the myth of the devil
without reifying the concept, that is, without seeing the devil
in time and space. When Luther, as a student in the seminary,
threw his inkwell at the devil, he was reifying the concept. In
the twentieth century it gives us a strange feeling to hear someone talking of the devil as an actual person in the flesh. An
elderly black woman who was the cook for some neighbors told
us that a younger friend of hers had been waiting for the bus in
a small crowd when "the devil spoke to her right there!" Her
young friend ran fast around the block to escape the devil. I
don't recall the rest of the story, but being a psychoanalyst I
assumed the young friend may have seen someone in the crowd
who cued off some reverie of sexual or other prohibited con-
tents and the devil was the best creature upon whom to project
it.

There is another strange contradiction in the treatment of
Satan, or the devil, which is the paradox in all three versions
of Faust. The devil, or Mephistopheles, the representative of
Satan, tries to persuade Faust *not* to sell his soul to Lucifer.
The devils had already done so, and they had afterward greatly
regretted their decisions. In answer to Faust's question in Marlowe's version, for example, Mephistopheles answers,

*Ibid., pp. 520–521.

O Faustus, leave these frivolous demands
Which strike a terror to my fainting soul!

And he states how much he regrets his own loss of the chance
to see the "face of God and taste the eternal joys of heaven."[*]

This surely says that an inner conflict goes on even in hell.
The group around their leader, Lucifer, already has a number
of famous names. The forms that this myth may take are infinite; the myths of the devil each of us brings to therapy are
unique. But the individual myths are variations on a central
theme of the classical myths, in this case Satan, which refer to
the existential crises in every person's life.

The devil's land of hell has been kept as part of our classical
vocabulary. In the myth of purgatory, we have seen Dante
exploring hell in company with Virgil. Hell is also that part of
the underworld which Odysseus had to visit to get directions
from his deceased father as to how to sail back to Ithaca in his
journey home. It is clear in these classics that one can learn
things of great value by visiting the underworld, the habitat of
the devil.

THE SOURCES
OF CREATIVITY

The devil, in some strange form, turns out to be essential to
creativity. In Dostoevsky's novel, *The Brothers Karamazov*,
Ivan has a discussion with the devil. The devil speaks, "No, you
are not someone apart, you are myself. You are I and nothing
more."

Ivan replies, "You are the incarnation of myself, but only
one side of me . . . of my thoughts and feelings, but only the
nastiest and stupidest of them. You are myself—with a different face. You just say what I am thinking, you are incapable of
saying anything new!"

[*]Marlowe, *Dr. Faustus*, p. 34.

This brings out one aspect of the devil—the fact that true originality, creating something which is unique, is denied him, though creativity cannot occur without him. He is the *negating* aspect of experience. The devil's reality lies in his opposing the laws of God, and this sets the dynamic necessary for all human experience. *The devil exists by virtue of the fact that he opposes God. Out of this comes the dynamic of human creativity.* Rilke was right when he said after his one and only session of psychotherapy, "If my devils are taken away, I am afraid my angels will take flight as well." This tension between the angels and the devils is essential for the creative process. Without the devil there would be stagnation instead of creative production. This is what William Blake had in mind when he stated that Milton in his *Paradise Lost* was "of Satan's party and didn't know it."

One way to avoid awareness of the struggle against the devil in our world is simply to deny it out of hand. This is the method of the cults. Rejuvenated by their new acquaintanceship with the religions from India and Asia Minor, the followers of cult leaders wipe out all those fears of what might happen and then concentrate in meditation on only the beliefs of the cult leader. Cult members close their ears and eyes to the clamoring of evil pounding at the door. We cannot wipe from our memories the gruesome logic in the mass suicide in Guyana in the summer of 1980, when 980 of the people belonging to this cult, all those present in the camp, who had come from America, committed suicide because Jim Jones, their leader, ordered them to do so. That is the logical climax of the activity of all cults which deny the conflict between good and evil.

It is possible to worship evil, which also makes the same mistake in reverse. There have been many "cults of the devil" during the last two decades, though they are not called that, just as there were cults of the devil at the time of the witch burnings in Salem.

We recall that Thomas Mann pictures the devil in his long dialogue with Dr. Faustus; the devil spoke mainly about art. It is the tension between the devil and the inspiration of the harmonious in the painter or musician or other creative person which leads to the creative act. In Beethoven's composing a symphony or Cézanne's painting Mount Sainte-Victoire that the struggle for originality—to sing the music or to paint the picture as they hear it or see it—is so intense. And if the artist succeeds, he or she has achieved the creative work by virtue of the struggle between negation and creation. Creation has won, defeating negation.

As the statement from Gnosticism at the head of this chapter tells us: the problems of freedom, moral strength, and creativity are intimately connected with evil. "O alas, how now do men accuse the gods," cries Homer in the *Odyssey*, "For they say evils come from us. But they themselves, by reason of their sins, have sufferings beyond those destined for them." Perhaps our greatest sin is our refusal to look evil and the devil straight in the face.

POE'S "RAVEN"

The conflict between the devil and God has been experienced by poets ever since human beings learned to communicate and is closer to us than we think. The American poet Edgar Allan Poe illustrates this in his well-known poem, "The Raven." He writes about the devil or demon in our terms:

> "Wretch," I cried, "thy God hath lent thee—
>   by these angels he hath sent thee. . . .
> . . . .
> "Prophet!" said I, "thing of evil!—prophet
>   still, if bird or devil!
> Whether tempter sent, or whether tempest
>   tossed thee here ashore,
> Desolate, yet all undaunted, on this desert
>   land enchanted—
> On this home by horror haunted—tell me

truly, I implore:
Is there—*is* there balm in Gilead?—tell me
—tell me I implore!"
Quoth the raven, "Nevermore."

. . . .

And the raven, never flitting, still is
sitting, still is sitting
On the pallid bust of pallas just above my
chamber door;
And his eyes have all the seeming of a
demon's that is dreaming;
And the lamplight o'er him streaming throws
the shadow on the floor;
And my soul from out that shadow that lies
floating on the floor
Shall be lifted—nevermore!*

Thus Poe described the struggle within himself against what he calls the demon and prophet. Poe's heart is "by horror haunted," his soul is doomed to lie in this condition. Except— and this throws clear light on the whole creative process—*Poe turns his agony into a poem.*

The creative process is characterized by joy one hour and agony the next. But if one wishes to experience the sense of joy, one must be willing to endure the agony of the journey into hell, more commonly called the dullness of hour after hour when inspiration is conspicuous by its absence.

John Steinbeck describes how "the despair came on me" when he was writing his great novel, *The Grapes of Wrath.* He was choking with trepidation about the work as he was writing it. "It's just a run of the mill book," he wrote in his diary. "And the awful thing is that it is absolutely the best I can do. . . . I've always had these travails . . . never get used to them."†

The Grapes of Wrath turned out to be a book for the ages.

---

*"The Raven," by Edgar Allan Poe, in *One Hundred and One Famous Poems* (Chicago: Cable, 1924).
†*New York Times Book Review,* April 9, 1989.

The specific topic of the Joads was universalized by Steinbeck in his struggles in describing these impoverished people; in our day it would be the homeless and the street people. He received a Nobel Prize particularly for this work, but he had to fight his devils every step of the way, his devils being expressed by fatigue, discouragement, and most of all despair about his ability as a writer.

MOBY DICK AND THE MYTH OF CAPTAIN AHAB

Moby Dick is a tale of the myth of the devil on a whaling ship, with Captain Ahab as skipper. This *Pequod* set forth for two years on a voyage to the far southern seas in search of the Great White Whale. Surely a classic, Melville's story is considered by many readers to be the greatest American novel. Melville gives us a picture of Satan in the person of Captain Ahab, an embodiment of that fallen angel or demi-god who in Christendom was variously called Adversary, Lucifer, Satan, Devil.

It is a marvelous story of the hunt for the white whale in distant oceans, and it grips us with the passion that fits its subject, the attraction of the devil in the person of Captain Ahab.* The Biblical name "Ahab" is taken from a king of ancient Judah who gave Jewish prophets much trouble; and he was especially attacked by Elijah.

The young man who relates the tale introduces himself simply with the phrase, "Call me Ishmael." This also fits a Biblical myth—it is the name of the little boy of four or five who is driven with his mother out into the unforgiving desert and sure starvation by Sarah, the first wife of Abraham.

*This section will often quote the late Dr. Henry Murray, to whom I am deeply grateful for his many insights about *Moby Dick*. I recommend those interested to read Dr. Murray's essay on *Moby Dick* in his collection of works, *Endeavors in Psychology*.

The quotations from the novel itself are from Melville, *Moby Dick* (Boston: Houghton-Mifflin, 1956). *Moby Dick* was first published in 1851.

At the beginning of *Moby Dick,* there occurs a Sunday worship service led by the pastor of the whaling church in New
Bedford. The pastor climbs up to his pulpit by his rope ladder,
which is the prow of a whaling ship, and there he delivers a
sermon to his seafaring and God-fearing congregation on the
story of Jonah, who was swallowed by the whale while he was
trying to escape God's command. Divine commandment is a
law at sea, and hence Jonah is brought back in the belly of the
whale.

Though the *Pequod* sails from New Bedford on its voyage to
the South Seas on Christmas day, the sailors do not see Captain
Ahab for several months. They only hear the sound of his pac-
ing—tap-tap-tap—all night long on the deck of the ship. His
peg leg was a result of his previous encounter with the great
white whale. But Captain Ahab's hatred, burning red hot till it
carried everything before it, is deeper than a lost leg. He is filled
with the devil's hatred of this great beast. He is to engage in a
battle like the wars of the gods on Mt. Olympus which caused
the whole world to go into convulsions and explosions which
the ancient Greeks could only endure with bated breath.

At Easter Captain Ahab appears and calls his sailors together
on deck. He there conducts a Black Mass, welding together the
spirit of the crew to engage in a life-and-death battle with
Moby Dick. This is clinched by the shouting crew as they all
drink grog from a horn, joining their captain in his war of
hatred against the arch-enemy, Moby Dick. All the sailors' ears
and eyes and strength are devoted to this volcanic struggle;
everything is subordinated to finding and killing the Great
White Whale. Henry Murray states, like almost every other
reviewer, that the White Whale is a myth of God.

Ahab is so filled with fierce hatred, so absorbed with the
life-and-death hunt, that he refuses to join another ship, *Rachel,* in the search for the son of the *Rachel's* captain, who had
become lost in the wilderness of the unending sea. The captain
of the *Rachel* could only shout back in response, "May God
forgive you!"

From the very soul of Melville, the experience of the heart of this quiet New England author, has come a character who represents the spirit of evil on this voyage of hatred and revenge. Captain Ahab embodies the spirit of Lucifer or Mephistopheles or the devil all in one in this peon to the anti-god. "Melville had learned on his own pulses what it was to be Narcissus, Orestes, Oedipus, Ishmael, Apollo, Lucifer. In this story he condenses from his own creative imagination the nature of Satan."*

The only one who was not convinced by the shared hatred of Moby Dick was the chief mate, Starbuck, a devout Quaker who believed he should shoot Ahab according to the laws of the sea but does not have the courage to do so. Ultimately Starbuck comes to love his fierce captain, committed to destruction though Ahab is. The devil has in this, as in any other conflicts, the strange power of evil. In Ahab we see the devil incarnate.

After a year and a half they sight the Great White Whale. For three days the battle ensues. The sailors, imbued with the spirit of their captain, absorb the powers of hell as they harpoon the great creature again and again. In the fight Ahab's peg leg is broken, another is quickly made, and this also is broken in the struggle against the Great White Whale.

After the second day, Starbuck, the mate, tries to persuade Ahab to call off the fight.

"Great God! but for one single instant show thyself," cried Starbuck; "never, never wilt thou capture him, old man—In Jesus' name no more of this, that's worse than devil's madness. Two days chased; twice stove to splinters; thy very leg once more snatched from under thee; thy evil shadow gone—good angels mobbing thee with warnings:—what more wouldst thou have?—Shall we keep chasing this murderous fish till he swamps the last man? Shall we be dragged by him to the bottom of the sea? Shall we be towed by him to the infernal world? Oh, oh,—Impiety and blasphemy to hunt him more!"

*Murray, *Endeavors in Psychology*, p. 85.

But Ahab answers,

"Starbuck, of late I've felt strangely moved to thee; ever since that hour we both saw—thou know'st what, in one another's eyes.

"Ahab is for ever Ahab, man. This whole act's immutably decreed. 'Twas rehearsed by thee and me a billion years before this ocean rolled. Fool! I am the Fates' lieutenant; I act under orders."

Yes, he does act under orders like Mephistopheles in Goethe's *Faust*, who also acted under orders from Lucifer. Later Ahab cries,

"Oh! my God! what is this that shoots through me, and leaves me so deadly calm, yet expectant,—fixed at the top of a shudder! Future things swim before me, as in empty outlines and skeletons; all the past is somehow grown dim."*

On the third day (the phenomenon is parallel with the last three days in the crucifixion of Christ), when the Great White Whale is again struck with harpoon after harpoon,

"Give way!" cried Ahab to the oarsmen, and the boats darted forward to the attack. But maddened by yesterday's fresh irons that corroded in him, Moby Dick seemed combinedly possessed by all the angels that fell from heaven.

Ahab cries,

"Oh, lonely death on lonely life! Oh, now I feel *my topmost greatness lies in my topmost grief*. Ho, ho! from all your furthest bounds, pour yet now in, ye bold billows of my whole foregone life, and top this one piled comber of my death! Towards thee I roll, thou all-destroying but unconquering whale; to the last I grapple with thee; from hell's heart I stab at thee; for hate's sake I spit my last breath at thee. . . . while still chasing thee, though tied to thee, thou damned whale! *Thus*, I give up the spear!"†

And Ahab hurls his last harpoon. He is driven so crazy by his passion for vengeance that he leaps upon the whale's body and

*Melville, *Moby Dick*, p. 422.
†Ibid., p. 430 (italics mine).

is entwined to the whale's back by his very own ropes. He sinks below the ocean waters, drowning in the great ocean of his hatred.

But this is not all. Infuriated, the white whale then attacks the ship. It lifts the prow high in the air and breaks the ship asunder. "Great God, where is our ship!" cried the men.

Moby Dick then fiercely drives the boats with the men clinging to them under the water. Then he attacks the stern, turning it on end so that it too sinks below the ocean's surface.

and so the bird of heaven, with angelic shrieks, and his imperial beak thrust upwards, and his whole captive form folded in the flag of Ahab, went down with his ship, which like Satan, would not sink to hell till she had dragged a living part of heaven along with her. . . .

Now small fowls flew screaming over the yet yawning gulf; a sullen white surf beat against its steep sides; then all collapsed, and the great shroud of the sea rolled on as it rolled five thousand years ago.*

The epilogue begins with a quotation from Job, uttered by Ishmael as he floats on a log:

"And I only am escaped alone to tell thee. . . .

"The drama's done. Why then here does any one step forth? Because one did survive the wreck.

"It so chanced, that after the Parsee's disappearance, I was he whom the Fates ordained to take the place of Ahab's bowsman, when that bowsman assumed the vacant post; the same, who, when on the last day the three men where tossed from out the rocking boat, was dropped astern. So, floating on the margin of the ensuing scene, and in full sight of it, when the half-spent suction of the sunken ship reached me, I was then, but slowly, drawn towards the closing vortex. When I reached it, it had subsided to a creamy pool. . . . Buoyed up by that coffin, for almost one whole day and night, I floated on a soft and dirge-like main. The unharming sharks, they glided by as if with padlocks on their mouths; the savage sea-hawks sailed with sheathed beaks. On the second day, a sail drew near, nearer, and picked me up

*Ibid., p. 431.

at last. It was the devious-cruising Rachel, that in her retracing search after her missing children, only found another orphan."*

CATHARSIS IN THE
STRUGGLE WITH EVIL

Like all great myths in literature, *Moby Dick* performs the task of giving the reader—indeed giving posterity—a catharsis from excessive anxiety and guilt. This we see in the experience of participation in a profoundly creative experience.

Henry Murray writes that for him reading *Moby Dick* is like listening to Beethoven's *Eroica.* In reading the mythic tale, we feel cleansed as if by a great religious experience, the destruction of Ahab, the embodiment of the devil. The world and life have a deeper quality that reaches down into a person's soul below even the customary "tomorrow and tomorrow and to-morrow" of Shakespeare's *Macbeth.* Love and joy and death confront one another in these depths of emotion.

In a letter to Hawthorne after he had finished *Moby Dick,* Melville wrote, "I have written a wicked book." Then when he heard that Hawthorne understood and liked it, he wrote back, "I feel like a new-born baby!" He had experienced the catharsis that one feels in creating something beautiful. The feeling is not just a "victory" over the devil or a wiping out of evil—these by themselves would lead only to sentimentality. It is rather the catharsis of feeling cleansed through one's battle with the devil, one's struggle with the recalcitrant words until one is able to express the vision in his or her own heart and mind. It was a cleansing of the fierce discord with the devil.

Not that the devil will not come back again. But rather that the author has learned in his struggle with the daimonic that he, the creative person, can meet evil and make of it something

*Ibid., p. 431.

joyous, beautiful, and health giving. One never finishes this battle once and for all. Goethe struggled for forty years before working out a creative ending for the last half of his *Faust.*

Melville's *Moby Dick* was written as an attack on the narrow, life-stifling, dark, and cruel repressions of Puritanism, which still festered in some of the churches and religion of New England. It was the same spirit which earlier had caused the burning of the "witches" at Salem. The name of the whaling ship, *Pequod,* was the name of a fierce tribe of Indians the New Englanders had exterminated, and it was this push toward extermination that carried over in New England to become what Melville attacked.

The dull, snowbound coldness of Melville's father and the quiet sweetness of his mother whom he never fully knew—these were some of the source of Melville's super-ego and of his dedication to these mythic depths. Freud suggests that continuous aggression is a sign of lack of eros; this lack characterizes the kind of Puritanism Melville attacked.

Such is the mythic catharsis of which every creative artist partakes. It is not surprising that the artists feel it in their own minds and hearts; their destiny requires they give it to others, to share with others the emotional wars and eruptions of which Melville writes. With *Moby Dick* Melville joins the great writers of the middle and last half of the nineteenth century—Kierkegaard, Schopenhauer, Nietzsche, and several decades later Freud and Spengler. *All of them saw that the error of the Enlightenment was that it lacked a devil.*

God is ultimately triumphant in *Moby Dick,* Satan's forces are vanquished, as it was foreseen on ancient Olympus. The victory is hard won, and the price of the life-and-death struggles ending in the sentence, as is the case in *Moby Dick,* "And I alone am left to tell the story." The mythic devil here stands for enduring the earthquakes and the volcanos which exude their fire and brimstone, but Good and Evil go on forever.

"Some may wonder how it was that Melville," writes Murray, "a fundamentally good, affectionate, noble, idealistic, and reverential man, should have felt impelled to write a wicked book."* Why did he aggress so furiously against Western orthodoxy, as furiously as Byron and Shelley, or any satanic writer who preceded him, as furiously as Nietzsche or the most radical of his successors in our day? These are questions we continually ask and never can answer. *But in the asking is the catharsis.*

I see this novel as an expression of the myth of wars between Good and Evil, when the character of Satan is a rehearsal of the wars of the gods, before Oedipus puts out his eyes or Prometheus suffers in bringing primitive man his learning, before Athena meets the daimonic in the *Oresteia,* before Socrates drinks his hemlock. Here is Satan, here are the necessary wars of the spirit. The eternal wars continue. As Joan of Arc hangs burning at the stake in George Bernard Shaw's *Saint Joan,* she cries out the great question, "How long, O Lord, how long?" This cry will be heard as long as people have the awareness of God and Satan, for out of this struggle come the qualities that make us human. Out of these depths comes great literature. We will never see it wiped away. The battle as shown in this myth still goes on as long as we are human and still gives us our most profound and joyful experiences.

*Murray, *Endeavors in Psychology,* p. 90.

PART IV

MYTHS FOR SURVIVAL

SIXTEEN

The Great Circle of Love

The state of mind which enables a man to do this kind of
work [science] is akin to that of the religious worshipper or
the lover.

Albert Einstein

LIBERATION OF WOMEN

They are—the Mothers.
  Faust (starting) . . . Mothers!
  Mephistopheles: Are you awed?
  Faust: The Mothers! Why, it strikes a singular chord.

Goethe, Faust

In preceding chapters we observed that the chauvinistic Peer
Gynt tried to find himself by gallivanting around the earth. But
he became increasingly more desperate until he confronted
death. He finally finds his genuine self only in the presence of
Solveig and her feminine love.

We have seen also in the myth of Briar Rose that the liberation of the princess did not occur for those unlucky princes who
exhibited only sheer male strength in trying to hack their way
through the thick hedges. But it did come in the presence of

the prince who did not force his way, the one who engaged in creative waiting until the hedge and thorns opened by themselves, when he and the princess could be genuinely present to each other.

In other myths, such as Goethe's Faust, the struggle of the myth is present if not resolved, namely, the myth of the equality of men and women.

In each of these dramas the liberation of both woman and man is possible only when each achieves a new myth of the other sex, leading to a new significant psychological relationship. They are both then liberated from their previous empty and lonely existence. *The woman and the man find their true selves only when they are fully present to each other.* They find they both need each other, not only physically but psychologically and spiritually as well.

In the Reformation a large part of our Western world became Protestant, and the Mother of Jesus was emphatically given a back seat, as is shown in the architecturally beautiful but barren churches of New England. Where was the Catholic Mariology with its warm, feminine art? It does not require brilliance to see the witch trials in Europe and America in this fifteenth and sixteenth centuries as overt attacks against the women of those countries. The most basic consideration is that *the two principles of rationalism and individualism, the myths on which the modern age is founded, are chiefly male, left-brain activities.*

The age of discovery in the fifteenth and sixteenth centuries was geared as well to male habits. Men ventured forth into the universe; women took care of the hearth at home. The Industrial Revolution consisted of heavy and powerful machines, which again appealed particularly to men. Imagine a woman in that day driving Goethe's locomotive from Bath to Liverpool! Ours is the age when capitalism flourished, with its factories and huge engines that could be manipulated by men and, until recently, only by men. These conditions left many women in the role of the stepchildren of our modern age. We surely were in need of an Ibsen to write *A Doll's House* in the last of the nineteenth century, showing what evils this period could do to the feminine half of our race.

One of the main reasons Alfred Adler withdrew from the group that met at Freud's house every Wednesday evening in the first decade of this century was that he differed with Freud's view of women. Freud had taken a condescending attitude toward women, using the Victorian method of flattery; he referred to them as the "fair sex," the "tender ones," and on that basis he understandably could never find an answer to his question, What do women want? Adler, on the contrary, said many times in different ways that "civilization will never be complete as long as one half of the people in it are considered inferior."

Otto Rank, following Adler's example, also withdrew from Freud's inner group, even though the master was proud of Rank and his work and gossip had it that Rank had been groomed for succession to Freud's throne. Disagreeing radically with Freud's broad references to women's problems by the derogatory term "penis envy," Rank believed that what motivates a woman is her "emotional and spiritual . . . craving for expression of her true woman-self in a masculine world which has no room or use for her."* Rank believed that the end result of psychoanalysis should be that the patient fulfill himself and *her*self. Rank used the term "self-realization" before any of us in America used it. He also emphasized "identity confusion" twenty years before Erik Erikson used the term, and he regarded sexism, the prejudice against women, as a "cultural disease."

Rank understood remarkably well the difficult position in which our culture placed women. He wrote in 1939 that the woman

must feel in this man-made world . . . not unlike Alice in Wonderland, strange and bewildered, for it is a world in the creation of which

*Otto Rank, *Beyond Psychology* (New York: Dover, 1941), p. 267.

she did not partake. . . . Just as they speak two different languages, so the sexes live in two different worlds linked like the motherland with her colonies by ties strong enough to keep the necessary cooperation between the two independent entities, separated by as yet uncharted seas.*

What has been lacking in our modern culture are myths and rituals to give significance to the woman's life apart from what she has in relation to a man, be he father or brother or husband. "What rituals can do is to transform necessary unremitting drudgery into something rich, satisfying, and filled with meaning," Bruce Lincoln tells us in his discussion of women's initiation in Navajo tribes. A ritual, we have said, is a myth transformed into action. This is observable in Indian tribes; the ritual expresses the myth by action of the body. Myth gives birth to rituals, and rituals give birth to myths. Women's role in the Navajos' initiation is the bearer of the young, the one who raises the crops and provides the food that sustains life, and each act is endowed with a myth of significance. "Each time a woman is initiated, the world is saved from chaos, for the fundamental power of creativity is renewed in her being."† Navajo rituals and myths give women's tasks meaning and elevate them above boredom, mindlessness, and despair. Among the Navajos this is no opportunistic stratagem to preserve male hegemony, continues Bruce Lincoln. Their myths form a ritual of sacrifice and an apotheosis—an acting out of the meaning and significance of the otherwise routine tasks the woman will do through her life. This kind of ritual demonstrates that *the myth for the Navajos is that woman saves the world from chaos*.

Liberation, for women and for men, means both are free to be what they inherently are. It means acting and living on the basis of your own being in your social group. Freedom from

---

*Ibid., p. 257. For those who wish to understand more of Rank's actual therapy, the diaries of Anaïs Nin are available in which she tells of her analysis with Rank in Paris.

†Bruce Lincoln, *Emerging from the Chrysalis* (Cambridge: Harvard University Press, 1981), p. 107.

artificial or cultural handicaps is freedom to develop as your body and your mind and spirit direct. Liberation includes tapping the unconscious powers, what have generally been accorded to feminine capacities such as telepathy and intuition.*

Men withhold liberation from women at the price of becoming slaves themselves. To have a slave makes you yourself participate in slavery; the master enslaves the peon but is enslaved by his own slave. No man can withhold liberation from women without losing it himself, and the same is true for women. But there is no freedom without responsibility. Thus the liberation of women means they also will assume responsibility in proportion to their freedom.

In our contemporary business culture, it is heartening to see that some corporate boards are finding that the feminine approach to problems, involving more empathy and sensitive understanding, can be of special help. Some women in business and politics, such as Margaret Thatcher and Jeanne Kirkpatrick, show that women can achieve success by being as tough as any man. But shall women meet the ills of a male-dominated culture by taking over the least desirable characteristics of men? This is certainly not the answer.

We recall the young woman in Briar Rose, whose dream in her therapy we described in Chapter 11, presenting women's special telepathy, "which was to demonstrate in the dream," concluded my patient helpfully, "that the woman was more intelligent and efficient than anyone gave her credit for being."

John Steinbeck in *The Grapes of Wrath* shows us a great and profound respect for Ma Joad, the archetypal "earth mother," who holds the migrant family together. In Steinbeck's world women have an innate understanding of cyclic immortality, and with motherhood woman comes into her own as a special elemental being. Thus the whiny young girl, Rose of Sharon, joins the ranks of the great Mother in the powerful closing passages of *The Grapes of Wrath*. Left destitute by seasonal

*Ibid.

rains and perpetual unemployment, the Joad family seeks refuge in an old barn, finding there a boy and another worker near death from starvation. Rose of Sharon has recently lost a baby and her breasts are swollen with milk. She and Ma communicate silently, on some intuitive level:

Suddenly the boy cried, "He's dying, I tell you! He's starvin' to death, I tell you." . . .

Ma's eyes passed Rose of Sharon's eyes, and then came back to them. And the two women looked deep into each other. The girl's breath came short and gasping.

She said "Yes."

Ma smiled. "I knowed you would. I knowed!" She looked down at her hands, tight-locked in her lap.

Rose of Sharon whispered, "Will—will you all—go out?" The rain whisked lightly on the roof.

Ma leaned forward and with her palm she brushed the touseled hair back from her daughter's forehead, and she kissed her on the forehead. Ma got up quickly. "Come on, you fellas," she called. "You come out in the tool shed."

Ruthie opened her mouth to speak. "Hush," Ma said. "Hush and git." She herded them through the door, drew the boy with her; and she closed the squeaking door.

For a minute Rose of Sharon sat still in the whispering barn. Then she hoisted her tired body up and drew the comfort about her. She moved slowly to the corner and stood looking down at the wasted face, into the wide, frightened eyes. Then slowly she lay down beside him. He shook his head slowly from side to side. Rose of Sharon loosened one side of the blanket and bared her breast. "You got to," she said. She squirmed closer and pulled his head close. "There!" she said. "There." Her hand moved behind his head and supported it. Her fingers moved gently in his hair. She looked up and across the barn, and her lips came together and smiled mysteriously.*

*Steinbeck, *The Grapes of Wrath* (New York: Viking Press, 1939), pp. 618–619.

THE CHARM OF MORTALITY

A great number of myths refer to life after death, such as the resurrection, the Neoplatonic concepts of immortality, the many Hindu myths, the Sufi, the new forms we may assume in future lives, and so on. We shall not deal with these myths of immortality here. Instead we shall direct our attention to the charm of mortality.

It is both significant and surprising in Greek myths that many times significant persons are offered immortality but choose mortality instead. One myth in which mortality is found to have charms is the story of Amphytrian. This myth is presented in modern times in a drama entitled *Amphytrian 38*, since such a multitude of versions of the myth have already been produced.*

The story goes as follows: Zeus has fallen in love with the wife of Amphytrian, a young Greek general in the Greek army. Zeus cannot tear himself away from looking down on earth at her shadow through her window. He moons around atop Mt. Olympus almost beside himself with his frustrated passion. Mercury takes pity on him and suggests that Zeus arrange a harmless maneuver of war so that Amphytrian will be called away, and in his absence Zeus can masquerade as Amphytrian and fulfill his yearning to make love with his wife. Zeus proceeds to do this. Everything goes according to plan.

But after Zeus completes the love affair, he and Amphytrian's wife have a conversation which greatly disturbs the chief of the gods. On his return to Mount Olympus he describes to Mercury what it is like to make love to a human being. Zeus is indeed troubled.

*The drama here referred to was written by Jean Giraudoux in 1938 in the present form and presented on the stage in New York as well as in Paris.

"Mercury, she will say, 'When I was young, or when I am old, or when I die.' This stabs me, Mercury. We miss something, Mercury.

"We miss the poignancy of the transient—that sweet sadness of grasping for something we know we cannot hold."

This arguing for the charm of mortality gives us pause. Our compassion for other people arises from our awareness that we too are on this spinning globe for three score and ten or twenty years, and then we bid goodbye to the world. Erich Fromm used to argue that fear of death is fear of not living out one's present life, which is akin to the above idea. There are assets to being mortal—that we experience our own loneliness, and as Zeus said, "the poignancy of the transient, the sweet sadness of grasping for something we know we cannot hold."

Our mortality then has a certain strange charm. Abraham Maslow once wrote to me after his major heart attack, "My river [the Charles River, which flowed past his back porch] was never so beautiful as after my heart attack. I wonder if we humans could love—love passionately—if we knew we'd never die." This is another asset of mortality: we learn to love each other. *We are able to love passionately because we die.*

I recall once taking a walk with the great theologian and philosopher, Paul Tillich, when he was in his late seventies and had not many more years to live.

"Paulus," I asked, "are you afraid of dying?"

His expression did not change as he answered, "Yes. Everybody is. Nobody has ever come back to tell us."

I continued, "What is it about death that you fear?"

He answered, "The loneliness. I know I never will see my friends and family again."

Whatever happens after we die—as Tillich says, no one has come back to tell us—we achieve a stimulus from the fact that we know we have only a few years to live on this earth. This awareness of being mortal challenges us to use these few years in a way that reaches deepest into our hearts and the hearts of those we love. There is, as Giraudoux tells us, a poignancy, an aliveness, indeed a vitality which is present in mortality.

The most famous choice of mortality is that of Odysseus in his long trip home from Troy when he is shipwrecked and spends seven years with the beautiful nymph, Calypso. She offers him immortality if he will stay forever with her. But he continually weeps in his desire to go home to Penelope.

Athena, the goddess who watches over the family of Odysseus, prevails upon Zeus to send Hermes to instruct Calypso to let Odysseus leave. When Hermes flies to the island and explains his instructions, Calypso becomes angry:

> "Oh you vile gods, in jealousy supernal!
> You hate it when we choose to lie with men—
> immortal flesh by some dear mortal side. . . .
>
> So now you grudge me, too, my mortal friend.
> But it was I who saved him—saw him straddle
> his own keel board, the one man left afloat
> when Zeus rent wide his ship with chain lightning
> and overturned him in the winedark sea.
> Then all his troops were lost, his good companions,
> when wind and current washed him here to me,
> I fed him, loved him, sang that he should not die
> nor grow old, ever, in all the days to come, . . ."

> The strong god glittering left her as she spoke,
> and now her ladyship, having given heed
> to Zeus's mandate, went to find Odysseus
> in his stone seat to seaward—tear on tear
> brimming his eyes. The sweet days of his life time
> were running out in anguish over his exile,
> for long ago the nymph had ceased to please.
> Though he fought shy of her and her desire,
> he lay with her each night, for she compelled him.
> But when day came he sat on the rocky shore
> and broke his own heart groaning, with eyes wet
> scanning the bare horizon of the sea.
> Now she stood near him in her beauty, saying:

"O forlorn man, be still.
Here you need grieve no more; you need not feel
your life consumed here; I have pondered it,
and I shall help you go."

But still Calypso cannot understand why Odysseus wants to
give up immortality and go back to Penelope:

"Son of Laertes, versatile Odysseus,
after these years with me, you still desire
your old home? Even so, I wish you well.
Can I be less desirable than Penelope is?
Less interesting? Less beautiful? Can mortals
compare with goddesses in grace and form?"

To this the strategist Odysseus answered:

"My lady goddess, here is no cause for anger.
My quiet Penelope—how well I know—
would seem a shade before your majesty,
death and old age being unknown to you,
while she must die. Yet, it is true, each day
I long for home, long for the sight of home.
If any god has marked me out again
for shipwreck, my tough heart can undergo it.
What hardship have I not long since endured
at sea, in battle! Let the trial come."

Now as he spoke the sun set, dusk drew on,
and they retired, this pair, to the inner cave
to enjoy themselves in love and stayed all night beside
each other.

When Dawn spread out her finger tips of rose
Odysseus pulled his tunic and his cloak on,
while the sea nymph dressed in a silvery gown
of subtle tissue, drew about her waist
a golden belt.*

*Homer, *The Odyssey,* trans. Robert Fitzgerald (New York: Doubleday, 1961),
pp. 87–88.

And so Odysseus chooses mortality even though he knows it means for him more years of being tossed in storms and his raft wrecked, and even though it means he must fight the rival gang of suitors when he returns to Ithaca.

We have said that in the moments when eternity breaks into time, there we find myth. Myth partakes of both dimensions: it is of the earth in our day-to-day experience, and is a reaching beyond our mundane existence. It gives us the capacity to live in the spirit. Who has not been moved by the majesty of the Corinthian pillars of the Temple of Zeus in Athens. Again we find ourselves repeating on hearing a Mozart sonata, "If I live to be a thousand years, I will never forget this moment!" Such moments are beyond time.

Nor does one need to travel over the earth. At sunrise in every meadow there are trillions of blades of grass, each with its drop of dew clinging to the green grass in the moment just before the sun rises; each drop of dew has, against its background of silver, a complete rainbow of colors. Trillions of diamonds in every meadow!

These incidents for that moment have the myth of eternity regardless of how brief they are or how many years we live. It is even a joy, when you are bored sitting in an airport, to enliven and beautify your existence by calling to your mind the many things of beauty and charm that you have seen or heard or experienced. We are all so much richer than we assume!

PLANETISM AND HUMANHOOD

Life will never be the same again. We will see the earth as it truly is, bright and blue and beautiful in that silence where it floats. . . . Human beings as riders on the earth together on that bright loveliness in the eternal cold know now that they are truly brothers.

Archibald MacLeish

It is the last phrase of MacLeish's statement that affects us most powerfully, that we "are truly brothers."* True, one reads that terrorism has not abated, that humans still kill humans in Africa, in the Near East, in the Orient, and in the Americas. The kidnapping of hostages has become a recognized form of warfare for some of the Third World nations which do not have powerful armies. We know that the great fact of brotherhood has not yet sunk into the awareness of the great mass of humanity.

But the exploring of the heavens is a myth out of which we can achieve a new international ethics and understanding, a new raison d'être for humanity. Though it has not yet changed us, we can believe that it will become a new myth out of which we may achieve a new international morality.

Russell Schweickart, one of the astronauts on the *Apollo 7* trip into space, tells us his feelings about these great events, and in doing so he gives us a remarkable narration and an authentic new myth.† He notes first the relation of his experience to the creation myth in Genesis, spoken in a previous flight:

In December of 1968, Frank Borman, Jim Lovell, and Bill Anders circled the moon on Christmas Eve and read from Genesis and other parts of the Bible, to *sacramentalize* that experience and to transmit somehow what they were experiencing to everyone back on Earth.

Rusty takes pains to point out that the astronauts are not heroes (though they may become heroes in the new myth) but they are neighbors, the people who live next door to all of us. In this way, Rusty makes his myth part of our community, whether we other members of the community do such novel things as fly in a capsule or stay at home. He, indeed, is part of the sacramentalizing of the planet.

Typical of myths, he talks about "you" as though all of us

---

*Archibald MacLeish interpreted the trips in space for the *New York Times Magazine* the day after the launching of *Apollo 7,* published in the *New York Times Magazine,* December 25, 1968.

†All quotations are from personal conversation with Russell Schweickart.

were with them on their lunar module, and in a mythic sense
we were.

You check out the portable life support system and everything seems
to work and you strap it on your back and you hook all the hoses and
connections and wires and cables and antennae and all those things to
your body. . . . And outside on the front porch of the lunar module
you watch the sun rise over the Pacific and it's an incredible sight,
beautiful, beautiful!

The astronauts depend on each other in ultimate ways, since
whether or not the two who were slated to separate would be
able to get back again, whether the lunar module will be able to
dock again on the command ship, depends upon each one con-
scientiously doing his part. The infinity of space makes this
interdependence a question of life or death. "Dave Scott is
your next-door neighbor, but he was never a neighbor like he's
a neighbor now," says Rusty of the bond that grew up among
the astronauts.

After these incredible experiences, Rusty asks the moral
question, "What does it all mean?" And he answers on a
mythic level below the obvious things: "I think that we've
played a part in changing the concept of man and the nature of
life."

This ultimate question and its answer give the myth its great
moral depth. Musing about this question, Rusty gazes down at
the earth looking so fragile from the perspective of the astronauts up in the stratosphere. The world is so small that the
spaceship can encircle it in an hour and a half, and

you begin to recognize that your identity is with that whole thing.
. . . You look down there and you can't imagine how many borders
and boundaries you cross, again and again and again and you don't
even see them. There you are—hundreds of people in the Mideast
killing each other over some imaginary line that you're not even aware
of. . . . And from where you see it, the thing is a *whole,* and it's so
beautiful.

Rusty wonders about the mystery present in all myths. Musing about why he is up there and not you or me, he asks, "Am I separated out to be touched by God, to have some special experience that others cannot have?" He firmly answers no. He feels he has experienced this trip that anyone else could have made with the right training. This is why, he says, "I've used the word 'you,' because its not me or the others on the lunar module. *It's life that's had that experience.*" All of these expressions make a myth of a new age, as Columbus and Magellan in their day contributed to the myth of the Renaissance.

Taking off from actual history, the myth then gives us images that come alive. The community which experiences the myth and the morality of the true myth are both there. Since human beings can now fly around the earth, the boundaries over which people war now become a deadly and cursed mistake, an insane and cruel destruction of our small, fragile, but beautiful earth.

Sir Fred Hoyle said in the very middle of our century, "Once a photograph of the earth, taken from the outside, is available . . . a new idea as powerful as any in history will be let loose."* We now have that new photograph. It was taken by the astronauts and printed in full page by countless newspapers and journals. It showed the Atlantic and the Pacific oceans, the China Sea and the Indian Ocean, the continents of Africa and South America, and all the countries of the Orient spinning on the surface of this earth. This photograph did leave an indelible impression on millions of peoples' minds—the picture of the earth emblazoned in dark blue and gold, turning serenely in its orbit, populated by people who are truly brothers and sisters.

Rusty Schweickart did not see the borders of the nations of Europe and Central America, which are nonexistent from this range. And Rusty felt, as we all did, that there was something ludicrous as well as tragic about the efforts of these countries,

---

*Sir Fred Hoyle in 1948, cited in P. Hussell, *The Global Brain* (Los Angeles: J. P. Tarcher, 1983), p. 16.

posturing like roosters, killing each other to preserve borders that no longer exist. The meaning of these great days and nights, merged together around the spaceship, was that scores of nations were trying to preserve boundaries which had become anachronisms. The moment of seeing that picture was the heralding of the time when at last it will be recognized, even though politicians may be the last to admit it, that what happens in Moscow also happens in Washington, that what occurs in London will also occur in Bombay. The moment in history has come when nation shall not lift up sword against nation and they shall study war no more.

The very dangers that we face, exemplified by nuclear bombs, are themselves commandments that we must learn to live together as brothers and sisters in a great family. From the Marshall McLuhan Institute in Toronto there had come a strange statement in the middle of 1982. The leader was quoted, "I'm delighted with the atom bomb." But before we could shout out our protest at such inhuman sentiments, we read the next sentence, "Something is necessary to bring us all together." And this is the danger we all face of destruction of the earth's atmosphere, the pollution of our oceans even as we explore the heavens. Since they are the same dangers for all of us, whatever our color or nationality, it behooves us to face them together.

We now do have a common enemy. It comes by way of our understanding this myth. The very technology for the destruction of our enemies also leaves us hostage to the destructive power we generate. We cannot turn the clock back (nor do we want to), but the control of nuclear energy is the requirement needed to bring us all together. The near tragedy of Three Mile Island and the actual tragedy of Chernobyl demonstrate the irrefutable fact that we are one world. When thousands of tons of lettuce and green vegetables had to be burned in Italy after the Chernobyl accident and tens of thousands of reindeer—almost the whole economy of the Laplanders in northern Sweden—had to be slaughtered because of the radiation contagion, we knew in our hearts we could never live separately again.

When headlines appeared in the *New York Times* after the accident, "Russia Asks the Help of the Scientists of the West," many of us were overtaken with a strange conviction: *this marks the beginning of the world in which the nations will no longer be border-ridden.* The new myth of the stars and trips to the planets will then have taken effect!

Radiation surely hasn't the slightest respect for fictitious borders. The efforts to keep these borders pure becomes, were it not so tragic, a strange joke—to protect borders which exist only in one's imagination! In the twenty-first century they will seem like anachronisms of the most destructive kind. This holds not only for radiation in Europe but for all the peoples on the crust of the earth.

As Rusty Schweickart has revealed, the power of myths is still with us. "And outside on the front porch of the lunar module, you watch the sun rise over the Pacific and it's an incredible sight, a beautiful, beautiful sight."

"And what's it all mean?" Here Rusty is forming a myth self-consciously, venturing his ideas on the most important point of all: "I think that in some ways there are other benefits which are more significant." As Rusty repeated, "I think that we've played a part in changing the concept of man and the nature of life."

We awake after a sleep of many centuries to find ourselves in a new and irrefutable sense in the myth of humankind. We find ourselves in a new world community; we cannot destroy the parts without destroying the whole. In this bright loveliness we know now that we are truly sisters and brothers, at last in the same family.

Index

reality of, 65
three facets of, 68
men, left-brain activity associated with, 288
menstruation, 200, 203
mental telepathy, 163
Mephistopheles:
    in Goethe's *Faust*, 34, 235, 236,
        237–243, 245–246, 248, 249–252,
        254, 255, 272–273, 280
    in Marlowe's *Doctor Faustus*, 223,
        225, 226, 227, 228, 231, 232
    see also Satan
mercy, 134
Merton, Thomas, 91
Merwin, W. S., 106
Meyer, Adolph, 69
Meyer, Michael, 169*n*, 170
Michelangelo, 209
Middle Ages, prominence of divinity in, 222
migraine, 259–260
Milken, Michael, 124*n*
Millay, Edna St. Vincent, 128
Miller, Arthur, 42–44, 261–262
Milton, John, 34, 274
Minkowski, Eugene, 203*n*
Mirandola, 220
Mnemosyne, 71
Moby Dick (Melville), 34, 277–284
money:
    as escape from depression, 238*n*
    ethical acquisition of, 131
    U.S. emphasis on, 48, 56, 60, 106,
        115, 119, 123–124, 131
monotony, 145, 146, 147
Moonies, 22*n*
morality:
    education in, 28–29
    individualistic view of, 110
    international, 298
    mythlessness and, 31, 59–60
    passion vs., 161
    see also ethics
mortality, 293–297
Moses, birth of, 38
motherhood, feminine abilities
        symbolized by, 243, 246–247,
        291–292
motivation, 61
Mount Olympus, divine conflicts on,
    278, 283

movies, 18, 26–27
Moyers, Bill, 123–124
Mozart, Wolfgang Amadeus, 218, 236, 297
Muktananda, 22*n*
Muller, Max, 25
murder, 100
Murray, Henry, 25*n*, 34, 271–272,
        277*n*, 278, 279*n*, 282, 283–284
Musgrave, Susan, 66
music, artist decline and, 262
mystery, myth and, 31, 73, 300
myth(s):
    archetypal patterns manifested in,
        37–38
    art vs., 28
    aspirations derived from, 61
    astrology as, 22*n*
    of care, 250*n*
    catharsis of, 221, 232–233
    as celebration, 50–52
    of change, 102–106
    consciousness vs., 37
    cults and, 22–24
    as cultural necessity, 15–16
    death and, 39, 217, 219
    denial of, 24–25
    of Eros, 39, 76–77, 134
    eternal values represented in, 26–29,
        39–40, 59, 60, 196, 297
    fairy tales vs., 196
    as falsehood, 23, 24–25
    of Faust, 217–222, 229–230, 253
    four functions of, 15–16, 30–31
    of freedom, 95
    Greek, *see* Greek myths
    healing power of, 81, 82, 84–87
    Hebrew, 28, 42
    history preceded by, 91–92
    individual identity and, 16, 26, 30,
        31–37
    lack of, 21, 63
    language and, 23
    of love, 39
    Mann on, 27, 31, 50, 73
    memory transformed into, 67–68, 70
    modern deterioration of, 15, 19
    mystery and, 31, 73, 300
    of newness, 101–104
    of Oedipus, 28, 37, 38, 43, 72–73, 75,
        78*n*, 81, 82, 84–86, 180–181, 284
    poets and, 106